Single Parenting For Dummies®

Cheat Sheet

Important Telephone Numbers

Contact	Phone Number
Neighbor	
Parental stress hot line	
Pediatrician	
Grandparents or other relative	
Parent's work and cell phone numbers	
Coparent's work, home, and cell phone numbers	
Poison control hot line	1-800-382-9097
The National Hopeline Network (suicide and crisis)	1-800-784-2433

Signs You or Your Child Need Therapy

- ✔ Extreme mood swings
- ✔ Fits of anger
- ✔ Extreme irritability
- ✔ Withdrawal from friends and family members
- ✔ Trouble at school, including poor grades and hanging out with a bad crowd
- ✔ Crying a lot
- ✔ Sleeping too much or too little
- ✔ Any signs of depression (given in Chapter 14)

Things You Should Do Today for Your Kids

- ✔ Spend one-on-one-time with each child, talking about her day and being a good listener.
- ✔ Hug your child and tell him you love him.
- ✔ Try to see the humor in things that happen and have fun with your kids.
- ✔ Answer your kids' questions as honestly as you can.
- ✔ Be a strong role model for your kids today.
- ✔ Praise and encourage each child.
- ✔ Respect your child's opinions.
- ✔ Respect your child's privacy.
- ✔ Keep any promises you've made to your child.
- ✔ Apologize to your child if you're in the wrong.

For Dummies: Bestselling Book Series for Beginners

Single Parenting For Dummies®

Children's and Single Parents' Bills of Rights

Children's Bill of Rights	Single Parents' Bill of Rights
Your child has the right to be told about the divorce by both parents at the same time; he should not hear about it from someone else before you talk to him.	You and your children have the right to be regarded as a *family*.
Your child has a right to hear why you divorced, explained simply with as much or little detail as your child can handle at her age.	You have the right to become an independent, fulfilled person with friends and a social life, in addition to being a parent.
Your child has the right to be loved and cherished by both parents.	You have the right to receive or pay fair custody or alimony payments.
Your child has the right to love and cherish each of his parents individually, without feeling guilty or being forced to take sides.	You have the right to spend time with your children and be involved in their lives.
Your child has the right to be protected from overhearing any arguments, verbal abuse, or bad-mouthing of one of her parents by the other.	You have the right to expect cooperation from your co-parent that includes sharing of major holidays, birthdays and other special days in a fair, equitable way.
Your child has the right to live in a clean, safe environment that is nurturing to his growth and development.	You have a right to live in a safe environment with adequate food; clothing and shelter.
Your child has the right to her own private space, even if it means one side of a shared bedroom.	You have the right to be included in all decisions regarding your children's education, medical/dental care and religious education.
Your child has the right to have his physical needs met, including nourishment, exercise, and medical, dental, and vision care.	You have the right to agree to disagree with your co-parent in order to keep conflicts to a minimum.
Your child has the right to have her emotional needs met, she needs praise, encouragement, and sympathy when she has had a setback of some kind.	
Your child has the right to expect both of his parents to be positive role models as he grows, matures, and copes with his future.	
Your child has the right to be treated fairly, courteously, and with respect.	
Your child has the right to have you welcome her friends into her home with respect.	
Your child has the right to an apology if you make a mistake.	
Your child has the right to expect you to keep your promises.	
Your child has the right to a stable life that includes a sense of continuity as he divides his time between two parents' residences.	

For Dummies: Bestselling Book Series for Beginners

Single Parenting

FOR

DUMMIES®

Single Parenting

FOR

DUMMIES®

by Marion Peterson, MFT, and Diane Warner

WILEY

Wiley Publishing, Inc.

Single Parenting For Dummies®

Published by
Wiley Publishing, Inc.
909 Third Avenue
New York, NY 10022
www.wiley.com

Copyright © 2003 by Wiley Publishing, Inc., Indianapolis, Indiana

Published simultaneously in Canada

For general information on our other products and services or to obtain technical support, please contact our Customer Care Department within the U.S. at 800-762-2974, outside the U.S. at 317-572-3993, or fax 317-572-4002.

Wiley also publishes its books in a variety of electronic formats. Some content that appears in print may not be available in electronic books.

Library of Congress Control Number: 2003101862

ISBN: 0-7645-1766-X

Manufactured in the United States of America

10 9 8 7 6 5 4 3 2 1

WILEY is a trademark of Wiley Publishing, Inc.

About the Authors

Marion Peterson, MFT (also known as *Marnie*), believes in *new beginnings*. Experiencing divorce, single parenting, and blended family life firsthand led to a new career. After spending many years as a registered nurse, she received a Masters in clinical psychology and became a Licensed Marriage, Family and Child Therapist. Marnie is also certificated in Scientific Marital Therapy and has organized and facilitated a group for Parents in Pain and has facilitated Women's Wisdom Groups on an ongoing basis. She has been actively supportive of a large singles program, facilitating groups for single parents and women in transition. She particularly enjoys witnessing the self-empowerment experienced by single parents and their families through psychotherapy.

She would love to hear your stories. You may contact her regarding her professional services, including her availability for conducting seminars and speaking engagements at:

Marnie Peterson, RN, LMFT
1756 Lacassie Avenue, Suite 200
Walnut Creek, CA 94596
(925) 933-8300

Diane Warner writes for magazines, newspapers, and web sites. She's also a professional speaker and has made hundreds of appearances on national television and radio, including stints on Discovery Channel, CNN, and Home & Garden TV. She lives with her husband in Tucson, Arizona and is the best-selling author of 21 books, including:

How to Have a Big Wedding on a Small Budget, 4th Edition
Big Wedding on a Small Budget Planner & Organizer
Beautiful Wedding Decorations & Gifts on a Small Budget
Picture-Perfect Worry Free Weddings
Best Wedding Ever
The Perfect Wedding Planner
Complete Book of Wedding Vows
Complete Book of Wedding Toasts
Complete Book of Wedding Showers
Complete Book of Baby Showers
Diane Warner's Wedding Question & Answer Book
Diane Warner's Big Book of Parties
Complete Book of Children's Parties

Diane Warner's Great Parties on Small Budgets
Puppets Help Teach
Puppet Scripts for Busy Teachers
The Unauthorized Teacher's Survival Guide, 2nd Edition*
The Inside Secrets of Finding a Teaching Job, 2nd Edition*
* Co-authored with Clyde Bryan and husband, Jack Warner

Visit Diane at her Web site, www.dianewarnerbooks.com, where you'll find free excerpts from her books, plus information about her availability for speaking engagements.

Dedication

We dedicate this book to our husbands: Paul Peterson and Jack Warner.

We appreciate all the love, patience, and support you've shown us through the years, but especially during the many months it took us to write this book.

Authors' Acknowledgments

A book like this doesn't come together without a lot of help. We wish we had room here to acknowledge each and every one of you.

We have many people to thank at John Wiley Publishing: Pam Mourouzis, Acquisitions Editor; Tonya Maddox Cupp, Project Editor; Mike Baker, Copy Editor; Jennifer Bingham, Copy Editor.

Special thanks to our agent, Jeffrey Herman, The Jeffrey Herman Agency, LLC. Without your help we wouldn't have been given the honor of writing this book.

A sincere thank you to Liz Hannigan, a true advocate of single parents, who has given up one evening a week for many years to facilitate the Single Parent Family Network. She has assisted us with surveys and opened the group so we could hear firsthand from so many single parents. We appreciate her support to the community and to us in the preparation of this book.

We want to acknowledge Cindy Elwell, founder of Divorce with Dignity, who answered our legal questions about divorce and child custody. She and her children graciously shared personal stories of their divorce recovery for this book.

We appreciate the help of the Women's Wisdom Group, who openly shared their intimate struggles and lovingly supported one another. Their courage and candor have inspired us.

Many clients' stories are woven into this book. Their names and scenarios have been changed to protect their privacy. Each and every client's experience has taught us something we needed to learn about life, love, and family relationships. Many of them took time to come in specifically to share for this Dummies book. Their time and support are greatly appreciated.

Our sons and daughters need to be acknowledged, too, because they have inspired us to reach out to other parents and kids. We are so proud of the fine grownups you have become, and also such fine parents, aunts, and uncles. You've made us proud, but humble, because we didn't get it all right as parents. Thank you Darren, Lynn, Bruce, and Marilee.

Publisher's Acknowledgments

We're proud of this book; please send us your comments through our Dummies online registration form located at www.dummies.com/register/.

Some of the people who helped bring this book to market include the following:

Acquisitions, Editorial, and Media Development

Project Editor: Tonya Maddox Cupp

Acquisitions Editor: Pamela Mourouzis

Copy Editor: Mike Baker, Jennifer Bingham

Acquisitions Coordinator:
Holly Gastineau Grimes

Technical Editors: Cliff Crain, MFT, Parenting Specialist at Center for Creative Living; Liz Hannigan, MA, CHT, Parenting Specialist at Center for Creative Living (925-829-4519)

Senior Permissions Editor: Carmen Krikorian

Editorial Manager: Jennifer Ehrlich

Editorial Assistant: Melissa Bennett

Cover Photos: PHX-Hagerstown

Cartoons: Rich Tennant, www.the5thwave.com

Production

Project Coordinator: Dale White

Layout and Graphics: Karl Brandt, Amanda Carter, Seth Conley, LeAndra Johnson, Stephanie D. Jumper, Tiffany Muth, Jeremey Unger

Proofreaders: Laura Albert, John Greenough, Angel Perez, Carl Pierce, TECHBOOKS Production Services

Indexer: TECHBOOKS Production Services

Publishing and Editorial for Consumer Dummies

Diane Graves Steele, Vice President and Publisher, Consumer Dummies

Joyce Pepple, Acquisitions Director, Consumer Dummies

Kristin A. Cocks, Product Development Director, Consumer Dummies

Michael Spring, Vice President and Publisher, Travel

Brice Gosnell, Publishing Director, Travel

Suzanne Jannetta, Editorial Director, Travel

Publishing for Technology Dummies

Andy Cummings, Vice President and Publisher, Dummies Technology/General User

Composition Services

Gerry Fahey, Vice President of Production Services

Debbie Stailey, Director of Composition Services

Contents at a Glance

Introduction *1*

Part 1: Surviving Your Change in Status *5*
Chapter 1: Winning the Single Parenthood Challenge 7
Chapter 2: Fitting a Onesy into a Twosy World 15
Chapter 3: Calling It Legalese Is Oxymoronic 33
Chapter 4: Crunching Time 53
Chapter 5: Crunching Numbers 71

Part 11: Keeping Close to Your Kids *99*
Chapter 6: Weighing in with Both Parents 101
Chapter 7: Talking Trucks and Tutus: Gender Issues 115
Chapter 8: Considering Your Kid's Point of View 135

Part 111: Challenging Your Maturity: Co-Parenting *165*
Chapter 9: Compromising: Knowing When to Fold 'Em 167
Chapter 10: Coexisting Peacefully with Other "Parents" ...199
Chapter 11: Keeping Cool When Resolving Co-Parenting Problems 209

Part 1V: Living Well Helps Your Kids Bloom, Too *225*
Chapter 12: You Don't Get Healin' without Grievin' 227
Chapter 13: Giving Yourself a Break Because You're Worth It 241
Chapter 14: Therapy Isn't Just for the Rich and Famous ...253

Part V: Finding Those Other Fish in the Sea *273*
Chapter 15: Dating Tips for the Middle-Aged Teen 275
Chapter 16: Blended Can Be Splendid 293

Part V1: The Part of Tens *309*
Chapter 17: Ten Questions Single Parents Most Frequently Ask 311
Chapter 18: Ten Great Resources for Single Parents 315

Index *319*

Table of Contents

Introduction 1

About This Book 1
Foolish Assumptions 2
How This Book Is Organized 2
    Part I: Surviving Your Change in Status 2
    Part II: Keeping Close to Your Kids 2
    Part III: Challenging Your Maturity: Co-Parenting 3
    Part IV: Living Well Helps Your Kids Bloom, Too 3
    Part V: Finding Those Other Fish in the Sea 3
    Part VI: The Part of Tens 3
Icons Used in This Book 4
Where to Go from Here 4

Part 1: Surviving Your Change in Status 5

Chapter 1: Winning the Single Parenthood Challenge 7

Taking a Look at Ten Challenges 7
    Adjusting to being a single parent 7
    Helping kids cope with trauma 8
    Becoming a strong person so you can be a strong parent 9
    Getting along with your ex 9
    Adopting a co-parenting plan 10
    Coping with legal issues 10
    Creating a single-parent budget 11
    Playing the "new and improved" dating game 11
    Facing remarriage and a blended family 12
    Knowing when you need professional help 12
Realizing You're Not the Only Single Parent in the World 13
Becoming Inspired by Real-Life Success Stories 13

Chapter 2: Fitting a Onesy into a Twosy World 15

Overcoming the Suddenly Single Syndrome 15
    Coping with divorce 16
    Coping with death 21
Being Single from the Start 23
    Voting for artificial insemination, in vitro, adoption,
        or natural conception 24
    Whoops 26

Kicking Up Your Single Heels 27
  Kicking the blues in the rump 27
  Kicking back with old chums 30
  Kicking around the possibility of new friends 31

Chapter 3: Calling It Legalese Is Oxymoronic **33**
Divvying Things Up After the Divorce 33
  Trusting your attorney 34
  Understanding all that itty-bitty fine print 36
  Calling a truce via a mediator 38
  Avoiding the judge's gavel 40
Wrestling for Your Rights 40
  Sharing the kids through custody 41
  Visiting the kids 42
  Adopting some legal problems 43
  Going down the test tubes 45
  Protecting your rights when dad's around 46
  Showing me the ali-money (and child support) 46
Adjusting Further: The Only Constant Is Change 48
  Changing status 49
  Changing income 49
  Changing employment 49
  Changing residence 50
  Changing health issues 51

Chapter 4: Crunching Time **53**
Simply Flying? Simplify 54
  Just saying "No" 55
  Prioritizing your responsibilities 56
  Getting the kids to pitch in 57
  Running hither and yon: Errands 59
  Dumping out your purse: Organizing 60
Doing Like Ringo Says and Accepting a Little Help 64
  Pools are cool — Car pools, that is 64
  Joining a babysitting co-op 66
  Whipping up a cooking club 66
Doing the Splits: Flexibility 67
  Negotiating with your employer 68
  Seeking alternative child care 69

Chapter 5: Crunching Numbers **71**
Avoiding the Five Biggest Single-Parent Money Mistakes 72
Doing the Math: Single Parent = Single Income 73
  Taking this job and shoving it 73
  Retraining for a better gig 74

Fudging a Budget Isn't Allowed 74
Living Comfortably on Less 79
    Nesting sensibly: Home sweet home 79
    That's my deductible?! 82
    Sending the kids off to grandma's 83
    Wheeling and dealing 85
    Cutting down on medical and dental expenses 86
    Cooking yummy vittles on a small budget 86
    Filling your leisure time for pennies a day 89
    Getting cheap goodies 90
    Bartering for stuff 92
Knowing When to Seek Help 92
    Taking advantage of government assistance 93
    Collecting child support 94
    Accepting help from a credit counselor 96
    Applying a financial advisor's advice 96

Part II: Keeping Close to Your Kids *99*

Chapter 6: Weighing in with Both Parents 101
Dealing with Ages and Stages 101
    Parenting by the numbers 102
    Staging a parenting exhibition 105
You Want What on Your Sandwich? Coping with Kids' Quirks 107
    Opening your ears 107
    Encouraging positive talk 109
Adjusting Your Schedule 110
Making Your Time Together Fun 112

Chapter 7: Talking Trucks and Tutus: Gender Issues 115
Digging On Dads 115
Marveling at Moms 116
Mothers and Sons, Dads and Daughters 117
    Single dad raising his 118
    Single mom raising her 121
    Talking about sex, no matter the gender 123
Avoiding Stereotypical Behavior 124
    Macho, macho man 124
    Saving yourself from the castle: Women 125
    Having sole — Custody, that is: Dads 126
    Throwing off your cape: The super mom myth 127
Fouling up: Avoiding the Biggest Mistakes 128
    Living vicariously through your kids: Dads 129
    Babying your children: Moms 130

Avoiding the warm, fuzzy stuff 130
Striving to become your teen's best buddy 131
Feeling guilty when you're working 131
Expecting your child to make your life better 131
Providing Role Models 132
Female 132
Male 133

Chapter 8: Considering Your Kid's Point of View **135**

Loving Them Up So They Feel Safe 136
Birth to age 2 136
Ages 2 to 5 137
Ages 6 to 12 139
Teenagers 140
Rebuilding physical security 142
Rebuilding emotional security 143
Divorcing your spouse, not your kids 149
Showing an Appetite: Craving Attention 150
Feeling deprived 150
Needing more of your time 151
Longing for time alone with you 151
Throwing a Fit About the Split? 152
What's a divorce? 153
Why can't you still be married? 154
Why do you hate Daddy/Mommy? 154
I'm to blame, huh? 154
Why did you divorce Daddy/Mommy anyway?
He/she didn't do anything wrong 155
Are you going to stop loving me, too? 156
What's going to happen to me now? 156
Can I go live with Daddy/Mommy? 157
Why do you cry all the time? Do I make you cry? 157
Wanting to Talk About Stuff 157
Feeling put upon 158
Feeling confused about the details 160
Calling for Help: Needing Professional Counseling 161

Part III: Challenging Your Maturity: Co-Parenting 165

Chapter 9: Compromising: Knowing When to Fold 'Em **167**

Avoiding a Leaning Tower of Co-Parenting: Designing a Sound Plan ...168
Putting pen to paper: What to include 169
Sampling a plan 172
Putting the Plan to Work 172
Agreeing on workable schedules 172
Maintaining continuity 174

Parents 1, Kids 0: Presenting a united front 178
Getting involved in your kids' activities 181
What's your take on discipline? 181
Creating new family traditions 187
Avoiding the Biggest Mistakes Made by Single Parents 190
Heaping more onto their plates 191
Encouraging your kids to be private detectives 191
Labeling your kids 191
Denying yourself a social life 192
Allowing your kids' traits to ring your bell 192
Expecting your children to deliver messages to your ex 192
Getting sucked into power plays 193
Being a poor role model 193
Allowing your kids to con you 194
Failing to establish boundaries 194
Pushing your ex's buttons 194
Refusing to consider professional therapy 195
Considering Your Kids' Bill of Rights 196

Chapter 10: Coexisting Peacefully with Other "Parents" **199**
Agreeing to See Grandparents 201
Grandma and Grandpa can help 201
Grandma and Grandpa's legal rights 203
Being Civil to Stepparents 203
Seeing the Good in Godparents 204
Setting Guidelines for Family Visits 205

**Chapter 11: Keeping Cool When Resolving
Co-Parenting Problems** **209**
Easing Transition Anxiety 210
Taking That Hex off Your Ex 212
Forgiving 213
Negotiating 214
Dealing with Co-parenting Problems 216
Resolving super-serious kid problems 217
Seeking help when your ex is causing trouble 218
Looking for co-parenting help in all the right places 222

Part 1U: Living Well Helps Your Kids Bloom, Too **225**

Chapter 12: You Don't Get Healin' without Grievin' **227**
Grieving with Grace: Good Luck! 228
Scaling Grief's Stages 229
Relating the stages to death 230
Relating the stages to divorce 232

Forgiving Yourself 235
Letting Go of Anger and Jealousy 237
    Puttin' out the fire 237
    Washin' that ex right outta your hair 237
Grieving at Three Feet Tall 238

Chapter 13: Giving Yourself a Break Because You're Worth It **241**

Cheering Yourself On 242
Putting Your Feet Up 243
Staying Fit and Frisky 246
    Weighing in on health 246
    Getting off your rump 248
Acting Like a Kid 248
Getting a Fuzzy Buddy: Pets 249
Giving Yourself Some Goodies 250
    Stocking up on yummy foods 250
    Buying a few new threads 250
    Going in for that makeover 251
    Adults only: Dinner and a movie 251
    Taking a daytrip 252

Chapter 14: Therapy Isn't Just for the Rich and Famous **253**

Facing Facts: You May Need Help 254
    Recognizing signs of depression 254
    Recognizing signs of anxiety disorders 256
    Transitioning: How well are you doing? 258
    Recognizing subtle hints from friends and family 258
Benefiting from Professional Therapy 260
    Three FAQs about therapy 262
    Picking from a smorgasbord of therapists 263
    Dealing with mental health insurance can drive you crazy 265
    Considering your options 265
    Evaluating the therapist 266
Jockeying for Support 267
    Joining a group 268
    Participating in family therapy 270

Part V: Finding Those Other Fish in the Sea **273**

Chapter 15: Dating Tips for the Middle-Aged Teen **275**

Looking at the Big Picture Before You Leap into Dating 276
    Viewing it from an adult's perspective 276
    Viewing it from a kid's perspective 279

Analyzing Your Expectations 281
   Searching for someone to marry 281
   Dating for the fun of it 281
   Looking for love in all the right places 282
Mustering Up Some Trust 285
Looking Your Fear Smack Dab in the Face 286
   Where would you like to go? 286
   Five outfits tried on and counting 287
   But enough about me 289
Cramming a Date Into Your Hectic Schedule 290
Scraping Up Enough Bucks to Date 290

Chapter 16: Blended Can Be Splendid **293**
Avoiding the Big R: Marrying on the Rebound 294
Considering a Prenuptial Agreement 295
Facing Blended-Family Struggles 298
   Bonding with stepchildren 299
   Battling stepsiblings 300
   Playing the name game 302
   Disliking a new stepchild 302
   Disagreeing on discipline policies 303
   Clashing about the cash 303
   Dealing with all the relatives 304
   Longing for privacy 304
   Misfiring on all cylinders 304
   Tripping over baggage 305
Following the Ten Stepparent Commandments 307

Part VI: The Part of Tens *309*

**Chapter 17: Ten Questions Single Parents
Most Frequently Ask** **311**
How Can I Adjust? 311
How Can I Heal? 312
How Can I Make Fair Child-Support and Alimony Payments? 312
How Can I Receive Fair Child-Support and Alimony Payments? 312
How Can I Make It on My Budget? 313
How Can We Develop a Co-parenting Plan That Works? 313
Where Can I Find a Single-Parent Support Group? 313
Where Can I Find Counseling for My Kids and Myself? 314
How Do I Get Back into the Dating Game? 314
What Factors Should I Consider Before Remarriage? 314

Chapter 18: Ten Great Resources for Single Parents 315

American Academy of Child and Adolescent Psychiatry (AACAP) 315
American Association for Marriage and Family Therapy 316
Big Brothers Big Sisters of America 316
National Center for Missing and Exploited Children 316
National Council for Adoption (NCFA) 317
National Organization of Single Mothers 317
Parents Without Partners 317
RESOLVE 318
Single Mothers by Choice 318
Stepfamily Association of America (SAA) 318

Index *319*

Introduction

*W*elcome to *Single Parenting For Dummies.* We've written this book especially for people who realize that you, as single parents, are a breed unto yourselves. General parenting books are fine, but what you need is an encouraging, user-friendly, practical book that deals with the special problems you're facing as a single parent. The 2000 census informed us that about ten million of you single parents are in the United States alone, and we think you could use a little help from friends.

Yes, we discovered a lot about you from the recent census, but we also know that when it comes to single parenting, things are a-changin'. No longer is an antiquated stigma attached to having a baby out of wedlock. In fact, the term illegitimate no longer applies to babies, for how can a precious gift of life, a human soul, be illegitimate? No matter how you came to be a single parent, you're finding that it's now totally acceptable, even admirable to be a single mom or a single dad. It's how you parent your child that counts, not how you came to be a single parent.

Our vision for this book is to give you a leg up on this single parenting thing, and in the process, we hope you come to think of us as your friends. Not that we have all the answers, because raising happy, healthy, well-adjusted kids is an art, not a science, but we sincerely care about you and the challenges you're facing, and we hope this comes across in this book.

You may be interested to know something about our experiences with parenthood, by the way; Marnie was a single parent, before remarrying and experiencing a blended family that includes her son and daughter and her new husband's son and daughter. Diane has been married only once and also has a son and daughter, but she was raised by a single mother, which gave her the opportunity to observe single parenthood from a child's point of view. We two *dummies* want to help you survive and thrive on a day to day, nitty-gritty basis, and to celebrate the fine, noble art of being a single parent.

About This Book

In typical Dummies style, we've arranged this book in small, digestible chunks addressing specific problems you may be having at the moment. This way you don't need to read the book cover-to-cover to find the help you need, but you can go straight to the heart of your problem and resolve it. That's not to say you can't enjoy and profit from reading the entire book, but we know that you — as a single parent especially — only have small snatches of time available in your busy schedule.

Foolish Assumptions

Because you've purchased this book, we're making these five assumptions:

- ✔ You are a single parent or someone you know is a single parent
- ✔ You want to be the best single parent you can be.
- ✔ You need encouragement.
- ✔ You have many general questions and problems.
- ✔ You have a few specific problems that need solutions immediately.

How This Book Is Organized

This book has 6 major parts and 18 chapters. Inside each chapter the contents are arranged in blocks of information. You can scan through a chapter until you come to a block that interests you, read that, and continue on until you come to another helpful block of advice. By the way, as you look through this book, you can enjoy the encouraging single parent success stories included in side-bars along the way. These stories are marked with the Anecdote icon.

Part I: Surviving Your Change in Status

This first part covers the five basic challenges you face as a single parent. You have a lot of stuff to handle, some of it you expected, some you did not.

Part II: Keeping Close to Your Kids

Here in Part II we come to the heart of this book: how to become the best single parent you can possibly be. We've interviewed hundreds of you, and we know from our research, training, and experience that this is what your heart longs for — above all other issues you may be facing at the moment.

Part III: Challenging Your Maturity: Co-Parenting

Here we come to the sticky part — letting others share the parenting responsibilities. How's your relationship with your ex? Is your ex a help or a hindrance? Can you resolve your differences for the sake of your child?

Part IV: Living Well Helps Your Kids Bloom, Too

Oh — so that's how it works? Do we mean to say that you're really a better, stronger parent after you get your own stuff together? Yes, that's exactly what we're saying.

Part V: Finding Those Other Fish in the Sea

If the idea of dating again scares you to death, especially as a single parent, you're not alone. Are you looking for a little once-in-a-while fun, or a long-lasting relationship? You may reach a stage where you're thinking about wedding vows and happily-ever-afters. And how about a blended family?

Part VI: The Part of Tens

This part offers two lists:

- ✔ Ten Questions Most Frequently Asked by Single Parents
- ✔ Ten Great Resources for Single Parents

You may dog-ear this section because you'll be referring to it often!

Icons Used in This Book

Icons bring things to your attention.

Whenever you see this icon, you find a little inside scoop on solving your problem.

This icon pops up to remind you of something important we don't want you to forget.

Why fall into the pit if you don't have to? Heed our warnings and you avoid trouble from the get-go.

This icon tips you off to the anecdotes that tell you how a single mom or dad succeeded and flourished.

Where to Go from Here

Read and enjoy this book and apply the practical, encouraging solutions to your own unique situations. It's our hope and greatest wish that you not only become a better parent, but a better person, because you applied the principles offered in this book. We challenge you to take the plunge — go for it! We're rooting for you!

If you're

- A father worried about how to talk to his daughter (or a mother talking to her son) about sex, jump to Chapter 7.
- Down to your last penny, see Chapter 5.
- Looking for love in all the wrong places, swim over to Chapter 15.
- Fighting for custody of your children, see Chapter 3.
- Feeling depressed and unable to overcome your grief, take a look at Chapter 12.
- Having trouble blending together after remarriage, see Chapter 16.
- Looking for helpful single parenting resources, look in Chapter 18.
- Wondering how to make this work with various and sundry other parents (your ex and his new wife, for instance), check out Part III.

Part I
Surviving Your Change in Status

"Normally, things don't get me down. But lately, just getting out of bed has been difficult."

In this part . . .

You're a single parent now and your life has changed. Change brings stress and stress brings struggle, and in this Part you find out how to survive some of the biggest struggles single parents face. These chapters offer guidelines, suggestions, and tips that will help you fit in as a onesy in this crazy joined-at-the-hip world of twosys, solve and understand your legal problems, and save time and money, so that you have some left over to spend on yourself and your kids.

Chapter 1

Winning the Single Parenthood Challenge

In This Chapter

▶ Discovering the main challenges single parents face

▶ Knowing you're not alone

▶ Getting inspiration from other single parents

*T*he single parenthood challenge is one you can rise to by adopting a survivalist attitude and implementing a few of the suggestions included in this book.

Taking a Look at Ten Challenges

As we researched for this book, we interviewed many single parents, asking them to rank their challenges according to their importance in their lives. Of course, each of you is fighting your own battle and the biggest challenge in your life may be completely different from your neighbor's, but here are the ten greatest challenges generally faced by single parents.

Adjusting to being a single parent

You, as single parents, are a lot like ice cream — you come in lots of flavors. The first flavor is "Cherries Jubilee," and it's for those of you who are ecstatic to be free of the ex. You're on such a high, in fact, your hearts are practically giddy with joy! Next is "Rocky Road," the perfect flavor for some of you who didn't sail through your divorce with quite as much ease, and your hearts are still heavy with hurts, guilt, and a sense of confusion. Of course, if your spouse died, you not only became an instant single in a world of couples, but you found that it's not easy to recover your emotional balance. You could use a scoop or two of "Heartbreak Healer."

Or, maybe you were just a little careless and became pregnant by accident. The relationship was on its way to no-wheres-ville, but you decided to have the baby and give him the best life a single parent can. You might find yourself in a "Pink Bubblegum" kind of mood.

Finally, we come to all of you overjoyed singles out there who became parents quite deliberately, either through adoption, artificial insemination, or "with just a little help from a friend." You fall into that rare category of singles who want to be parents, but aren't that crazy about having a significant other hanging around the house. We know a lot of you who fall into this category, and you're adjusting to single parenthood extremely well. We admire you for your "S'More Spirit."

So, whether you became a single parent by accident or on purpose, our goal is to help you be as happy, well-adjusted, and satisfied as you can possibly be with your single-parent status. Sure, you hit obstacles — maybe, you're feeling a little blue now and then, or maybe your old friends don't seem to fit into your life right now, especially all those happy couples with their weekend plans. But new friends and lots of happy times are in your future.

You can find encouraging tips throughout this book, especially in Chapter 2 where you find out how a onesy can adjust in a twosy world.

Helping kids cope with trauma

Regardless of how you happened to become a single parent, you want close relationships with your kids. In fact, we venture to say that's probably one of the reasons why you bought this book. We know you — we've talked to so many of you — and we see how you're striving to help your kids get back to normal. Your kids' lives may be recovering from a "train wreck" at the moment, as they deal with the death of a parent or the trauma of your divorce, but they're resilient characters, and they bounce back because you're there for them. You find gobs of help in Parts II and III of this book.

We admire you greatly for the love and concern you have for your children. As a matter of fact — we salute you!

Becoming a strong person so you can be a strong parent

It takes a while for most single parents to figure out that you can't be the parent you really want to be until you're strong, healthy, and fit yourself. By that, we mean mentally strong, emotionally healthy, and physically fit — it takes all three.

Did you know that you're a very special person? Oh yes, being a single parent is pretty special, too. But you're also a unique, one-of-a-kind individual; if you give all your energy to your kids, you won't have any left to nurture your inner self.

So, pump yourself up and give yourself a pat on the back! And how about a little grin — at least once in a while? Don't you know that a sense of humor is the oil that keeps that engine of yours running? It doesn't hurt to spruce up the bod a little either, you know, with a few new threads, or a makeover. Treat yourself to a few of your favorite things; food, entertainment, travel, or something totally indulgent — like a full-body massage and dinner at the Four Seasons. You don't have to spend the big bucks either. You can come up with dozens of ways to lift your spirits that don't cost a dime. How about a walk in the park or a day at the beach? Or, you can call a friend to go work out or take that day hike you've been thinking about all winter. Check out Chapter 13 to find great ways to give yourself the break you deserve.

It may be difficult for you to do something for yourself instead of something for your kids — so take the challenge. You'll be a better parent for it.

Getting along with your ex

Here's a big issue — getting along with your ex. In our experience, we find that most single parents fall into one of these four categories:

- ✔ You and your ex are pretty good friends with few obstacles in your path.

- ✔ You and your ex get along okay. You're not exactly doing handstands over the relationship, but at least you've worked things out, if only for the kids' sake.

- ✔ You and your ex aren't on the best terms — a lot of issues still need to be overcome, such as jealousy, bitterness, or just plain old-fashioned anger. There's so much to be angry about — money stuff, sticky legal wranglings, or the whole child custody–child support issue. If this is going on with you and your ex, the relationship needs a little help over the rough spots, and we're here to lead the way.

✔ You and your ex are not talking at all or talk only through lawyers. If this is your situation, maybe you can change to help the children, but sometimes these relationships never get better. You benefit from seeking out professional support for you and your children.

You can find help on legal issues in Chapter 3 and ways to solve the co-parenting challenge in Part III of this book.

Adopting a co-parenting plan

Here we arrive at the single-parent buzz-word-of-the-month: *Co-parenting*. What is co-parenting? Why is it important? How does it work? If we were to describe successful co-parenting, here's what we'd say:

"Co-parenting is sharing parenting responsibilities and keeping your child's best interests in mind." In other words, work out an arrangement that's in the best interest of your kids (where have we heard that phrase before?), yet workable within your schedules. A co-parenting plan involves agreeing on a discipline plan, presenting a united front, and involving your kids in joint activities, such as family sports, school functions, or church get-togethers. Make smooth, seamless continuity within your children's lives one of your main goals.

It's not that "the family that plays together stays together," or anything as pie-in-the-sky as that, it's just that — and here it comes again — *for the sake of the children,* give co-parenting a chance.

We've devoted an entire section of this book to the co-parenting issue, so check out Part III for help with sharing parenting responsibilities, discipline, and resolving some of the problems that crop up — you know, all those pesky things, like getting along with your ex and creating a buffer zone, if necessary.

Coping with legal issues

No other segment of society faces as many legal issues as single parents do. If you've adopted a child or conceived via artificial insemination, you've already signed enough legal documents to paper your living room. The biggest culprit of all, however, is the divorce issue, resulting in reams of stuff to be debated, agreed upon, and eventually, signed. We cover everything from the alimony and child support payments to the child custody issue to who-gets-what-and-who-pays-what-bills. Our hearts go out to you, believe us. Our goal is to guide you through this legal maze, and we offer a few practical shortcuts.

We've devoted an entire chapter to the legal stuff. Check out Chapter 3 for help with such things as alimony payments and custody rights, plus all that itty-bitty fine print!

Creating a single-parent budget

As if you don't have enough going on in your lives already, the money crunch is also a big issue. Naturally, you want to provide a quality standard of living for you and your kids, but it can be a difficult challenge, especially for those of you who have gone from a two-parent to a single-parent income. So, is there such a thing as a single-parent budget that works? Yes, there is, and it's our pleasure to pass along a few helpful tips.

For starters, you may decide now is the time to earn more money by making a career change or, possibly, retraining for a better gig. Or, you can increase the amount of your disposable monthly income by:

- ✔ Eliminating or restructuring your debts.
- ✔ Collecting delinquent child support payments.
- ✔ Spending less on everything including child care, housing, meals, and transportation.

Right now you need to get the money monkey off your back, and when you do, you can relax in the freedom that comes from living within your means and having a little jingle left in your jeans at the end of each month. We have a cage for your monkey — you find it in Chapter 5!

Playing the "new and improved" dating game

If the idea of dating again scares you to death, you're not alone. It helps to take your fears, lay them on the table, and take a good look at them. What are they, and are they really as scary as they seem? Maybe it's easier than you think to jump back into this thing called the *dating game*.

Some of you only want to date for the fun of it, but many of you are seriously looking for a long-term relationship, or someone to marry. In either case, the big question is how to find someone to date. Someone with similar values. Someone with compatible interests. Look around — it's mostly a matter of following your heart and getting involved in activities that are *fun* for you. That way you can meet others with similar interests.

Time and money are also major issues. A single parent doesn't exactly have cookie jars filled with fifty-dollar bills. And how the heck do you cram a date into your hectic schedule? Finally, if you do find someone special, someone you care about, can you ever trust again? Fortunately, other single parents have hacked through this jungle before you and left a safe path for you to tread. They've even left a few helpful road signs for you to follow along the way. Take a peek in Chapter 15 for insight on the new and improved dating game.

Facing remarriage and a blended family

If you're thinking about getting married again, perhaps to someone who's also a single parent, you need to be aware of the pitfalls. Remarriage can be wonderful if you're doing it for the right reasons, but don't remarry because you're on the rebound. And whatever you do, don't remarry for the children's sake.

You make a lot of sacrifices for the *sake of the children,* but remarriage should never be one of them.

So, what should you know before taking this big step? Well, to begin with you need to understand why women are slow to take the plunge, while men often remarry within eighteen months. You also need to listen to the experts — their advice is invaluable. At the very least, get a little premarital counseling beforehand.

Blending together as a family is a little tricky, too, but forewarned is forearmed, and you can find out a lot from other single parents who've remarried and done a beautiful job melding their families together. Remarriage is a huge issue — so we've devoted an entire chapter to this topic. Check out Chapter 16.

Knowing when you need professional help

If you fall off the back porch and break your arm, you know you need to get to the emergency room or at least see your doctor pronto. It's a no-brainer — not only are you in pain, but you'll never wear a long-sleeved shirt again with that bone jutting through the skin!

On the other hand, it's not quite as easy to know when you need professional counseling. Fortunately, we list ten warning signs in Chapter 14 that may help you recognize when you need a little help. What a blessing to live in a country where trained professionals are available with compassionate advice and support when you need it. You can receive this kind of help in a number of different ways: one-on-one counseling, through support groups, or family therapy programs.

Realizing You're Not the Only Single Parent in the World

The recent census told us a lot about single heads-of-household, and the statistics should be encouraging because they prove that you're not the lone ranger — you're in good company. Here are a few interesting statistics that came out of the census:

- ✔ Almost 10 million households are headed by a single parent, which is 9 percent of all U.S. households, up from 8 percent in 1990.
- ✔ Single fathers head up 2.2 million households, which is 1 household in every 45.
- ✔ Single mothers head up a little over 7.5 million households, which is 7 percent of all households in the country, up from 5 percent 30 years ago.
- ✔ Single father households rose by 62 percent from 1990 to 2000. In fact, single father homes rose from 1,254,540 in 1990 to 2,190,989 in 2000. Wow! No wonder we're seeing so many of you single fathers around town!

Do you get the picture? You're definitely not alone — not with 10 million of you out there, all facing similar challenges. So, take heart! There's hope for you!

Becoming Inspired by Real-Life Success Stories

What's more inspiring than a true story of someone who has solved a problem? Other single parents have been there and done that, and are eager to share their success stories with you. You can find these stories sprinkled throughout this book.

They're on your side and so are we! What a privilege to write a book like this one — practical, encouraging, and filled with the latest ways for you to conquer the single-parenting challenges in your lives.

Chapter 2

Fitting a Onesy into a Twosy World

· ·

In This Chapter

▶ Dealing with being unexpectedly single

▶ Adjusting to becoming a single parent by choice

▶ Finding the fun in singleness

· ·

*H*ow does it feel to be a onesy in a twosy world? Twosies are everywhere you look: A romantic carriage ride seats two, a spin on the Ferris wheel seats two, and when was the last time the maitre'd asked, "Table for one?" Yes, this onesy thing can be uncomfortable at times.

If you became a single parent intentionally, you may be adjusting pretty well to your onesy life. However, if you became a suddenly single parent due to death or divorce or by accident, you may be having a little more trouble making the transition. Regardless of how you became a single parent, you're probably still adjusting to your new status. Well, you've come to the right place. In this chapter, we cover all these situations and help make your transition into single parenthood a bit easier. Whether you became a single parent through death, divorce, or accidental or planned parenthood, you find ways to cope by chasing away the blues, restoring your self-esteem, making new friends, and putting a little fun back into your life.

Overcoming the Suddenly Single Syndrome

Losing your partner through death or divorce is an unthinkable event! In fact, these two losses are at the top of the list of life stressors. Although death is the more painful and final form of loss, divorce can feel like death, too. After all, a divorce *is* the death of your marriage. Your life will never be the same again, but you *will* get through it because you have no choice; your children need you more than ever. Try to get by one day at a time. If you suddenly lost your spouse because of an unforeseen divorce or a tragic accident, you may even have to get by one *hour* at a time!

Escaping codependency

Kim's husband had such a serious drinking problem that it led to physical abuse. She sucked it up for years, becoming more and more *codependent* (a condition in which a person supports, either overtly or inadvertently, the addictive behavior of another). Finally, she couldn't take it anymore. Her friends had been urging her to attend a 12-step Al-Anon program (a support program for those living with an addictive person) where she could get some support and, hopefully, break away from the codependency. She agreed to attend this program and eventually made the painful decision to end her marriage — one of the most difficult decisions a codependent spouse can make.

After Kim made this decision, her greatest heartbreak was realizing that her four-year-old daughter, Alice, wouldn't have the stable, secure, traditional childhood she had always wanted her to have. So, Kim determined that she would provide the most safe, secure, loving, single-parent home she possibly could for her daughter, but her plan came with a hitch: With only one income now instead of two, Kim could no longer afford to live in the family home where Alice had lived all her life. (You can read more about money in Chapter 5.)

Although Kim had an excellent education and a decent job, she decided that she and Alice needed the support of living closer to her parents. Selling her home in New Jersey and moving back to New Hampshire proved to be a huge undertaking, and although housing costs were lower in New Hampshire, finding a comparable job and purchasing a home wasn't any easier. In spite of the job situation, Kim was determined to find a new job that would qualify her for a home loan. She found a job that wasn't perfect, but she felt she could always look for something better later on. Her main goal was to get Alice and herself settled and secure in a home of their own.

Kim decided on a condo for several reasons: It was in a gated community, she would have close neighbors and feel safe, no yard work or exterior maintenance was required, and a swimming pool and exercise room were big pluses. Although she vowed not to ask her parents for financial help, she was grateful when her father offered to cosign the mortgage papers.

As Kim looked back on her life a year later, she was amazed that she managed to make a major move, find a new job, and buy a home. She stuck with the 12-step program where she continued to receive support and made some good friends. Meanwhile, Alice was adjusting well — her dad phoned her on a regular basis, and she loved spending time with her grandparents, aunts, uncles, and cousins.

Kim realized that breaking loose from her codependency and being on her own not only gave her a sense of freedom, but it also made her feel worthwhile — more "grown up" than she had ever felt in her life. Hurray for Kim and Alice!

Coping with divorce

Some divorces have been a long time coming and aren't much of a shock to the couple by the time they actually decide to split. Other divorces are more traumatic because they happen suddenly. You don't wake up one morning and suddenly say to your spouse, "Hey, let's get a divorce today," but you've probably been ignoring the warning signs so that the actual decision comes as a blow. In either case, adjusting to the aftermath isn't easy, especially if separation anxiety sets in.

A divorce is painful and emotional. Anger is often present and most couples find it difficult to let go of their past, forgive each other, and move on with their lives. A divorce is a loss that causes genuine grief — the same kind of grief you feel if someone close to you dies.

As you struggle to cope with your new status as a divorced person (more about this topic in *Divorce For Dummies* by John Ventura and Mary Reed published by Wiley Publishing, Inc.), you also struggle to cope as a divorced parent because divorce turns your children's world upside down. You see the shock and loss on their faces, which calls you to action. You *must* put them first at this time in their lives — they need your love, support, and assurance now more than ever.

Here are ways to comfort and assure your children:

- ✔ **Hug them, tell them you love them, and explain that their other parent loves them and always will.** Situations involving the other parent can be a bit tricky though. Reassuring the kids is important, but guard against lying or distorting the truth. Certainly you should tell them that the other parent loves them if the statement is outwardly apparent; otherwise, you may want to make your reassurance more accurate. You can say something like the other parent loves them in his or her own way.

- ✔ **When your children ask questions about your divorce, try to answer their questions as honestly as you can, without getting too down and dirty or too specific.** For example, when they want to know when you two will get back together, explain that it isn't going to happen. Never give your children false hope that reconciliation may occur. However, assure them that you and your ex are *both* still their parents and that they'll never have to choose between you.

- ✔ **Explain to them that they didn't cause the divorce — it wasn't their fault.**

- ✔ **Explain to them that nothing they can do or say will put the marriage back together.** They didn't cause the divorce, so they can't undo it.

- ✔ **Tell them that you don't expect them to change — you want them to stay just the way they are.**

- ✔ **Assure them that you're there to take care of *them;* you don't expect them to take care of *you,* no matter how down or moody you may seem at times.**

✓ **Apologize to them for not being as good a listener as you should have been, especially when the divorce was fresh and new and you were trying desperately to adjust.** Assure them that you'll try to be more available to them every day from now on.

✓ **Try to maintain continuity in their lives by nurturing the same friendships; attending the same church, day care, and school; and following the same routine as always.**

SingleMOTHER is an organization with local chapters that's very supportive of divorced, widowed, and never-married single mothers. Check out Chapter 18 for contact info and more sources of support for single mothers and fathers.

The *dumper* (the spouse who initiates the divorce) suffers just as much guilt as the *dumpee* (the spouse who gets dumped). This guilt can drive the dumper to shortchange himself when it comes to the divorce settlement — he's willing to settle for less than he deserves, not only in terms of the couple's assets but also in terms of custody or visitation rights. Don't relinquish your rights out of guilt! Many adults in the United States have been divorced once or twice, at least. So don't feel like you're some kind of bizarre mutation — you're in good company!

A divorce raises many questions:

✓ What's wrong with me? Could I have made the marriage work if I'd tried just a little harder?

✓ Should we have tried a marriage counselor or just one more marriage counselor?

✓ Should I have just sucked it up and stuck it out for the kids' sake?

✓ Why do I feel like such a failure?

✓ What do I tell the children?

✓ How do I deal with the anger?

✓ Will I ever feel like a normal, happy person again?

Here are a few positive things for you to think about when you ask yourself these types of questions and as you consider how the difficult aspects of divorce wear on you and the kids:

✓ **Tell the guilt to go!** There's nothing wrong with you. You tried as hard as you could to hold the marriage together, so don't blame yourself. Cut yourself a little slack. Make lists of your past achievements and your good qualities as a person, and treat yourself to something fun once in a while.

How about a day at the spa? Or a shopping trip? Or lunch with a friend at your favorite restaurant? You're special, and you deserve to be happy.

✔ **Remind yourself that being part of a marriage in which you have to suck it up for the kids' sake is no way to live.** You deserve better, and so do your children.

✔ **Grab your kids and get involved in something physical.** How about an impromptu softball game with their friends in the park? Tennis lessons for all of you? A day at your local water park? A charity walk-a-thon? The important thing is to get out of the house and move your bod around a bit — it's been slumping in that recliner long enough.

✔ **Gather up all the photos of your ex and put them out of sight, except any photos your kids would like to display in their rooms.** In fact, hide any mementos that remind you of your ex — this clean sweep will help finalize your emotional divorce, which is different from your legal divorce. When you finalize your emotional divorce, you're on your way to a healthy, happy new life.

✔ **Don't let any negative feelings you have toward your ex poison your kids' feelings toward their other parent.** Even though you may be harboring feelings of anger or bitterness toward your ex, don't badmouth him or her in front of your children. Whenever you criticize your ex, you're attacking your child's genes. If you're having trouble resolving your pain and resentment, check out Chapter 11 where you can find healthy solutions to the co-parenting challenge.

✔ **Please, please stop wearing your wedding ring.** That band of gold on your finger has been a symbol of eternal love, and although that love is long gone, you may not be able to take it off. There are many logical reasons for this state of affairs:

- The ring feels comfortable, and you would feel naked without it.

- Wearing a wedding ring makes you feel protected from unwanted suitors. (Ready for a suitor? Jump to Chapter 15.)

- Your ring is a sentimental object that reminds you of happier times.

- Your ring has a three-carat diamond, and nobody else is going to get his or her hands on it!

- Deep down in your heart, you may be holding out hope that you and your ex will still get back together, and the physical act of removing your ring seems so final.

Whatever your reason for holding onto your ring, we want to encourage you to remove it because doing so helps you heal and look to your future. So why not slip that ring back into its box? Why not be proactive and save yourself emotional turmoil?

By the way, you can always cash in that rock for a nice chunk of change or place it in a marvelous dinner-ring setting. It's your call.

✔ **Don't sleep with your ex.** If you do, you'll just create more emotional ties that need to be untied later on. A night of passion isn't worth the emotional pain that will come from it.

Your anger may be justified, but try to let it go in healthy ways, or it can make you sick. You may be angry with your ex, or you may be angry with yourself for putting up with the lies or infidelities for so many years. In either case, here are some ways to get rid of your anger:

✔ **Talk about it:** Tell your friends and family members how angry you are, and include your children. By letting your kids know you're angry, you give them permission to express their anger. This is good because it helps normalize their feelings and realize they're not alone.

✔ **Meet with a professional therapist:** Just a few sessions may be all you need. Tell the therapist how you feel.

✔ **Join a divorce support group:** Tell the group how angry you feel, and listen to their stories. You'll soon realize that you're not alone. (Chapter 18 has a bunch of single-parent resources.)

✔ **Do the exercise thing:** Physical exercise can be a marvelous release, so take your anger out on a volleyball or a golf ball or go for a run. The rhythmic pounding of your feet releases anger in a wonderful, healthy way.

✔ **Write about your anger:** Put together a journal, a diary, or a letter addressed to your ex. Tell your ex how mad you are, how unfairly you were treated, and how angry you felt when you were lied to, insulted, or abused. Write down everything you're feeling — don't hold anything back. When you reread what you've written, you may be surprised to see hidden emotions you didn't even realize you were harboring. Finally, when you've got all that anger on paper, build a nice little ritual fire in your fireplace and burn that stuff up. The act of physically destroying your anger can bring a powerful sense of closure that will help you heal.

✔ **Reassess how you're healing:** This step may be particularly necessary if you lost your spouse more than a year ago and you're still feeling hurt and angry on a daily basis. Could your anger actually be a symptom of depression? Do you long to feel light and easy again? Everyone has a different timeframe, but you may need a little professional therapy to help you over this rough spot, or maybe a much-needed vacation would help. But, wherever you are in your healing process, don't make the mistake of stuffing your feelings.

Here's a great word of advice from Liz, a facilitator of a single-parent support group in the San Francisco Bay area: "The best revenge is to go on and have a happy life!" We dare you! Don't let the past hold you back.

Coping with death

If your spouse has died, we know you're carrying a heavy load right now. Some of the following may sound familiar:

✔ You may be in shock and not functioning normally.

✔ You feel responsible for your children. How do you explain death to a child? How can you comfort your children when you're barely hanging on yourself?

✔ You feel drained and don't have the energy to carry on with your daily routine.

✔ You don't know what to say to friends and family members who call or drop by.

✔ You can't stop watching for your spouse to come walking through the front door, just like always.

✔ Your future seems bleak. How will you cope as a single parent? How can you fit in as a single parent when you're used to being married?

If you've lost your spouse because of death or divorce and you're having trouble with the grieving process, take a look at Chapter 12.

Everyone has *expert* advice for you, but just let it float on by. Friends and family members think that they have the answers, but they don't always know what's best for you. They mean well, so listen to them, but filter their advice through your own common sense.

It takes time and a lot of tears to heal and to be able to think straight after you've lost your spouse. Meanwhile, here are a few things you can do:

✔ **Accept invitations to lunch or dinner:** Even though you may not feel like getting dressed and leaving the house, you need social contact. Accepting a little support from your friends and family members doesn't hurt.

✔ **Be creative:** Try out some interesting new recipes or enroll in a water-color class.

✔ **Get plenty of exercise:** Exercise in a social setting is the best way to go. If you enjoy tennis, get back into it and work out a little of your anger and frustration by slamming that ball past your opponent's head for a win.

✔ **Talk about your spouse:** *When you're ready,* reminisce about all the good times, the funny things that happened, and your spouse's wonderful qualities.

We know that you're deeply hurt and sometimes you feel like your heart will never mend, but with as much pain as you're feeling, don't forget that your children are hurting, too. Comforting your children after the loss of their mother or father when you're equally devastated is one of the hardest things you'll ever have to face. However, putting your children first will give you a sense of purpose and something constructive to do at this time in your life.

There are bereavement therapy groups for children, teens, and adults. You can use all the help you can get, so contact your local hospice, church, or hospital to inquire about these free and helpful support groups.

Here are some positive things you can do to help your children heal:

- **Sit down and comfort your children:** Hold them and cry with them. As you do, you not only comfort them, but you also receive solace from them in return.

- **Encourage your children to participate in the grieving rituals:** If they're shielded from the sorrow (or even from the memorial service and burial), they feel left out and resentful. These feelings may cause grief and delayed healing.

- **Talk to your children every day:** Reassure them of your love.

- **Talk about the good times:** Help your children heal by talking about all the good times you had as a family before your spouse died. These discussions help you heal as well.

- **Be sure that your children have plenty of photos and snapshots of their dad or mom displayed in their rooms, plus keep other reminders and mementos throughout your home.** Ask your kids if they'd like to have an article of clothing that belonged to their mom or dad. Your child can even be encouraged to wear the item when he sleeps, which is a great way to help your child through the grieving process.

- **Get involved in your kids' lives:** Attend their activities and try a few new family diversions, such as miniature golf, a new children's movie, or a daytrip you'll all enjoy.

We know a beautiful young mother who became suddenly single when her husband was killed in a plane crash. As she described her grief, we wondered how she made it. She said, "As soon as the kids left for school every morning, I'd take a roll of paper towels, get in the car, and drive to a cliff overlooking the ocean. I needed a place where I could cry in private. I'd cry until I soaked every sheet of the paper towels. I did that day after day until one day, I finally realized I was healing and beginning to enjoy my life again."

ANECDOTE

Biological clock

On her 36th birthday, Pam woke up in a cold sweat. Something was drastically wrong, and she knew what it was. Pam had always planned to get married, settle down, and have four children. All her girlfriends were married with children, but here she was still single and in a shaky relationship.

Pam was above average in looks and intelligence. She was a college grad with a good job and a secure future. She had spent years in therapy making sure that she was emotionally intelligent enough (that is, not so neurotic that she wouldn't be able to develop and maintain a good married relationship). She worked hard at being a good partner and had given her current four-year relationship everything she had to make it work. However, he didn't seem to want to make that final commitment.

Before her feet hit the bedroom floor on the morning of her birthday, she decided to take destiny into her own hands. She even wrote out a priority list. She made an appointment with her gynecologist for a check-up, but unfortunately, her doctor found that her tubes weren't open, so she would require surgery in order to conceive. She went through with the surgery, but it was a bitter day when she found out that she still wouldn't be able to conceive in the normal way. However, she still had the option of in vitro fertilization.

Now she had to convince her partner. She invited him out to dinner at their favorite restaurant. The dinner conversation was direct on her part but very tentative on his part. He didn't like the idea at all, and not only that, he felt both of them would be better off if she moved out — although he wanted to remain good friends.

Pam eventually did move out and considered her chances of meeting a nice man to marry and father her child within the next year or so — she didn't think the odds were very good! In vitro fertilization seemed like her best option. She talked it over with her mother and sisters. They were supportive, although they had some cautious reservations. They had never known anyone who had done in vitro, but they knew Pam was serious.

Finally, she decided to go for it! She went to a certified sperm bank at a large medical center where she went through lengthy interviews and examinations to see if in vitro fertilization was a possibility for her. The center offered no guarantees, and the fee had to be paid up front, but nine months after her 36th birthday, she had a fertilized egg implanted in her uterus. The in vitro fertilization worked on the first try. Nine months after that Pam gave birth to her own healthy daughter whom she named Rose. Pam is a loving and patient working mom who still hopes to meet a nice partner. In the meantime, she and Rose are healthy and happy together.

Being Single from the Start

You can become a single parent by adopting, becoming pregnant through artificial insemination or in vitro fertilization, or conceiving naturally with a partner's help.

Voting for artificial insemination, in vitro, adoption, or natural conception

Making the conscious decision to become a single parent through one of the means listed above is a life-changing opportunity for self-growth and empowerment, which is why your decision needs to be made for the right reasons.

Are these the right reasons to have a child outside of marriage?

- You don't want to go through your life without being a parent.
- You want to be an awesome mom or dad and you want your child to know that he is truly loved and wanted.
- You're prepared to provide a loving and safe home for your child.
- You aren't fazed when friends or family members criticize or disapprove of your choice.

You can become a single parent by choice in a number of ways:

- **Adoption:** Adopting a child, especially a child currently in the foster-care system, has become very trendy with many celebrities who advocate this idea. Rosie O'Donnell, lauded television talk-show host, has probably done more to raise public awareness of this concept than any other 50 people combined.

- **Artificial insemination:** Single women are also taking advantage of artificial insemination to become pregnant. This popular method enables the single woman to become inseminated with sperm from a known or anonymous donor. Statistics show that approximately 10 percent of sperm-bank clients are single women who want to become mothers.

  Single men may become fathers through artificial insemination as well. It's a concept teasingly called "rent-a-womb," but technically known as *surrogate motherhood*. The man's sperm is used to impregnate a willing woman who carries the child to full term, delivers, and then turns the baby over to him.

- **In vitro fertilization:** In vitro fertilization is another popular, though expensive, option. In this procedure, the woman's egg and the man's sperm meet for the first time in a petri dish — talk about a blind date! The sperm may be from a known or unknown donor. Conception doesn't always take place on the first try, but when it finally does, the embryo is placed in the woman's womb where the pregnancy continues in a normal way until the baby is born.

- **Natural conception:** A single woman may become a parent with the help of a partner willing to help her conceive and become a single parent, even though he may have no interest in the responsibilities of fatherhood.

If you became a single parent by choice, your life is undoubtedly filled with joy. After all, you pursued this goal, and the end result has brought you great fulfillment. However, even though you're feeling joyful and fulfilled, you still need to adjust to being a single parent.

✔ Now that you're a single parent, your childhood and college friends may have deserted you, unless they're parents, too. The case of the mysteriously vanishing friends isn't your fault; it's natural fallout when a person becomes a parent and can't bop around town like he used to. Take a look in Chapters 13 and 15 for ways to have fun, make new friends, and date someone interesting, if that's what you'd like to do.

✔ Raising a child isn't a part-time job, so you're suddenly saddled with a lot of responsibilities you're not used to having. You're probably feeling tired and overwhelmed at times to the point where you think that you'll never have another moment for yourself. All new parents feel these same frustrations, but when a mom and dad can share the duties, the duties are cut in half; you're carrying it all on your own shoulders.

You'll have good days and bad days — try to go with the flow. Eventually, the good days outweigh the bad ones.

Yes, becoming a single parent requires adjustments in your life. For example, we know of one single woman who adopted an 11-year-old foster child and was immediately excluded from the fun stuff she used to do with her clique of girlfriends. She and a group of single college friends (none of whom had kids) always ate lunch at a four-star restaurant one Saturday a month and followed it with an afternoon of shopping. They also flew to Puerto Vallarta for a week in the sun or indulged in a singles' cruise in the Caribbean once a year.

When a single person becomes a parent, he needs to realize that it's not that different from a group of childless couples who did everything together for years, until one of the couples has a baby and develops different interests. Unless the new parents get babysitters or have some other kind of child care available, there just aren't that many social activities they can do together anymore. It's nothing personal — just a fact of life.

So, how does a single person adjust to being a new parent?

✔ **Get the word out as soon as the child comes into your life:** Send out scads of birth or adoption announcements. Give friends and family members a chance to congratulate you, celebrate with you, and support you if they would like. If people want to know what they can do to help out, have a list of ideas ready to go. Can you use at-home help for a while with the new baby? Would a few hot meals be nice for those first few weeks? Take advantage of loving relatives, such as grandparents or aunts and uncles, who want to express their love for your child. If the grandparents don't live nearby, develop surrogate grandparents, such as an older couple you know in the neighborhood or through church.

✔ **Don't give up on your old friends:** Invite one or two friends over for lunch occasionally or get a sitter and do something social with the gang once in a while. Grab a bite to eat or check out a movie. Nurture these friendships. Who knows? Several of your buddies may become parents themselves one of these days, and you'll have a lot in common.

✔ **Get involved with other parents:** Find some folks (single or not) who have kids the same age as yours. You can meet parents at your children's swim lessons, during their T-ball games, or in neighborhood play groups. And don't forget that many activities are fun for both adults and children. A day at an amusement park, an afternoon of miniature golf, or a camping trip with other parents and their kids are all good stuff.

✔ **Keep your eyes open for people in a similar situation:** Other single parents may be experiencing the same roller-coaster ride. To have a friend, you need to be a friend, and we're willing to bet that some deep friendships are waiting for you if you just watch for the opportunities.

If you're trying to become a single mother through adoption or conception, contact Single Mothers by Choice. See the details in Chapter 18.

Whoops . . .

In the best of all worlds, every child would be intentionally and lovingly conceived at the right time, with the right person. But then again, some of us wouldn't be here to tell the tale if that were the case. Where would our civilization be if those were the criteria for every new life?

Accidental pregnancies are nothing new, but more of these pregnancies occur now than ever before due to the sexual revolution that has swept through a large part of the world since the 1960s.

If you're one of these singles who became a parent by accident, the question is: How are you going to adjust to your new life as a single parent? Your individual situation will play a role in determining how you answer this question.

✔ If the pregnancy was accidental, it probably caught you short of funds. After all, having, much less providing for, a baby isn't cheap these days. You may need to borrow cash from family. Is that so bad? Of course not. If they're willing to help out, be willing to accept their generosity and understanding. If you happen to be a college student at the time, you can also apply for financial assistance for everything from tuition to child care.

✔ We hope and pray you had support from your friends and family as you went through your pregnancy (or as you're going through it right now if that's the case). If not, try not to be discouraged. You have your whole life and many happy times ahead of you. Raising your child will be a joy, and he or she will return your love and bring you even greater joy.

✔ Have your buddies deserted you? Or are a few sticking by you and trying to help out? If so, you're fortunate, but meanwhile, get involved with other single parents who are in the same boat (see Chapter 18).

✔ If you're raising your child alone while working fulltime, and you have no help from family or friends, we know you're running on empty a lot of the time, but it won't always be like this. A day will come (sooner than you think) when you'll get your strength back and feel like a normal person again. When you reach that point, you'll be in the mood to get involved with other single parents on a social basis.

Seek out a knowledgeable, reputable attorney to protect your rights and those of your child — whether you become a single parent by accident or by choice. See Chapter 3 for ways to cope with the legal aspects of adoption, artificial insemination, in vitro fertilization, and natural pregnancies.

Kicking Up Your Single Heels

So, you're a onesy in a twosy world? So what? You're not the only single parent in town. You may be amazed to know that there are over 10 million single-parent households in the United States alone — 77.5 percent headed by single mothers and 22.5 percent headed by single dads. But often, onesies (especially those folks who used to be twosies) do need to make a few social adjustments.

If you're feeling a little lonely, you can take some simple steps to overcome these feelings.

Kicking the blues in the rump

As a single parent, the way that you're coping with your singleness probably falls somewhere on a scale of one to ten. Where do you fall on this scale? Are you doing pretty well — say an eight, a nine, or even a ten? Congratulations! Or are you mucking around down in the lower numbers? When we say "mucking around," we picture you in one of these scenarios:

✔ You're not sleeping well.

✔ Nothing tastes good anymore.

✔ Getting out of bed in the morning is a real bummer.

- ✔ Simply packing lunches and getting ready for work drains most of your energy.

- ✔ Dressing the kids and getting them off to school is excruciating.

- ✔ Work is a drag.

- ✔ Thinking about the future isn't fun — it looks grim.

- ✔ Friends and coworkers seem to be avoiding you.

- ✔ Even your cat hides under the bed when you get home from work.

Sound familiar? You need to realize that if you've become a single parent due to death or divorce, going through a grieving period isn't unusual. Elizabeth Kubler Ross, a noted psychiatrist, has described the stages of grief with the acronym DABDA. You can skip stages, backtrack, or experience more than one stage at a time. After you get back to your normal, happy self and look back on what you've been through, you'll probably come up with your own description of the grieving process you went through. Meanwhile, being able to recognize these five common stages of grief may help:

- ✔ **Denial:** Yes, it's more than a river in Africa. You're numb and you feel cold. You can't think, much less make a decision. It may encourage you to know that this stage may help you buy a little time until reality can seep in at a rate you can tolerate.

- ✔ **Anger:** You're incensed and full of rage, and you have a right to be mad at the world and your partner who abandoned you. Even if your spouse died, you may still be angry with him or her. Or, even if you were the dumper, so to speak, you may be grieving and angry because you didn't want your marriage to end the way it ended.

- ✔ **Bargaining:** You're thinking, "This whole thing may be a mistake. I'll become a better person, and you'll come back." This process is torture, but these feelings comprise a common stage of grieving for people of all ages who experience separation and loss.

- ✔ **Depression:** Reality sets in, and although anger and denial are still hanging around, you've dropped into a pit of sadness. Maybe you're sleeping a lot, or very little. Maybe you're hardly eating a thing, or on the biggest eating binge of your life. Maybe your energy level has disappeared, or you may be bursting with nervous energy. You're frustrated, irritable, and confused. And, as if all that isn't enough, you feel brain dead. Not to worry. The damage isn't permanent! But please don't make any big decisions right now. You need time to recover. We know this is a difficult time in your life, but you have to reach the depths before you can heal (as we discuss in Chapter 12). Take a look at the warning signs on the tear-out card in the front of this book. Hang this card on your refrigerator so you can watch for any signs that may pop up.

Serious depression needs immediate attention. If the depression has lasted longer than six weeks or if you, your friend, or your child experiences the following symptoms, immediately call a family doctor, a mental-health professional, the hospital, or a local suicide prevention hotline (that number is in your phone book).

- Constant crying

- Can't think of one good thing she's ever done

- Always exhausted, even when he wakes up in the morning

- Can't sleep or wants to sleep all the time

- Abrupt changes in appearance, risk-taking behavior, activities, or weight

- Extreme apathy (acting like she doesn't care)

- Feels helpless or beyond help

- Talks about or displays a preoccupation with death

- Suicide notes

- Direct threats

✔ **Acceptance:** Finally, acceptance begins to seep in. This healing acceptance brings back some of your equilibrium. You notice that you're able to think a little more clearly. You begin to reach out for comfort, and you even give comfort to others who are also hurting.

You can try one of these remedies; they may help you heal more quickly:

✔ **Make a list of the things you used to do back in the old days and add them to your schedule:** You remember the old days when you were happy, don't you? What kind of activities did you enjoy before? Visiting an art gallery? Then visit one again. Taking line-dancing lessons? What's stopping you? Get your boots to scootin'.

Speaking of the old days, do you remember these lyrics: "You've gotta accentuate the positive — eliminate the negative"? As corny as it may seem, psychologists have found that following this advice works. Try not to think negative thoughts or speak negative words — make a conscious effort to think and speak positively. This idea has worked for golfers for years. If a golfer stands on the tee box and says to herself, "Don't shank the ball! Don't shank the ball!" What do you think she'll do? She'll shank the ball. But what if she visualizes a perfect swing in her mind, sets her sights on a spot in the middle of the fairway, and says to herself, "Hit the ball straight and far, landing it right in that dark green patch in the middle of the fairway"? Well, that's what she's likely to do — all because of her positive thoughts.

- ✔ **Smile more:** Showing your pearly whites relaxes your jaw and makes you feel better — physically and emotionally. But wait 'til you see what it does for others — including your kids. They respond in kind.

- ✔ **Make a list of your past accomplishments:** Print it out in large, bold letters and hang the list where you can see it every day.

- ✔ **Write down all the things you like about yourself — or at least *used* to like about yourself:** Are you a different person than you were before? No, of course not. You're the same person deep down inside — you're a nice, likable person with a lot of positive qualities.

- ✔ **Spruce up your appearance:** Buy a new wardrobe, change your hairstyle, or go to the cosmetics counter at your local department store and get a makeover. When you look in the mirror, you need to like what you see.

- ✔ **Invite a furry friend into the house:** If you and your kids have never had a pet, now may be the time for a trip to the animal shelter. Studies have shown that having a pet helps reduce stress and can even add a few years to your life.

- ✔ **Help someone who's worse off than you are:** Yes, as impossible as it may seem, some folks do measure up to this description. Get involved in your church, a charity, or a volunteer group that reaches out to others. If you don't want to join something, look for ways to reach out to one person at a time. Find someone in your neighborhood who's hurting or sick or who could use a meal, a gift basket, or a simple visit. The important thing is to climb out of that depressing rut you've been stuck in lately. By the way, it's good to let your children get involved in however you decide to volunteer your time.

Sometimes you just can't do it alone. If you're feeling depressed most of the time, or you're having trouble functioning in your role as single parent, check out Chapter 14 for a list of signs that you may need a little help from a professional therapist.

Kicking back with old chums

If you're recently divorced or widowed, you may be feeling frustrated with your personal relationships. Friends who were always there for you in the past don't seem to call or come around anymore. What really hurts is to see couples you used to socialize with going off on daytrips, weekend jaunts, and vacations without you. You may never feel more like a onesy than when your best friend carries on about the awesome trip she and her family are planning to Orlando for spring break. You know deep down in your heart that if you hadn't lost your spouse to death or divorce, your family would be included in the plans.

So where does this leave you? Wallowing in your tears? No! You need to find another single parent and plan a dynamite trip with your own kids. What's stopping you? Onesies need each other and can have just as much fun as the twosies in this world. Give it a chance — you'll see.

If you're looking for ways to get back into the dating scene, take a look at Chapter 15 for some good places to meet someone fun to date, whether you're hoping for a long-term relationship or you just want someone to socialize with once in a while.

Kicking around the possibility of new friends

So you need to find a few new friends with similar interests? Does this seem like an impossible challenge? It isn't.

Take these positive steps to find new friends:

- ✔ **Look for casual or organized groups of single parents like yourself.** Churches and community organizations are great places to start. Chapter 18 presents detailed information.

- ✔ **Look for clubs, classes, or organizations that are interesting to you.** You can find mixed groups of single and married parents with similar interests. Many of these mixed groups plan daytrips, weekends, and once-a-month social activities. Local newspapers, magazines, radio announcements, and church bulletins are just a few places to find this kind of information. You can also ask your friends for suggestions.

- ✔ **Hang out with people who like you and are supportive.** These folks should pump you up and make you feel good about yourself. Avoid anyone, including past friends and family members, who are critical of your choices or your lifestyle. Watch out for positive, uplifting people at work, at church, in your neighborhood, or at social functions.

- ✔ **Start entertaining in your home.** Ask a few other single parents over for a potluck dinner or a game night or to watch a sports event or a movie. Other parents are looking for friends, just like you are, and they may include you in their future plans, too.

- ✔ **Get involved in your children's sports activities.** You can meet other parents with kids the same age as your kids.

- ✔ **Don't sit around on the weekends feeling sorry for yourself.** Take a little time during the week to make plans for the upcoming weekend. Ask another single and his child to go with you to the circus on Saturday afternoon, or get a babysitter and take in a movie with another lonely soul on Sunday night. By filling your weekends with fun stuff, you're bound to pump up your social life and make new friends.

Chapter 3

Calling It Legalese Is Oxymoronic

In This Chapter
- ▶ Getting cozy with your divorce settlement
- ▶ Standing up for your rights
- ▶ Wading through the ongoing legal problems

Any single parent will tell you that navigating the legal system is the pits. It's like tiptoeing barefoot down a path littered with broken glass and trying not to get cut. What you need is a pair of heavy-duty, steel-toed combat boots, and that's what we provide for you in this chapter. We know that many single parents have to tread this path at some point in time, so our goal is to make the journey as painless as possible.

You may currently be separated from your spouse or in the process of working out a divorce agreement. As you make your way through this potential minefield, this is our challenge to you: Be strong and courageous as you deal with the conflicts, negotiations, and paperwork necessary to assure the best outcome for you and your children. Or you may have recently become widowed, or maybe you've become a single parent by choice or by accident. In any case, we have combat boots that come in all shapes and sizes. You *can* do this! *Divorce For Dummies* by John Ventura and Mary Reed (Wiley Publishing, Inc.) can help.

If you're not getting a divorce, skip to the section called "Wrestling for Your Rights," found later in this chapter.

The information in this chapter should *not* be considered legal advice. The purpose of this chapter is to point out legal questions that may require professional advice from an attorney.

Divvying Things Up After the Divorce

We know that you want to be the best single parent possible, but we also know that you'll never relax and get on with your life until you feel comfortable with the terms of your divorce. Here are a few ideas to consider.

The uncontested divorce

Scott and Elizabeth decided that they were going to be civilized, reasonable, and hip about the dissolution of their marriage. They read a book about how to get a divorce for $750, and the advice sounded good, although neither one of them would have given two cents for their marriage for the past few years.

They drew up an exhaustive list of things they agreed on. They were so comfortable with their agreement that they decided they only needed one attorney to review it and help them with the divorce procedures. So Elizabeth took their agreement to an attorney and asked him to make it legal. The attorney told her that it would be a good idea to have Scott hire his own attorney to look it over as well.

The next thing they knew, letters and phone calls flew back and forth between the two law offices, and over a two-month period, the legal fees mounted as they received itemized bills from their individual attorneys for letters and timed phone calls.

Finally, Elizabeth and Scott wised up. They had a face-to-face talk and agreed that they still liked their original agreement that covered the division of their property and the child-care provisions. Scott fired his attorney, and the first attorney helped them successfully maneuver their uncontested divorce through the court. However, by this time, the whole thing cost a lot more than the original fantasy figure of $750.

Trusting your attorney

Make sure to find an attorney you like, respect, and trust. You have to know, without a doubt, that your attorney is on your side, fighting for you. How can you find an attorney you trust? Here are some guidelines:

- **Do some research:** Ask around and get referrals from your divorced friends.

- **Look for a divorce or family-law specialist:** Many attorneys have extra training and certification that qualifies them as a certified specialist in family law, which means that they know all about child custody, child support, property division, alimony, and so on. Check with your state bar association for referrals.

- **Look for an attorney with many years of experience:** You can check out the *Martindale-Hubbell Law Directory* for this info, as well as an attorney's age, peer ratings, educational background, and other interesting stuff. You can find this directory in your local library, courthouse law libraries, or any law-school library. An online version is also available at www.martindale.com.

✔ **Talk to several lawyers before making your decision:** Just chatting with an attorney about your situation usually costs very little. Have a list ready before your appointment so you don't forget to ask the really important questions.

✔ **Compare costs:** Attorneys bill their clients in a variety of ways. Some lawyers have fixed fees, others charge by the hour, and still others charge *contingency fees,* which means you only have to pay if you win in court or receive a settlement. Lower-income clients may be able to get a lawyer *pro bono,* which means that a lawyer will help you at no cost. You can find out if you qualify by calling a large law firm, or look in the phone book under *Legal Aid.* By the way, negotiating with an attorney about fees is perfectly okay.

✔ **Determine how the attorney expects to be paid:** Some attorneys require a *retainer* (a partial payment) up front. If you don't have the upfront money to get things started, look for an attorney who'll accept payment by credit card or who will set up an installment plan that fits your budget. Find out exactly how your lawyer will bill you after the retainer has been settled. Will the attorney bill on an hourly basis and send invoices once a month? Are payments due at certain times? While you're at it, find out whether you're expected to pay for phone calls, postage, copy services, or other incidental expenses.

✔ **Find out who will actually represent you:** Be sure that the attorney you're considering will handle your case herself unless you don't mind being turned over to an associate.

✔ **Look for an attorney with a caring attitude:** Find someone who's able to counsel you, as opposed to a lawyer who wants to get to the bottom line so she can meet with her next client. You need an attorney who can take time to listen to you — someone who has a heart for her clients.

As caring and compassionate as your attorney may be, he's not a professional therapist. He's there to give you legal advice, do the legal research and paperwork, negotiate on your behalf to the best of his ability, and generally maneuver you through the legal system. He's not there to solve your emotional problems. If you need professional counseling, hire a professional therapist to help you through this rough time in your life.

Here are four things to expect from your attorney:

✔ **Competence:** He should have the skills and experience required to handle your case.

✔ **Respect for you as a client:** The attorney and her staff should treat you with respect, taking time to explain everything and answer your questions in a relaxed, unhurried manner. She should return your phone calls within a reasonable length of time and should never talk down to you or disrespect you in any way.

✔ **Honest progress reports:** He should keep you updated at least once a week with verbal progress reports on everything that's happening with your case and provide an honest assessment of your chances of succeeding.

✔ **Detailed monthly billing:** Itemized statements should include what you owe to date, what the attorney has done, and how many hours she has spent on your case. Any miscellaneous costs should also be spelled out in plain English (or Spanish or Nepalese . . . whatever!).

Understanding all that itty-bitty fine print

Here are a few legal terms that tend to pop up during a divorce settlement. Having a handle on these terms in advance really helps — you won't feel so feeble-witted. This list doesn't feature legal definitions; we simply provide easy-to-understand explanations that may give you a leg up on divorce speak:

✔ **Alimony:** Alimony is money paid by one spouse to the other spouse in scheduled payments or in lump sums from time to time. Many people think of alimony as payments from the ex-husband to his ex-wife. However, women making payments to their ex-husbands has become quite common (which many men think is *way* cool). Alimony is also known as *spousal support.*

✔ **Assets:** This is the dollar value of all your stuff — cash, property, investments, and anything else of monetary value (when you subtract what you owe, that's your *net worth*).

✔ **Automatic wage attachment:** These three little words are a good thing if you're the one who's supposed to be receiving these payments. The court orders your ex's employer to take child-support payments out of his or her paychecks and send them to you, if you're the custodial parent.

✔ **Best interests of the child:** You've probably heard this phrase a lot; if you haven't, just wait. Judges use this legal standard when they make decisions about who gets custody of your child, who provides financial support, and who gets to visit your child (and the terms of the visits). Hopefully you and the judge will agree on these crucial decisions — if not, you probably won't be a very happy camper.

✔ **Child custody:** Two major types of child custody exist — legal and physical custody. Each of these types of custody may be either sole or joint.

 • **Sole legal custody:** One parent is the legal guardian of the child and makes all major decisions including those involving medical care, education, and religious training.

- **Joint legal custody:** Both parents are the legal guardians, and they share all major decision-making responsibilities.

- **Sole physical custody:** One parent has physical custody and responsibility for the child's daily care.

- **Joint physical custody:** Both parents share physical custody of the child on an agreed-upon schedule (such as one week with one parent, and the next week with the other; or school days with one parent, and non-school days with the other).

✔ **Child support:** This term refers to the money the non-custodial parent pays to the custodial parent to be used for the child's daily living expenses and special needs that come up from time to time.

✔ **Community property:** In *community-property states,* a couple's assets and debt obligations are divided equally when they divorce unless the court decides that this situation is unfair for some reason. In this case, most community-property states have the option of using *equitable distribution,* which considers how long the couple has been married, their health, ages, earning potential, and other similar factors. If the judge opts for equitable distribution, hope like heck that the split favors you.

✔ **Contested divorce:** This kind of divorce ends up in court, where the judge decides on the issues you're arguing over. (Not your warm-and-fuzzy style divorce.)

✔ **Emancipation:** When a child reaches a certain age (usually somewhere between 17 and 21), he or she becomes legally independent, or emancipated. When the child is emancipated, most states don't require the non-custodial parent to continue making payments to the custodial parent for his or her support. A child may also be considered emancipated if he or she gets married, enters military service, or becomes self-supporting through fulltime employment. The parent paying child support usually views emancipation as freedom, but the custodial parent often thinks that this idea stinks (especially when the child's college-tuition bill arrives).

✔ **Family court:** This court deals with family-related legal problems including divorce, alimony, child support, custody, adoption, spousal support, modifications in child support or custody, enforcement of payments previously established by the court, and other matters related to children. Family courts are also committed to protecting children from neglect or abuse. A family-court judge has powers similar to those of any other judge.

✔ **Guardian ad litem:** The court appoints this person to work out an agreement that protects the rights and best interests of a child in a divorce settlement. This person is usually an attorney and only steps in when you and your spouse can't agree on who will have custody of your child.

- ✔ **Injunction:** This permanent restraining order prevents one person from harming another. Some temporary restraining orders do the same thing but also keep the husband or wife from squandering all the money, taking the children, or removing the goodies from the house during divorce negotiations. A *temporary restraining order* is also known as a TRO, just in case you care.

- ✔ **No-fault divorce:** Either spouse can initiate this divorce without permission from the other. This kind of divorce is comfortable (if any divorce can feel comfortable) because one spouse can't point the finger at the other and say, "It's all *your* fault." The term *irreconcilable differences* is usually good enough in the eyes of the law, as opposed to one guilty party and one innocent party. In other words, the couple doesn't need to prove what their differences were during their marriage, but can simply state irreconcilable differences as their legal reason for seeking a divorce. We learned as kids to say, "It wasn't *my* fault," and now it actually works for us as adults.

- ✔ **Uncontested divorce:** This divorce can be warm and fuzzy. No formal litigation, court dates, or any of that other disgusting stuff is necessary. All you and your soon-to-be ex need to do is draw up your own agreement about who gets what, who pays for what, and who has what responsibilities for the children. After you put your agreement together in a neat and tidy court-approved format, the court reviews it — just to be sure that the terms are fair and reasonable.

- ✔ **Visitation:** The court sets up a visitation schedule for the non-custodial parent to see his or her child regularly. The right to visit the child is automatic unless good reasons (called *extenuating circumstances*) exist as to why the individual shouldn't be allowed to see the child. Hopefully you can come to some sort of agreement concerning visitation; otherwise, the court will step in and order the terms of the visitation.

While you're in the process of dealing with all the legal stuff anyway, have your will changed to make sure that your child is taken care of in case of your death, including naming a guardian.

Calling a truce via a mediator

Hiring a private mediator can be a brilliant decision for certain couples — especially couples who don't want to pay individual attorneys to put on their armor and go to war. Rather than drawing a line in the sand, hire a mediator to help you work out an agreement. Mediated divorce agreements often last the longest and work the best because everyone involved agrees to the terms. Plus, mediation spares the children from the pain caused by their parents' angry, contentious divorce settlements.

What's a *private mediator,* you ask? This person meets with you in private at your convenience. Some private mediators, such as mental-health professionals, have a special talent for mediating when emotional conflicts are involved. But, if you're more concerned about the particulars of current family law in your state, you may want to look for a mediator who's an attorney or a retired judge. If you're totally messed up — a highly technical term that means you have emotional conflicts *and* family law questions — you can hire an attorney-therapist team.

During the mediation process, the mediator encourages the couple to communicate so an agreement can be worked out. The mediator may meet with the couple individually or together, but when they're together, the mediator ensures that each person has uninterrupted time to express herself. After listening to both sides, the mediator may suggest creative ways to resolve differences so an agreement can be put in writing. Check out Table 3-1 for the scoop on some of the advantages and disadvantages of mediation.

Table 3-1	The Pros and Cons of Mediation
Advantages	*Disadvantages*
Gets the couple talking to each other (which may be a novelty for them).	May not work if emotions are so out of control that the couple can't think straight during the meetings.
Assures the couple that they each. have plenty of time to get their points without interruption	Doesn't usually work well if one spouse is loud, dominant, and controlling and the other spouse won't speak up in the face of the assertive spouse's onslaught.
Softens the trauma the children may suffer when they overhear the verbal arguments that often arise during divorce preparations and proceedings.	No disadvantage.
Encourages new and creative solutions the couple may have never considered.	Because the parties aren't under oath, nothing keeps one or both spouses from lying.
The final agreement is more likely to stick because both spouses have aired their problems and agreed to compromise before the agreement becomes final.	Almost never works unless both spouses are willing to give it a fair chance.
Helps the couple communicate and get along better after the divorce is final.	No disadvantage.

Unfortunately, mediators may not be able to save the day in every situation. If one of you is seething with revenge, ongoing physical abuse is an issue, or someone is sneaking around, hiding assets, withdrawing funds from joint bank accounts, or doing other nasty stuff, you may have no choice but to take the adversarial route.

Avoiding the judge's gavel

Most couples prefer to settle things without going to court. This option saves time, money, and emotional stress. Here are a couple sensible ways to go about it:

- ✔ **Try to have a warm, fuzzy divorce that needs no formal litigation.** Sit down, talk things over, and draw up your own divorce agreement (a *marital settlement agreement*). Then let the court review your handiwork to see if it's fair. If the court signs off on the plan, you're out of your misery. If you need a little help drawing up your agreement, hire an affordable, independent paralegal to prepare and file the papers.

- ✔ **If the two of you can't agree, the judge may recommend a *settlement conference* where a court-appointed mediator will help you come to an agreement.** The court usually provides these mediators as a free service. (The judge wants you to settle out of court just as much as you do.)

We think that we're safe in saying that most couples aren't completely satisfied with their time in front of a judge. Most participants don't come away with the idea that their judgment day was a victory for good over evil. So try to do whatever you can to avoid placing your future in the hands of someone else.

Wrestling for Your Rights

You have rights, and your child has rights, but you may have to fight for them. You should receive the alimony you deserve, and you should have sole custody of your child (if that arrangement is fair and reasonable). If you're not the sole-custody parent, you should have the right to visit your child according to an equitable schedule.

If you've adopted a child or become a single parent through artificial insemination or in vitro fertilization, you need to have a legal agreement that protects you and your child. If you became pregnant naturally, you and the natural father should also draw up a legal agreement that protects you and your child from any future legal problems that could result in your child being temporarily or permanently taken from you.

Sharing the kids through custody

If you and your ex agree from the get-go about the custody thing, you have nothing to negotiate. You've probably decided that one of you will have sole custody or that you'll share joint custody of your children. However, if you're *not* in agreement, you have some work to do. If you can't agree, the judge may decide custody according to what's in the *best interests of the child.* Judges take these things into consideration:

✔ Which parent has the strongest emotional bond with the child?

✔ Who does the child prefer to live with?

✔ Which parent has been serving as the child's primary caregiver?

✔ How many hours per day does each parent spend with the child?

✔ Which parent takes care of the child's medical and dental care?

✔ Which parent prepares the child's meals on a regular basis?

✔ Does the child perform better in school when being cared for by one parent over the other?

✔ Which parent can provide the safest home environment?

✔ Which parent has changed residences less often?

✔ Which parent has greater job stability?

✔ Which parent will be able to provide continuity in the child's life (staying in the same home, attending the same church, going to the same school, having the same friends, and so on)?

✔ Does either parent have a history of child abuse, drug use, or alcoholism?

✔ Which parent has the best driving record?

✔ Which parent does the child go to for comfort or advice?

✔ What does the custody evaluation report say?

The judge may order a *custody evaluation report* to help determine custody; this evaluation may be made by a mental-health professional such as a social worker or psychologist.

If you're getting nowhere fast and talking to your ex is like talking to a can of tuna, you may need the help of a court-appointed mediator or conciliator. Or you can submit your dispute to binding arbitration. In *binding arbitration,* a third party (often an attorney or therapist) listens to each of you, interviews witnesses, reviews the evidence, and then makes a ruling. Submitting to binding arbitration is pretty sticky stuff and not a fun time because your kids are your life and you want the best for them. By submitting to binding arbitration you're avoiding litigation in court in front of a judge; however, you must agree beforehand that you will abide by the decision and know that you are not allowed to appeal the decision.

Visiting the kids

If parents have joint custody of the children, which happens 20 percent of the time, visitation rights aren't an issue. More and more parents are opting for joint custody for this very reason. Not only do visitation rights become a non-issue, but the non-custodial parent also tends to feel less *divorced* from the kids. Joint custody also builds stronger bonds between the child and each parent. Unfortunately, if the parents have extremely bitter feelings towards one another, joint custody usually doesn't work out — at least not without wearing battle armor most of the time. A constant verbal barrage isn't good for the kids either. One key to having a divorce that does minimum harm to the child is having a divorce with a minimum of long-term bickering and tension between the adults.

In cases where the mother or father has sole custody, a written agreement regarding the visitation rights of the non-custodial parent is necessary. Mothers have full custody most of the time in the United States; therefore in most cases, the mother grants visitation rights to the father.

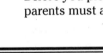

Before you pick up a pen and sign anything, here are visitation issues both parents must agree upon in advance and get in writing:

Widows and widowers

If your spouse has died, leaving you as a single parent, here are some helpful words of advice:

1. Make an appointment with your financial advisor to go over your finances, including everything from setting up a budget you can live on, to increasing your income, to reorganizing your investment portfolio.

2. Meet with your insurance advisor to go over your current policies, including changes in your beneficiaries.

3. Make changes in your health insurance coverage, especially if you've lost your coverage due to your spouse's death.

4. Contact Social Security to take advantage of any benefits due you because of your new status.

5. Meet with your attorney to go over your will, including beneficiary changes and appointing a legal guardian for your children in the case of your death.

✔ How many day or evening visits per week will the non-custodial parent have?

✔ How many weekend visits per month will the non-custodial parent have?

✔ How many school vacation days will be spent with each parent?

✔ What about holidays and birthdays? Which holidays and birthdays will the child spend with which parent?

Grandparents and other family members also have the legal right to visitation; take a look in Chapter 10.

Don't sign anything until you understand and agree with what you're signing.

Adopting some legal problems

United States adoption laws and regulations are not uniform from state to state, and they constantly change. This situation places a lot of responsibility on individuals involved in adopting a child. It means that you must read up on the current laws and regulations in your area and that you need advice from an attorney who specializes in adoption law (or from your local adoption support group).

These major kinds of adoptions occur:

✔ **Independent private adoption:** Many single men and women choose this route, especially if they already know of a birth mother willing to give up her baby for adoption. Have an attorney check out specific rules and regulations for you.

✔ **Agency adoption:** Some agency adoptions work well for single men and women, but others don't. Agencies also vary in the type of children they have available for adoption. An *agency* is a business or government organization authorized to act for others. Two types of adoption agencies exist:

• **Public:** Those that help in the adoption of children who, for one reason or another, have become wards of the state.

• **Private:** May be profit or non-profit agencies. Help individuals adopt children that are not wards of the state.

One of the most important adoption issues that you need to understand and settle early on (regardless of whether you choose an independent or agency adoption) is whether the adoption will be *closed* or *open*. The terms closed and open have become quite controversial, and very strong opinions are associated with each style.

✔ **Closed adoption:** The traditional style of adoption where information is protected from disclosure (kept secret). Advocates of closed adoptions feel that it's better for the child not to have contact with the birth parents or any other relatives (such as the grandparents) after the adoption is final.

✔ **Open adoption:** A more progressive style of adoption where certain information is shared. An open adoption is sometimes called an *experimental adoption*. This type of adoption may allow contact between the birth mother and the adoptive parents, not only before the birth of the baby, but also after. Open adoption may also permit contact between the birth father and the adoptive parents and his baby. Advocates of open adoptions feel that this style of adoption is healthier.

Here are the six legal steps required for adoption in most of the United States:

1. **Notice.** Everyone and anyone who may be involved in the adoption is required by law to receive legal notice informing them that the adoption proceedings are going to take place. If the child is illegitimate, the birth father must also be notified. In the eyes of the law, the birth father has certain legal rights to custody of the child, so he must be notified.

2. **Petition.** The prospective parent prepares this document, which requests permission from the court to adopt the child. The document includes all kinds of information about the prospective parent, the natural parents, and the child. Written consent must accompany the petition.

3. **Written consent.** The adoption agency or the child's natural parents execute this document to provide their consent to the impending adoption.

4. **Hearing.** This meeting takes place in a closed courtroom. The court examines the prospective parent's qualifications and then grants or denies the petition.

5. **Probation.** Most states require a probationary period following the hearing during which the child's new relationship is monitored carefully to be sure that the child and the parent are happy with the situation. If everything works out, the parent is finally issued a permanent adoption decree.

6. **Birth certificate.** The court seals the child's original birth certificate and issues a new certificate that includes his or her new name, date of birth, and other information (including the name and age of his new parent).

Don't take anyone's word for anything. It's important to follow the law to the letter when it comes to adopting a child. Although you have the right to act as your own attorney, we advise that you solicit the help of an attorney who's experienced in adoption law in your area, then do what he tells you to do, sign what he tells you to sign, and ensure that all documents are recorded, if applicable.

Going down the test tubes

Legal issues have always arisen in connection with adoptions, but recent reproductive technologies have opened up a whole new world of legal issues. When you become a single parent through *artificial insemination* (where a man's semen is introduced into a woman's vagina or uterus without sexual contact) or *in vitro fertilization* (where the woman's egg and the man's sperm are placed together in a petri dish, conception takes place, and the embryo is placed into the woman's womb), you need to resolve a number of issues within signed agreements. And what a coincidence — we cover some of these issues in the following sections.

When we talk about *donated sperm* in the sections that follow, the sperm may be used for either artificial insemination or in vitro fertilization.

The bottom line is this: You need to have prepared and signed legal contracts in your soon-to-be-parental hands before you go forward with any of these procedures, which means you should hire a knowledgeable, reputable attorney to draw up the documents for all parties to sign. This is true whether you plan to be artificially inseminated or become pregnant through in vitro fertilization.

Who's your daddy? Insemination from an unknown donor

If you were (or plan to be) impregnated by an anonymous donor's sperm, double-check that the donor signed a release when he donated the sperm. This issue should never be a problem when dealing with a sperm bank because most banks require a written release that absolves the donor from any claims on the child (as well as any liabilities or responsibilities for the child after it has been born). Just ask to see the form.

He's your daddy: Insemination from a known donor

Aha! Things can get a little tricky at this point. If you know the donor, the likelihood that he'll see the child after it's born is greater, which can trigger some kind of positive parental feelings toward the child on his part. So having a signed release in advance from a known donor is really important. It prevents any claims to the child in the future.

Who's your mamma? Going the surrogate-mother route

This process, also known as *rent-a-womb* or *surrogate motherhood,* is where a man wants to become a father and pays a willing woman to carry his child through to delivery, at which time the baby is turned over to him. The woman may become pregnant with the man's sperm through natural conception, artificial insemination, or in vitro fertilization. If you go down this road, you need to have a very tight contract prepared and signed prior to the procedure that protects you from any future claims to the child by the mother after she gives birth.

However, even with a solid legal contract, problems may still arise. The courts haven't always upheld surrogate-mother contracts.

Protecting your rights when dad's around

You may have become a single mother by choice or by accident during intercourse. However you got here, the father knows that you're having his child. Here are some ways to protect your rights when the natural biological father is in the picture:

- ✔ **Single mother by choice with the help of a friend:** If you enlisted the help of a friend to impregnate you, with full knowledge that he wants no responsibility for the child after its birth, you still need a legal agreement signed by both of you. In this agreement, you absolve him of any future financial, emotional, or legal responsibilities for the child, and he relinquishes any claims to the child as well. You need this agreement in writing to protect your rights to the child in case the father decides to become involved in the child's life in the future.

- ✔ **Single mother by accident:** If you become pregnant accidentally and want to keep the baby, you'll need a legal release from the biological father that relinquishes his claim to the child after its birth. However, if the father wants to be involved in his child's life, or the father wants to help support the child financially, he has certain legal rights. You need to seek the help of an attorney who'll put your agreement in writing. The agreement must be signed by the birth mother and father and recorded, if applicable.

Seek out good, professional advice ahead of time regarding the birth certificate. Do you want the biological father's name on the certificate? Important legal issues are involved in many of the decisions you face.

Showing me the ali-money (and child support)

Every state has its own ideas on whether an ex-spouse deserves *alimony* (spousal support) and the amount and duration of alimony payments. If children are involved, the state almost always favors the child before the ex-spouse, meaning that child support comes before alimony. Some states combine alimony and child support into one payment, which is called *family support*. (Tax repercussions may be associated with receiving alimony and child support. Check it out with a tax attorney or a Certified Public Accountant.)

The *dumper* (the person who initiates the divorce) suffers just as much guilt as the *dumpee* when a relationship turns sour. This guilt can cause the dumper to not pursue all of his or her rights when it comes to the divorce settlement. The dumper may settle for less than she deserves — not only in relation to the couple's assets, but also when dealing with child-custody or visitation rights. Don't relinquish your rights out of guilt!

Heading off alimony issues

When you're in the thick of negotiating your divorce agreement, thinking of every issue that could pertain to spousal support (especially all the really bad stuff that could happen to you in the future) is difficult. Table 3-2 lists a few crucial points that you need to talk out and put in writing before you sign the agreement.

Table 3-2	Potential Reasons for Alimony
Problem	*Solution*
You get sick and can't work.	You need to agree that your ex will pay for your support while you're ill and help out with any unexpected medical expenses not covered by insurance.
You lose your job and can't find another one.	You need to include a provision in your agreement that increases your alimony payments until you find another job.
Your ex has future pension payments.	Don't you deserve a fair share? Of course, you do! You were married to your ex when the 401-K or SEP account was created in the first place, and you watched it grow through the years, so your investment should be rewarded when the time comes.

A relatively new field has exploded in the past few years. *Certified Divorce Planners* aren't usually attorneys, but they are specially trained and certified to help plan financial settlements for divorcing couples. A planner can scope out the couple's stock holdings for embedded capital gains, set up alimony schedules, and make sure that the spouse who keeps the house doesn't get *hosed,* among other functions.

Taking care of child-support conditions

Child-support issues can also become muddled when you need to plan for every contingency that may arise in the future — especially if something unexpected happens. Fortunately, states keep child support and other matters relating to the children of divorce open (under the court's jurisdiction) as long as the child is a minor. So, if your situation changes, you can always go back and ask for a change in the terms of the child-support agreement.

Uniform Parentage Act doesn't provide aprons

The anonymous sperm donor is often a college student, a hospital employee, or another male in need of a few bucks who the sperm bank has paid to contribute his sperm. Many cases have come up in which the woman was married when she was artificially inseminated, but when she and her husband divorced, he tried to absolve himself of any future financial (or other) responsibilities for the child by insisting he isn't the *natural father.* What a crock! In most instances, the courts have come to the rescue by declaring the husband to be the father. In fact, the United States has adopted the Uniform Parentage Act, which says that the husband is the legal father and treats the donor as if he never existed.

But why not get in front of future potential problems by including a little provisional verbiage in your original agreement?

Adjusting Further: The Only Constant Is Change

You can only count on three things in this life: death, taxes, and child-custody agreements that don't hold up forever. Just when life is going smoothly, something happens that conflicts with your original divorce or custody agreement.

For example, you may remarry and want to move out of state. What happens to the joint custody of your children? You can't ask your ex to tag along so your kids will still have him around. Or what happens if your boss dropkicks you out the door?

An unexpected move or the kind of unplanned free time that doesn't include a paycheck are just two examples of situations that can cause problems with alimony, child custody, child support, and other terms in your original divorce or custody agreement. How can you work around these pesky problems? The answer is simple: If you feel that changing the original agreement is necessary, return to the court and request the modification. This procedure isn't spooky or scary — people do it all the time, so don't freak out.

If you do decide on a modification, you can employ the services of the attorney who helped you draw up your original agreement or hire a different attorney. The choice is yours.

Changing status

The most common change in status is when a parent remarries. A custody or visitation agreement may need to be modified when one parent remarries and the new marriage

✔ Changes a parent's ability to fulfill the terms of joint or sole custody or visitation

✔ Interferes with existing spousal- or child-support payments

✔ Requires a major move (especially one that's out of state)

✔ Causes a drastic change in the child's home life (such as poor treatment by the stepparent or the presence of any new stepsisters or stepbrothers)

✔ Means that the child will be raised in a different religious environment

A parent's status may also change if the parent

✔ Gets arrested and put in jail

✔ Becomes addicted to alcohol

✔ Uses illegal drugs

✔ Becomes a danger to the child

These drastic changes in status may require more than a few modifications to your original agreement and could even result in a temporary or permanent *restraining order* (a court injunction that prevents one person from harming another).

Changing income

If your income drastically changes to the point where you can't support yourself, much less your share of your child's support, a modification can be made in your child support agreement that requires more financial support from the other parent. This modification may only be temporary until your income recovers.

Changing employment

Losing your job suddenly isn't that uncommon, and it may be another reason to modify your child-support agreement. If you're the one making payments, the court should require you to pay less until you find another job.

Victim no more

At age 24, Jean took control of her life. She had been abused by her father and watched her mother stay in the marriage for the sake of the children. When her husband admitted he was having an affair, she decided she'd be a victim no more. She's still rather pleased with her quick comeback upon hearing the news, "I don't care what she's given you, as long as it isn't contagious." She assertively demanded that he sign the paper giving her full custody of their two-year-old daughter.

Jean still remembers a very kindly gentleman in the district attorney's office who took her through all the bureaucratic steps. He coached her on what to do when future glitches occur. Although her ex-husband moved across the country, she's always received child-support payments.

The first five years after her divorce, Jean was on and off welfare. She received some office training and landed a job as a department-store manager. Unfortunately, the position didn't pay as well as welfare, and there were lean years when the fear of running out of toilet paper haunted her.

Jean always put her daughter first, and with only her mother to depend on for help, she took an 18-month training program to become a licensed vocational nurse. The program offered her a path to job security and a little more income. But she didn't stop there. Jean slowly began to take the prerequisite courses to become a registered nurse. She juggled work, school, and single parenthood. In fact, one of her fondest memories was when she and her daughter would sit at either end of the kitchen table studying together.

Today her daughter is a straight-A high-school student, and Jean is a registered nurse in a neonatal intensive-care unit. She admits that her next hurdle is to overcome her fear of being hurt. She wants to lose a few pounds and meet a nice man for companionship, and more.

Jean is vivacious and enthusiastic, and she says that she's earned her gray hair at age 39. But she's a victim no more!

But, if you're the sole-custody parent and you switch jobs to one that messes up your daily schedule, you may need to modify your custody agreement. If you're working crazy hours now, and you and your kids are rarely home at the same time, you may need to ask your ex for a little help.

WARNING!

Judges tend to frown on a job change that causes your kids to be home alone during the day.

Changing residence

Moving from one residence to another (especially if it's a long-distance move) can really throw a kink into your joint-custody or visitation schedule. Most non-custodial parents strongly object when sole-custody parents move quite a distance away, especially if they move out of state. If a non-custodial parent moves, visitation agreements should remain the same. The non-custodial parent will simply face greater inconveniences and expenses when visiting the child.

In change-of-residence cases, the judge modifies your agreement *in the best interests of the child.* If you, as sole-custody parent, move from California to Texas, and the original visitation agreement is impossible to fulfill, the judge can change that agreement by compensating the non-custodial parent for all the time he or she misses with the kids during the school year by awarding more time over holidays and summer vacations. In theory, at least, the changes are supposed to work out for everyone involved — especially for the kids. Try to ride with these modifications and look for the bright side.

Changing health issues

Everyone is subject to illness, accidents, and sudden disabilities. Staying spunky and healthy year in and year out would be nice, but life ain't like that, buddy. So, if you face a health crisis, make a few adjustments to the original divorce agreement, especially in the case of child custody.

If you're temporarily sidelined due to bad health, ask for a *temporary modification* to your original child-custody agreement. This type of change will usually turn your children over to their other parent *only* while you're laid up. You can even ask the judge to specify a date or a certain event at which point this modification will end and your children will return to your custody. After you're well and feeling like your old self again, you'll have your kids back at the breakfast table begging for their favorite smiley-face pancakes, so don't worry.

Chapter 4

Crunching Time

. . . .

In This Chapter

▶ Simplifying your life

▶ Accepting a little help from your friends

▶ Anticipating a need to be flexible

. . . .

*W*e have a surprise for you — so shut your eyes! And don't peek! It's a gift — all wrapped up with gold foil paper and tied with a shiny satin bow. Wanna guess what it is? Here are a few hints:

✔ It's something you really need.

✔ It's something you've been wanting for awhile.

✔ It's something valuable — so valuable, in fact, that even Bill Gates can't afford it!

✔ It's something that will bring a little peace and quiet into your life.

✔ It's something that will make you smile!

✔ It's something that will bring enormous joy to you and your children.

Okay, are you ready? Open your eyes and unwrap your gift. Are you surprised? We thought you'd be! We've given you the precious gift of *time!*

Throughout this chapter we show you ways to multiply your time. As a single parent, you have waaaaaay too much to do and not enough time to do it. And if you're recently divorced or widowed, you're on your own now so you have to accomplish twice as much as before in the same amount of time. You may have taken on the responsibility of a fulltime job for the first time in a while or you may have started working longer hours. What you need is to add hours to your day, and we know how you can do exactly that.

Simply Flying? Simplify

One of the most difficult jobs in America today is that of a single parent. Whether you're a single dad or a single mom, it's not easy to juggle the responsibilities of your career, your home, and your kids. It's difficult, in fact, for a married couple to juggle these three time-consuming obligations, but going it alone is beyond ridiculous.

If you're the typical single parent, for example, your day may go something like the sample day in Table 4-1.

Table 4-1	Typical Day for a Single Parent
6:00 a.m.	Alarm goes off.
6:30 a.m.	Awaken the children and try to interest them in breakfast.
6:45 a.m.	Dress the children and pack their bags for day care.
7:00 a.m.	Get dressed yourself, blow-dry your hair, and shave or apply your makeup.
7:30 a.m.	Leave the house.
7:40 a.m.	Drop the two-year-old off at your friend's home.
7:50 a.m.	Drop the four-year-old off at preschool.
8:00 a.m.	Arrive at work.
Over your lunch hour:	Pay four bills; pick up your allergy prescription at the downtown Thrifty Drug, along with a package of Pampers; gobble down your brown-bag lunch at your desk in the few minutes you have left after running your errands!
5:00 p.m.	Leave work.
5:15 p.m.	Pick up the four-year-old from preschool.
5:30 p.m.	Pick up the two-year-old.
5:40 p.m.	Return home and start preparing dinner while searching through the mail for the child-support payment, which isn't there . . . again!

6:30 p.m.	Serve dinner.
7:00 p.m.	Do the dishes, empty the garbage, pack your brown-bag lunch for tomorrow, and feed the cat.
7:30 p.m.	Give the children their baths, read to the children, and get them both to bed.
8:00 p.m.	Straighten up the house, change the cat's litter box, turn on the sprinkler (because it's your watering day), do a load of wash, clean the bathroom, and iron your shirt for work tomorrow.
10:20 p.m.	Settle down on the sofa at last to watch a little TV and try to relax.
10:30 p.m.	Head for bed because you can't keep your eyes open!

And this is a good day! A bad day is something else entirely. A bad day is when you have an unstoppable headache, you receive a frantic call at work that your daughter is running a high fever at preschool and must be picked up immediately, then, as Murphy's Law would have it, this is the day your two-year-old decides she hates her "bad, bad" stuffed raccoon and tries to flush it down the toilet! You finally collapse into bed after midnight, only to awaken every hour to check on your daughter's fever. It's a great life!

What you need to do is simplify, and here are four ways to start.

Just saying "No"

You've got to force yourself to say that word! Try it! Put your tongue on the roof of your mouth and practice. You can't be everybody's everything every day of every week like you used to be. This is the new you.

Every time you say "no" to others, you're saying "yes" to your kids and yourself.

Let's look at a couple of scenarios: You get a call from a neighbor, asking if you would like to help host a baby shower for a mutual friend. Or — this one's a doozy — you get a frantic call from your ex, asking you to buy your child a birthday gift *from him*, because he's working overtime and won't have time to get to the store.

Say no at least once in a while to

- ✔ **The TV.** The boob tube, the idiot box. Need we say more?
- ✔ **Telephone calls.** Subscribe to caller ID. If the ID shows Unknown Caller or a company name, let the call go to your answering machine. Heck, if it shows your mother, let the machine get it!
- ✔ **Your neighbor.** Say that although you don't have time to co-host the shower, you'll be glad to blow up a few balloons or address the invitations.
- ✔ **Your ex's plea for you to shop for him.** Explain that you're also busy and suggest he order the gift from a Web site.
- ✔ **Your pastor.** When he calls to ask you to teach Sunday School next Sunday, explain that you're running on fumes lately and that you're afraid to overload your schedule — but maybe another time?

Prioritizing your responsibilities

It all comes down to *priorities*. What are the most important ways for you to spend your time at this stage in your life? If you take a good look at your schedule, you may find that you're overloaded with weekly *must do* responsibilities and you need to drop a few, at least for now.

As a single parent, you just don't have time do everything that's on your list, even though you want to. Here are a few important activities you may need to prioritize:

- ✔ Working full time.
- ✔ Attending every one of your daughter's softball games and practices.
- ✔ Teaching piano lessons from ten to noon on Saturday mornings.
- ✔ Serving as chair of your neighborhood watch program.
- ✔ Enjoying your weekly Friday poker nights with the guys.
- ✔ Having your widowed Mother over for dinner every Sunday.
- ✔ Playing in the men's summer soccer league.
- ✔ Babysitting your sister's kids one night a week, so she and her husband can have a romantic night out.

Whew! We know you have a big heart, but this is way beyond bionic!

Here's an idea: take a piece of paper and divide it into two columns by drawing a line down the center of the page. Label the left column "can't possibly give up" and the right column "can give up if I have to." Then, honestly and sensibly, enter your weekly duties in one column or the other.

You'll be surprised how many things you *can* give up — you just never thought it through before. For example, you may decide to forsake the piano lessons, the neighborhood watch duty, and the Friday night babysitting sessions, which would leave you with your daughter's softball schedule and your Mom's weekly visits. This is still puh-lenty, don't you agree?

Children don't have enough dreaming time because they're hugely over-scheduled with activities. Give your kids — and yourself — a break by cutting down on a few of their gigs. If your child is taking piano lessons, ballet lessons, and tae kwon do, in addition to playing T-ball and receiving private tutoring, she has at *least* three too many responsibilities each week! Your child needs time to wrestle with his dog when he gets home from school, run through the sprinkler for an hour if he feels like it, or just lie on the grass and gaze at the clouds! This will develop his imagination and give him a sense of inner calm. Sounds good, doesn't it? I bet you want to give it a try yourself.

Don't ignore the piddly stuff either — you can simplify your schedule in many little ways:

- ✔ **Replace your live houseplants with easy-care silk plants.**

- ✔ **Have your hair cut and restyled into something you can take care of yourself.** No more weekly hair appointments. (Or even trim it yourself.)

- ✔ **Cut down on telephone time.** Even though a friend expects to chat for a half hour or so, explain as nicely as you can that you have a couple things you *really* must get done before dinner or bedtime, so you'll need to talk more another time.

- ✔ **Wash the car half as often.** You can always park in the back lot at work. That way your buddies won't be tempted to compare your grime with their shine!

- ✔ **If your home requires a lot of maintenance, consider selling it.** Move into something smaller and easier to care for.

- ✔ **No more weekly professional manicures and pedicures.** Start doing your own nails, unless you're going to a wedding or on a very special date! (Chapter 15 has more dating information.)

- ✔ **Stop surfing the Net, delete worthless e-mail messages without opening them, and forget those mindless chat rooms.**

- ✔ **Give your housecleaning a break once in a while and stop worrying about trivial stuff.** We know you've always been known as Mr. Clean, but you're a single parent now.

Getting the kids to pitch in

Delegate doable chores to your children. They're plenty capable of taking on some of the little things you do around the house every day, and even though they may complain, a structured schedule actually gives them a feeling of being part of a team. Kids need this structure, especially if they've recently suffered the trauma of divorce or losing a parent.

Depending on their ages, your kids can

- ✔ **Clean their rooms.**

- ✔ **Make their beds.**

- ✔ **Put their toys away.**

- ✔ **Bring their dirty clothes to the laundry room and put their clean clothes away.** Ask them to carry clean clothes from the laundry room instead of taking them to the children's' rooms yourself. (Furnish your older kids with a supply of large safety pins. Every time they take off their dirty socks, get them in the habit of pinning the socks together. That way the socks stay paired.)

- ✔ **Lay out their school clothes the night before.**

- ✔ **Help make their school lunches, if they brown-bag it.**

- ✔ **Help out in the kitchen before and after dinner.** Kids can set the table, clean vegetables, slice strawberries, clear the table, load the dishwasher, empty the garbage, and put food away in the refrigerator — even a three-year-old can plunk the catsup bottle back in the door of the fridge.

- ✔ **Wash the family car.** So what if it isn't a perfect job and they get a little wet in the process? At least you don't have to do it!

- ✔ **Take care of the household pets.** Ask your kids to bathe pets (if they're *washable* pets, that is), feed and water them, change the litter box, and take them for walks.

- ✔ **Clean the house.** You can ask your children to sweep the kitchen and bathroom floors, vacuum, dust, pick up clutter in the family room each night before bed, empty all the wastebaskets in the house, clean mirrors and windows, and so on.

- ✔ **Help with the yard work.** Kids can handle watering, weeding, mowing, raking, and keeping the lawn and flower bins looking sharp.

If you have several children, alternate their daily chores. Make up a chart that shows which child is responsible for which chore each day.

We've both raised kids ourselves, so we know how tempting it can be to forego the delegating and do the chore yourself! When you're in a hurry, it's frustrating to take the extra time to teach your child a household chore. By the time you give him instructions, then follow up to see that he did a good job, you could have done the chore three times yourself! However — and here's the good part — faithfully delegating chores to your kids will pays off in the long run. Your kids practice a skill, and they become responsible and valuable members of your family. Your kids will become proficient at their tasks eventually; all you need is as little patience at the start.

Are you a perfectionist? If so — and you know who you are! — try to break the habit. Perfectionism is a tremendous time thief! You're probably the one who follows your kids around the house, straightening up the bedspreads after they've already made their beds in the morning. And we suspect you also alphabetize the canned goods in your kitchen pantry and take all the ornaments off the Christmas tree and re-hang them so they'll be evenly spaced! Are we right? If so, please try to relax and go with the flow. The bedspreads will get tossed off when the kids go to bed tonight anyway, and Christmas can be *just* as much fun with a lopsided tree! Really!

Running hither and yon: Errands

It takes a little practice to get used to the idea of structuring your errands to save time.

- ✔ **Realize that every errand doesn't *have* to be done today.** So, what if you need to pick up your navy blue suit from the cleaners for work tomorrow? There *are* other clothes in your closet. And that prescription that's ready at the pharmacy? Are you really down to your last pill, or could you combine the pharmacy and the dry cleaners into one errand tomorrow?

- ✔ **Keep a running list of errands and cluster as many together as you can.** Not only does this save you driving time, but it also saves on gas.

- ✔ **Check out your local vendors — if any deliver, especially for free, take advantage of their home delivery services.** See if your dry cleaners and drug store deliver. Or, how about your corner grocery store?

- ✔ **Do something constructive while you're waiting.** We all know the drill: hurry up and wait. You can easily spend an hour in your doctor's waiting room, or a half hour waiting for your hairdresser to finish with his previous customer. Here are a few things you can do to fill in those waiting gaps:

  - Make necessary calls using your cell phone.

  - Update your to-do lists.

  - Balance your checkbook.

  - Catch up on your correspondence.

  - Pay a couple bills.

  - Clean out your purse.

  - Bring your laptop along so you can reply to your e-mails or get a little work done while you wait.

  - Take a power nap while no one is looking — you'll feel refreshed.

We know a mother who keeps a "To-Do-To-Go" bag filled with things she can do while waiting. One year she dumped her Christmas cards, address book, and a pen in her bag and not only addressed all her cards, but wrote personal notes in each one as well. Try this — or really give yourself a break by saying "no" to Christmas cards and sending New Year's notes instead to a very few close friends and relatives who live out of town.

Dumping out your purse: Organizing

You can probably free up several hours each week by being more organized. Every family can reap this reward if they just take a little time to get their stuff together, but for a single parent, it's not a choice. You've *got* to get organized, even if you've never tried it before — now is the time to try out this clever new concept!

The grocery store can be a drag

Emily is a single mother with good intentions. To save time, she decided to grocery shop only once a week — on Saturday mornings when she was relatively fresh and could think straight. Every Saturday, she packed up the kids and trekked down to her neighborhood grocery store for a week's worth of bread, milk, toilet paper, and all the other supplies she needed for her family. But as hard as Emily tried to remember everything she needed on Saturday morning, she always ended up stopping after work during the week for something important she forgot to buy.

Finally, it dawned on her why her Saturday morning shopping trips weren't saving time after all: She realized that her grocery list was pretty sketchy — she was counting on remembering things she needed while she was in the store — plus she couldn't concentrate because the kids were constantly begging for a certain kind of cereal, ice cream bar, or candy.

So, she made a major decision. No more weekly trips to the grocery store. She decided to spend one Saturday morning a month shopping for that month's groceries and supplies. And this time

she not only made up a detailed list, but also got her cookbooks out, planned a menu ahead of time, and wrote down every ingredient needed. Then, she walked through her home peeking into the refrigerator and cupboards to see what she was low on, and added those items to her list. She also checked her calendar to see what birthday and anniversary cards she needed for the month.

Then she made the biggest decision of all — a babysitter for the kids one Saturday morning each month. That way she could actually think while she was at the store and, hopefully, eliminate those annoying trips to buy things after work.

Her new plan not only worked, but it saved money. Instead of her local neighborhood grocery, she drove a few miles farther to a discount warehouse-style grocery store where the prices were a little better. And Emily discovered another unexpected benefit — no more stress over what to fix for dinner! Her menu was set for the month; she knew she had all the ingredients for each meal. Emily relaxed when she got home from work each day and actually enjoyed fixing dinner.

Here are five great ways to organize your home and add precious hours to each day:

Uncluttering the place

Take a look around — where does clutter seem to accumulate in your house? In your hall closet? In your kitchen cupboards? How about your home office? Every home is different, but take an honest look around and see what can be organized in a more logical way.

✔ **Add rods to all your closets.** If your closets have the standard single rod, raise it and add another rod below it. The closet will hold twice as many clothes and they won't be crammed together.

✔ **Place hooks over the closet rods.** Hooks hold belts, scarves, baseball caps, and anything else that can be looped onto the hooks.

✔ **Add shelves in the closets.** Place one above the present shelf, and several shorter ones down each side of the closet.

✔ **Attach pouched shoe bags to the backs of doors.** Hang these on the doors of your bedroom, bathroom, and closet to hold items you use every day, such as a hairbrush, shampoo, your dog's leash, the flashlight, all those remote controls, and so on.

✔ **Organize your kids' rooms.** We know you don't even want to look in there, let alone organize it, but after you get things under control, your kids will (hopefully) find it easier to keep their rooms clean.

  • Buy a half dozen colored plastic crates or large wicker baskets — place them around your kids' bedrooms, or where your kids keep their toys, books, stuffed animals, sports equipment, or dirty clothes. Wall shelves and bookcases work well too.

  • If your children have more stuffed animals than they can count, get the animals off the floor by placing them in a stringed hammock suspended close to the ceiling across the corner of the bedroom. Stringed hammocks are available at toy stores.

  • Designate one shelf for each child's schoolbooks and homework — wow, will that ever save time every school morning!

  • If your kids have way too much stuff, throw the tattered toys, books, and clothes in the trash, then donate outgrown clothes and duplicate games or toys to a charity. Include your children in these decisions, and take them along to the Salvation Army, which is a great way to teach them generosity and social responsibility.

Streamlining your laundry room

It's where you clean your clothes; now you can clean the room itself!

Go pro

If you don't have time to get organized, and it's not really your favorite thing anyway, you can hire a professional organizer who will come into your home and do it for you. A pro can help you sort the clothes in your closet, for example, into three piles: stuff to throw away, stuff to give away, and stuff to keep. And they work so fast they can organize an entire home in one day! You might want to give one of these amazing magicians a try.

✔ **Organize a basket or bag for each type of laundry load.** Make sure you provide a big basket for the everyday stuff such as towels, sheets, underwear, and socks. You can set up separate baskets for colored and white permanent press loads that require a cooler temperature or other special handling.

✔ **Eliminate ironing.** String up a clothesline in your garage or basement to hang damp clothes on hangers. Then follow these steps for a nearly ironing free existence:

1. Wash clothes on the permanent press cycle.

2. Add fabric softener (preferably Snuggle Ultra).

3. As soon as the wash cycle is finished, lift the clothes into your dryer and put them through an air-only cycle.

4. Here's the trick: Remove the clothes from the dryer *before* the dryer has kicked off.

5. Place each item of clothing on a hanger.

6. While you're hanging a couple garments on hangers, let the dryer continue turning until you lift another couple items out.

The key is to be close by when this little maneuver is taking place; otherwise, the clothes sit in the washer or dryer too long and we all know what that means — lots of wrinkles that need to be *ironed* out. Ugh!

✔ **Create a plan for your clean clothes.** Following these steps will save you more time than anything else:

1. Label one laundry basket — or ordinary cardboard box — for each room in the house. Your daughter Jenny gets a box marked JENNY. Your kitchen gets a basket marked KITCHEN.

2. When folding laundry, each item taken out of the dryer gets placed directly into its designated basket.

3. Carry full baskets to their destination and unload. And here's an added perk — each child who's able carries his own basket to his own room and puts his clothes away. You'll really love this system, especially when you're on your way out the door to your daughter's soccer practice and Ashley can't find her soccer socks. Take a look in the box marked ASHLEY and that's probably where you'll find them!

Keeping track of your kids' after-school stuff

Their stuff can quickly become a pile of homework, toys, and galoshes. Put an end to all that clutter! Put up colorful hooks on the wall for your kids to store their backpacks and coats. Place a basket under the hooks for their boots and bike helmets. Color-code the hooks and baskets so that each child has his own color.

Putting your desk into some kind of order

Okay, so your desk can quickly become a pile of bills, receipts, and pens. Stop the madness!

✔ **Designate a basket, drawer, or cubbyhole specifically for your bills — and bills *only*!**

✔ **Keep a supply of envelopes, return-address stickers, and stamps together in another cubbyhole or basket.**

✔ **Name your desk drawers.** No, not Fred or Bill! Name the drawers so you can sort what goes into them:

  • **Drawer one:** Toss *really* important stuff in here. The invitation to a birthday party will probably be in the No. 1 drawer, because that needs immediate attention — you need to buy a card and a gift, for one thing.

  • **Drawer two:** Toss *pretty* important stuff in here. When you finally have a minute to reply to your elderly aunt's letter from two weeks ago, it will probably be in your No. 2 drawer.

  • **Drawer three:** Toss the you'll-get-to-it-someday-if-you-have-the-time stuff here. The discount coupon for Jake's Pizza on the other side of town, that you never go to anyway because they skimp on the cheese, can sit indefinitely in your No. 3 drawer, and you'll never miss it! See how this cool plan works?

✔ **Furnish your desk with its very own, never-move-from-this-spot-or-you-die office supplies.** If these items still mysteriously disappear from your desk, that means you need to go out and buy duplicates or triplicates. That way you'll have what you need in the kitchen by the phone, and your kids will have supplies in their rooms. Your desk tools won't *need* to be borrowed.

Creating a calendar that actually works!

It's already *what* month?

- ✔ **Put everything on one calendar.** If you're like most parents, your wall calendar doesn't have *everything* noted on it. For example, you may post your daughter's school schedule on the bulletin board, with field days underlined. Or, you may have your son's football practice schedule attached to the refrigerator door.

- ✔ **Get a year-at-a-glance calendar to keep you on track.** The standard month-by-month calendars don't work for those people who only concentrate on the current month and forget to glance ahead at the upcoming months. As bizarre as it may seem to some of you, it *is* important to know *this* month what's happening *next* month!

Doing Like Ringo Says and Accepting a Little Help

Single parents need a little help from their friends from time to time, especially when it comes to running taxi service for your kids, babysitting for each others' children, cooking meals for each other, and other timesaving tricks.

Pools are cool — Car pools, that is

Although carpooling has been around since Henry Ford, most parents don't take full advantage of this marvelous timesaver. Most of you could be carpooling a lot more. Car pools can be used for transporting the kids to and from school, sporting events, church activities, music lessons, camp, and so on.

1. Ask for a list of other parents whose children are enrolling in the same activity as yours.

2. Get on the phone and start calling those parents who live close enough together to form a car pool for that particular activity.

   Try to get enough parents involved so that each parent drives the kids to practices only once every week or two.

Be sure you know something about the person who'll be doing the driving. Ask around and get a few references before entrusting the safety of your child to someone you don't know well.

Jim's colorful calendar

Jim is a single dad in the San Francisco Bay area who was going nuts trying to keep track of his own schedule, his son's school and sports schedules, and holidays and vacations. When Jim and his wife divorced, his wife kept custody of their daughter, a college freshman, and Jim kept sole-custody of their fourteen-year-old son. Jim had never had trouble keeping track of appointments, but when he received full responsibility for his son he found it difficult to coordinate their schedules.

Jim's solution was to buy a year-at-a-glance erasable wall calendar, along with a supply of colored dry-erase pens, stickers, and stars. He uses the pens to color-code his calendar. His son's football practices are marked on the calendar with blue ink, his games in red, school vacations and early-out school days are marked in green. Anything unusual happening at work,

such as an all-day conference or a business trip, is marked in black. Jim uses the colored stars to mark special events, such as birthdays, anniversaries, or weddings. Finally, yellow butterfly stickers indicate out-of-town guests and visits from his daughter.

The calendar is quite a colorful sight, but it works for Jim and his son. They like the fact that they can easily see what's on the schedule in the months to come, and it's given Jim the feeling of being back in control. No more scrambling around at the last minute to buy a gift or make arrangements for his son when he'll be gone on a two-day business trip. Sure, his friends and family members tease him when they come by for a visit, but he just grins and suggests they should try it before they knock it. Sounds like a winning idea to us!

Here are ways to maximize the concept:

✔ One parent drives the children *to* the event every week, while the other parent drives the children *from* the event.

✔ One parent drives the children to and from the event every other week.

✔ One parent drives the kids to and from events during the week, while the other parent provides transportation for weekend events.

✔ Ask your child's other parent to drive the kid to his game once in a while — and stay to attend the game as well. Perhaps your ex will take over this duty a couple times a month, if she lives close by, or your child's grandparents, aunts, or uncles can get involved, too. Meanwhile, have the other parent videotape the game so you can watch it later, especially if your child wants you to see his fantastic home run or touchdown! By the way, giving yourself permission to miss a few games can be empowering to your kids who realize you trust them to do their best, whether you're there or not.

Just because you'll be attending your child's basketball game anyway doesn't mean you need to arrive early for the pre-game practice. Use carpooling to get your child to that early practice. That way you don't arrive until game time, and you save an hour or more of precious time every game day.

Joining a babysitting co-op

The biggest advantage of a babysitting co-op is saving money, but there's another reason why one of these co-ops is an awesome idea for a single parent — it will add hours of free time to your life. This is the way it works:

- ✔ **Several parents get together to form a co-op, which is a way to babysit each other's kids for free.** For example, you have your neighbor's girls over for a Saturday afternoon play time with your children, which can be exchanged for equal babysitting time when you need to get away.

- ✔ **The parents alternate serving as the "bank," which means that one of the parents keeps track of members' credits and debits.** Every time you babysit someone's children for four hours, you receive four hours credit, which are placed in your account in the "bank." When you ask another member of the co-op to have your daughters over to play with her kids for two hours, two hours are debited from your account.

- ✔ **To keep strict track of the hours, some co-ops use paper *credits* and *debits* signed by both parents at the end of each babysitting session.** These credits and debits are given to the banker who records them.

Of course, you can always pay a sitter to stay with your children while you run errands or take a break, but the co-op idea is much less stressful for the kids. Instead of "being babysat while Dad leaves us at home to go do something fun," they "get to go over to Jordan's house to play a video game."

Because most single parents have fulltime employment that already requires paid child care during workdays, it's nice to have a "babysitting account" to draw from in the evenings or on weekends. And, of course, the money you save is a bonus!

Whipping up a cooking club

Cooking co-ops are catching on in our country. Talk about a timesaver! How would you like to have dinner delivered to your door two nights a week? What a treat.

Here's the way it works:

- **Get together with two other single parents to form a cooking co-op where you take turns cooking the main meal.** This means that when it's your night to cook, you cook dinner for all the families, including your own. Some single parents cook on the weekend, preparing dishes that can be frozen until their mid-week cooking day, when they are popped in the oven to cook or heat up before delivery.

- **Set limits on the menu.** Get together with other members to decide that all meals should be healthy and balanced. You can decide that all meals come with meat, one starch, one vegetable, and a salad. And you can declare what's off limits too; for instance, no spicy foods, no desserts, ethnic foods only on a limited basis, and so on.

- **Limit the co-op members to a certain geographic radius, within two or three miles.**

- **Plan the meals so they stay within a comparable cost range.**

- **Choose three nights a week for these dinner exchanges.** Some co-ops pick Mondays, Tuesdays, and Thursdays, eating leftovers on Wednesdays, then eating out or cooking single-family meals the other nights.

- **Set up reasonable delivery times, depending on when each parent gets home from work.**

- **Pack food in disposable pans, zip-top bags, or reusable plastic containers; bag green salad items separately, so everything stays crisp until the last minute.** Some co-ops have pitched in to buy a supply of aluminum serving pans and other containers that rotate from house to house as they are used to deliver food.

If you like the idea of having hot meals ready when you get home from work, but you're not really into a cooking club, how about taking advantage of your slow cooker? If you don't own one — go out and buy a *large* sized cooker. Look through the little cookbook that came with your slow cooker or check out *Slow Cookers For Dummies* by Tom Lacalamita (Wiley Publishing, Inc.).

Doing the Splits: Flexibility

Now that you're a single parent, you need to be flexible in a lot of ways, and your job needs to be flexible as well. If your current job is too demanding, stressful, and time-consuming, if it requires extra hours above and beyond your forty-hour week, maybe it's time to look for something less demanding. If your kids are still covered by your ex's health insurance, you have the freedom to look around for a job that opens up your schedule, whether it offers health benefits or not.

Believe it or not, some companies out there promote work/life balance for their employees. Companies on the cutting edge, like the University of Arizona, offer workers flexible schedules so they can "have a life." This concept is more than just a feel-good program, because it actually increases productivity.

You can also negotiate with your present employer for a better work schedule, or you may even be able to find a different employer who offers child care at the work site.

Negotiating with your employer

If you're thinking about looking for another job that's less stressful and time-consuming, why not give your current employer a chance before you make the leap? You may be surprised what your current boss will do for you — after all, you're a valuable employee. Additionally, your boss may have some helpful suggestions.

Here are a few options your boss may throw out:

- ✔ **Four ten-hour days, instead of five eight-hour days.**

- ✔ **Work from home one or two days a week.** Sometimes you can even get a four-day workweek out of this deal, with two days in the office and two days working from your home.

- ✔ **Work from home fulltime.** Wow! Wouldn't that be fantastic? Thousands of workers work from home already, with more signing on every year. Search on www.google.com for information on *telecommuting*. Become informed on the subject so when you approach your boss, you know how it works. Read the telecommuting story "Kathy, the work-from-home mom" in this chapter.

- ✔ **An alternative position in the company.** You might be offered one that pays a little less, but is less stressful and requires no overtime.

- ✔ **Flextime.** This means you still put in your forty hours, but on your schedule, not theirs. That way you can stay home if your child is sick, get to work late occasionally if an emergency comes up, take off for your child's dental appointment, and generally allow for all those Murphy's Law catastrophes that come along in the lives of single parents.

- ✔ **A job-share position.** In this type of position, you and your coworker perform one job. This may mean you work three days and she works two, or vice versa. Or, she may work the even-numbered weekdays and you the odd-numbered days. This is an idea that's already taken hold in many professions, especially in hospitals and special education classrooms, where job burnout is high.

Working from home

Kathy is the mother of two boys, one in junior high and one in high school. Fortunately, they're really awesome, well-behaved, high-achieving kids. And they love the fact that their mom works at home.

Kathy performs the same job she used to commute for. She works for a medical clinic; her duties include transcribing data into patients' files, keeping the books, and calling patients who are behind on their payments. She and her boss came up with a system where data is sent to her on cassette tapes twice a week and the daily billing data is sent to her via e-mail attachments. At 9:00 a.m. and 2:00 p.m. every day, Kathy calls her boss to check in.

When it's time for the boys to get home from school, Kathy lays snacks on a table along with a list of chores for the day. If she doesn't want to be disturbed, she attaches a note to the front door. The note explains that she's taking an important call or working on a tight deadline, so that the boys know they need to be quiet and not interrupt her until a certain time.

This schedule has worked out well for Kathy, her boss, and her boys. Even though it's a tad inconvenient at times, she feels it's worth it. Talk about a win-win situation!

Seeking alternative child care

If your current child-care arrangement requires a lot of driving to drop kids off and pick them up, why not look for a better plan? Well, you may not want to rock the boat at this stage in your life — if your child has been coping pretty well where he is, why change? Right?

Not necessarily. This could be another case where you're making an enormous sacrifice *for the sake of the children.* Is it possible that your kids might be just as happy someplace close to home? Or closer to your job site?

This has nothing to do with the cost, you understand, which we'll talk about some other time, but this is strictly for *your* sake — to save you precious time every workday. The kids would rather spend less time in a car and more time at home, too. Take a look in Chapter 5 for a variety of child-care options.

Here are some alternatives to think about:

> ✔ **Does a neighbor provide licensed child care out of her home?** If so, your child may be able to spend time with other kids he already knows from your neighborhood.

✔ **Is child care offered at your place of work?** That would not only save you driving time, but it would keep you close by in case your child becomes ill during your workday.

✔ **Do you know a child-care provider who will come to your home?** Perhaps a friend or relative would love to make a little income while caring for a child who already means a lot to her personally.

✔ **How about sharing the cost of an in-home child-care provider with a friend who also needs child care for his children?** You could have the provider come to your home or your friend's home. By splitting the cost, you may be able to avoid transporting your child to a day-care center or preschool every day.

✔ **Do you have a spare bedroom where you can house a college student in exchange for that student taking care of your children while you're at work?** Of course, this idea will only work if you and the student are away from the house at different times of day.

✔ **Have you looked for a child-care center or preschool close to your home or work, or on the drive in between?** The important thing is to waste little time driving out of your way to deliver and pick up your children.

Chapter 5

Crunching Numbers

. . . .

In This Chapter

▶ Reviewing some financial pitfalls

▶ Figuring out ways to make a little more moola

▶ Creating a single-parent budget that works

▶ Adjusting to a smaller income

▶ Looking for assistance

. . . .

Money problems are the pits! Is anything worse than the feeling you get when a young waiter gives you his sad puppy-dog face and says, "Sorry, but your credit card was rejected"? How humiliating. But the situation can get even more embarrassing: Your friend (the one you're *treating* to a birthday lunch) hears the comment, and you only have $1.23 on you at the moment.

Or how about the few days before payday when you run out of money for the kids' school lunches? You scrounge around the house for spare change, searching the junk drawer and the bottom of your purse until you finally round up enough nickels and dimes to get by until you get paid.

You may think that you're the only single parent in town who's *this* tight on money every week, but you're not alone — really. In fact, money is the biggest problem for most single parents. It's like a monkey clinging to your back day and night. A lot of traditional families and wealthy single parents struggle with these same monkeys — just because they have the big bucks doesn't mean they spend them wisely.

Providing a quality standard of living for yourself and your kids is a difficult challenge, but it *is* possible. The user-friendly, practical solutions that we offer in this chapter can help get that monkey off your back once and for all and give you a sense of freedom and a peace of mind you've probably never experienced before. No more angst, no more sleepless nights, and no more heartache — *everything* in your life can seem just right when you're finally living within your means.

In this chapter we show you ways to avoid the five biggest single-parent money mistakes, how to increase your income, and how to live within your means by setting up a workable budget. You can also find out where to get a little help, from government assistance to the advice of credit counselors and financial advisors. Our goal is to get that stinky old monkey off your back, put him in a cage, and lock him up for life.

Avoiding the Five Biggest Single-Parent Money Mistakes

No one's perfect, and we all make poor money-spending decisions from time to time, but single parents are notorious for falling into one or more of these money traps:

- **Confusing wants and needs:** Your first priority should be to take care of your family's *needs*. The *wants* come later — if you have any money left over.

- **Using credit cards to buy stuff:** Unless you're able to pay the balance off within the grace period, stay away from the plastic. Calmly put the card down, keep your hands where we can see them, and slowly step away from the sales counter. If you can't pay off your credit cards *totally* every 30 days, you're buying things you can't afford. In other words, you're living above your means.

- **Spending guilt money on your children:** When your kids beg for something at the mall, don't give in. Keep that ATM card safely tucked away. If your kids have faced a lot of upheaval due to a divorce or the trauma associated with the death of their parent, don't try to compensate by spending big bucks on pricey entertainment. You can't *buy* your kids' love, and you can't replace what they've lost, so forget the cruise with the famous mouse and instead treat them to a day at the zoo (or something even less expensive like hiking at a state park). What your kids need is your love and your time, neither one of which costs a dime.

- **Spending without a plan:** You get your paycheck, cash it, and start spending money with no thought of saving for emergencies. What's wrong with this picture? You can avoid falling into this trap by setting up a spending plan (a *budget* for all you budding accountants) in advance. Even if you don't follow the plan to the letter, you at least have guidelines in place.

- **Living in a financial state of denial:** Many single parents strive to maintain their previous standard of living with less income at their disposal. You can only dip into your savings so many times until your balance is zero, so listen to the wakeup call and face reality — as unpleasant as it may seem right now.

Doing the Math: Single Parent = Single Income

If you're a recently divorced or widowed parent, you've basically gone from two incomes to one. In the case of divorce, you may receive alimony or child-support payments or make these payments, but the basic idea still holds true.

You want statistics? Well we have them. One year after her divorce, a single mother's income drops to 67 percent of her pre-divorce income. A divorced father is a lot better off: His income only drops a little to 90 percent of his pre-divorce income, mainly because of his alimony or child-support payments. But, in either case, you try to maintain the same standard of living for you and the kids on less income. Obviously, accomplishing this feat is impossible, but you may not fess up to this fact until you're buried under mega-bills and maxed-out credit-card debt. Fessing up to the problem is a good first step. Until you become the master of the obvious, you have no hope of solving your financial woes.

When your income seems to drop out from under you, one of the first things to reconsider is how you're making that money.

Taking this job and shoving it

If you became a single parent on purpose, you probably had a little time to think things through and make a career change before becoming a parent. But you may feel trapped in your job — especially if the single parenthood thing kind of snuck up on you. Take an honest look at your current career:

- Do you enjoy it?
- Do you respect your employer?
- Does your employer respect you?
- Are the hours compatible with your kids' schedule?
- How's the pay?
- Any chance for a raise?

If more of your answers to the questions were negative than positive, give these ideas some thought:

- **Ask your current employer for a raise or a promotion before looking elsewhere.** You may be surprised by what your employer will offer you.

- **If your current employer is a dud but you like the type of work you're doing, look for an employer who offers you more.** Better pay, more benefits, and if you can find these goodies, flextime, onsite child care, or other programs make your life easier.

✔ **If you're sick of your position, but you want to stay in the same general field, check out other jobs.** For example, if you've been working as a pharmaceutical assistant, but you're tired of dealing with cranky customers who constantly nag you about their puny insurance coverage, consider a position such as medical records clerk.

Retraining for a better gig

What if you could snag a better gig by going to school for six months or so? Sound interesting? Education is the best way for single parents to increase their incomes. Take a look at the *Occupational Outlook Handbook* by the U.S. Department of Labor and the Bureau of Labor Statistics. It offers information about various careers, their growth projections, the training required, and the average pay around the United States. The government updates this amazing handbook every year. You can find a copy in the reference department of your library or in electronic format by visiting www.bls.gov/oco/home.htm for job opportunities in your state or country.

Consider these programs as well:

✔ **Job-training programs offered by individual states and provinces:** Check with your state or provincial government to see if grant money is available to help train you for a better, higher-paying job.

✔ **Welfare to Work:** This program is designed for single parents with low incomes who want to complete their education. Read all about Welfare-to-Work at www.usdoj.gov/jmd/ps/wtw.htm. It's administered through your county Department of Social Services.

✔ **Extended Opportunities Programs and Services (EOPS):** This program provides help for individuals attending college, including free child care. See a related success story in the "Going from welfare to work" sidebar, later in this chapter. EOPS is administered through individual colleges and universities, so use a search engine to locate a college or university in your city or state.

Fudging a Budget Isn't Allowed

We can hear you asking, "What's a budget?" If your spouse always handled the bills, and a budget is as foreign to you as speaking Latin, you need to become acquainted with this handy tool. A *budget* is a record of your monthly income and expenses, and the object is to get these two categories to balance. Novel idea, huh?

We live in a paycheck-to-paycheck, buy-today-pay-tomorrow society, so the idea of budget guidelines is a bummer to a lot of people. You may think of adhering to a budget as being on a constant diet where you never get to eat the things you love. Not true. You can set up a workable budget that provides a happy and satisfying standard of living for you and your kids. The first thing you need to understand is that your budget should be based on *after-tax* dollars — your *spendable income*.

We don't offer tax advice in this chapter except to suggest contacting your accountant about the tax ramifications of being a single parent because a ton of consequences exist. And don't wait until tax time to get some advice because you need to know about these tax breaks beforehand so you can take advantage of them all year long.

In Table 5-1, we provide some suggested percentages to allot toward each category of your single-parent budget. Don't be discouraged by these percentages, however, because your financial situation may require a bit of juggling. Consider them merely as *guidelines.* The table uses an *after-tax, spendable income* of $24,850 for the sample budget.

Table 5-1	Sample Budget for $24,850 After-Tax Annual Income		
Category	*Total*	*Yearly $ Total*	*Approximate Monthly $ Total*
Housing	36%	8,946.00	745.50
Food	12%	2,982.00	248.50
Child care	12%	2,982.00	248.50
Transportation	11%	2,733.50	227.80
Entertainment/ recreation	5%	1,242.50	103.54
Insurance	5%	1,242.50	103.54
Debts	4%	994.00	82.83
Clothing	4%	994.00	82.83
Medical/dental	4%	994.00	82.83
Charity giving	2%	497.00	41.42
Miscellaneous	2%	497.00	41.42
Savings (designated)	2%	497.00	41.42
Savings (emergency)	1%	248.50	20.71
TOTAL	100%	24,850.00	2,070.84

Use the percentages in Table 5-1 as guidelines for creating your own personalized budget. The accompanying figure is blank so you can make copies and insert your information. Then, after you have your budget all figured out and lookin' good, hang it on your refrigerator where you and your kids can see it every day. Keeping it handy can help you stay on track, especially if budgeting is a new concept for you.

Take a look at our breakdown of each individual budget category:

- **Housing:** Your total housing expenses should include your mortgage payment (composed of principal and interest, plus taxes, homeowners insurance, and PMI insurance, if applicable) or rent and utilities. To get a monthly estimate of your utilities, take the total of all your utility costs for a year and divide by 12.

Budget for after-tax income per year of $ _____

Category	Percent	Yearly Total in Dollars	Monthly Total in Dollars (approximate)
Housing	%	$	$
Food	%	$	$
Child care	%	$	$
Transportation	%	$	$
Entertainment-Recreation	%	$	$
Insurance	%	$	$
Debts	%	$	$
Clothing	%	$	$
Miscellaneous	%	$	$
Medical/Dental	%	$	$
Savings (Designated)	%	$	$
Savings (Emergency)	%	$	$
Charity giving	%	$	$
	100%	$	$

- **Food:** Your food budget should include almost everything you purchase at a grocery store, including food items, paper goods, cleaning supplies, and any other nonfood products you normally purchase when you shop at a discount food store.

- **Child care:** The amount budgeted toward child care should include every expense involving your child's before- and after-school care, plus school tuition if applicable. Your child's future college tuition is not covered here. Hopefully your ex will help pay. Your child may receive scholarships, grants, and loans.

- **Transportation:** Your transportation allotment includes your car payment (or lease payment), auto insurance, gas, oil, repairs, maintenance, and *depreciation* (the amount your car drops in value as it ages).

- **Entertainment/recreation:** This category covers all the fun stuff in your life, including vacations, daytrips, eating out, club dues, sporting equipment, movies, concerts, hobby expenses, camping trips, tickets to a ball game . . . you get the idea.

- **Insurance:** This category includes all your insurance expenses, except for your homeowners insurance (included under *housing*) and your auto insurance (included under *transportation*).

- **Debts:** This is your budget for paying off credit cards and other loans, such as any college loans (not including your home mortgage or car loan).

See the "Retraining for a better gig" section, mentioned earlier in this chapter, for information about government assistance with college expenses. Also contact the financial aid office at your child's university.

- **Clothing:** To determine what your family normally spends on clothing, you need to total up all your clothing expenditures for a year and divide by 12. The problem is that very few of us keep all our receipts, plus it becomes academic anyway when you realize that you *must* stay within your allotted clothing budget per month now that you're a single parent. In other words, you only have so much money to spend in this category, so you need to learn how to live with it.

- **Medical/dental:** This category is your fund for paying insurance deductibles and co-pays for office calls, prescriptions, eye exams, glasses, dental work (including those infamous braces!), and over-the-counter medications.

- **Savings (designated):** These savings are for *known* expenses that pop up at odd times during the year, such as homeowners-association dues, professional dues, Christmas funds, yearly termite inspections, and so on. When November rolls around, for example, and you're anxious to start your Christmas shopping, you need to have enough saved so you can pay cash for all your gifts.

- ✔ **Savings (emergency):** This fund should build until you eventually have enough to get by for at least three months if you should lose your job, become hospitalized, or have other emergency expenses that pop up. If you're overloaded with credit-card debt, the idea of saving anything may seem laughable to you, but you *must* save a little every payday in spite of your debt.

- ✔ **Charity giving:** You may want to assign a lot more than 2 percent of your income toward charitable giving, but we had to pick some number, and 2 percent seems to work. Here's a handy little nugget of info that you can use to stretch your charity budget: Many people work as volunteers for their church or favorite charity instead of giving cash. You can also write off many donations on your taxes (talk to your friendly neighborhood accountant).

- ✔ **Miscellaneous:** This category includes your children's allowances (if applicable), coffee money at work, haircuts, cosmetics, gifts, and so on.

If you've never been in charge of the budget before, you may want to apply a trick that many single parents use to prevent overspending between paydays: They use an envelope system. Here's how it works:

1. **Label one envelope for each cash category.**

   Many people use cash for Food, Entertainment/recreation, Clothing, Child care, and Miscellaneous.

2. **On payday, get small bills from the bank and place the designated amount in each envelope.**

   For example, if you get paid once a month, load up your Clothing envelope with $82.83 in cash (according to the budget in Table 5-1).

3. **When it's gone, it's gone. That's all there is folks.**

   No "borrowing" allowed. If you run out of entertainment money, you can't dig into the Child care envelope because you'll be short when you have to pay the preschool. See how it works?

What if the Food envelope runs short? Rob from your Entertainment/recreation envelope. If that envelope is empty, raid your larder for canned food and try to be more careful next month. This may result in thinned-down tomato paste poured over spaghetti noodles, or some odd combination of canned spinach and canned beets, but it works.

This system is also a great way to teach your children the value of money because they get to see and actually handle *real* money for a change — many people are only used to dealing with *invisible* money (ATM debit cards, paper checks, electronic transfers, and so on).

Living Comfortably on Less

Yes you can have a happy, fulfilled life that closely resembles your previous live-on-more lifestyle. Sure you may need to cut down on your standard of living a little (especially with the big stuff like the size of your home and the age of your car), but if you stick with us, you can find ways to pay less for lots of things.

Nesting sensibly: Home sweet home

Take a look at your current housing expenses, including your rent or house payment plus everything you need to operate your home (taxes, utilities, insurance, and maintenance). Does the total of all your housing expenses exceed 36 percent of your after-tax income? If so, you need to look for ways to lower this total.

Here are some popular ways single parents have lowered this expense:

- **Refinance your mortgage at a lower interest rate:** Spread your payments out over a longer period of time. While you're at it, consider refinancing for an amount that enables you to pay off your credit cards, which will do away with those payments and give you a tax write-off at the same time. Credit-card interest isn't deductible on your income tax, but mortgage interest is.

- **Consider selling the family home:** If you can't afford the family home you lived in before becoming a single parent, this option may be necessary. We know how painful this decision is. If you opt to sell your house you can

    • Buy a smaller home, a condo, or a duplex — one side of which you can rent out for extra income.

    • Use the cash to get back on your feet financially and rent for a while.

- **Share your housing expenses with another single parent:** This option can work whether you stay in your current home, sell it and buy a different home, or rent a home or apartment. It makes sense for several reasons: You can share the utility bills, cooking and cleaning responsibilities, and babysitting duties on and off during the week.

- **Move in with a relative:** We know this choice isn't first on your list (in fact, you may cringe at the idea). But life is hard, and facts are facts: Over 1.8 million single parents live with relatives. It can be the *temporary* answer to your housing crisis too.

✔ **Become an apartment manager:** In exchange for your services of renting apartments and dealing with tenants' complaints and problems, all your housing expenses are usually free.

✔ **See if you qualify for subsidized housing:** If your income is really in the cellar right now, check with your local housing authority to see what may be available in your town.

✔ **Apply for a Habitat for Humanity home:** If you have a stable income, but you can't afford the down payment on a home, you may qualify. A single parent can put in *sweat equity* (doing some of the work yourself) to become a homeowner. Call the Habitat for Humanity office near you or visit www.habitat.org.

✔ **Sign up for housing that features income-based payments:** This concept is popular (especially for single parents), so you may be put on a waiting list for these types of co-ops, condos, or apartments. For government subsidized housing, contact your local Department of Social Services or Housing Authority. For privately subsidized housing, look in your yellow pages under Apartments or Condominiums.

✔ **Cut down on the cost of your utilities:** You have many options at your disposal to lower these bills. Here are a few:

- **Electricity:** Turn off lights when you leave the room. Light up the corner of the room you're using at the moment. Replace incandescent light bulbs with fluorescent bulbs. Avoid the so-called long-life light bulbs — they actually cost you more in the long run because they use more energy. Call your power company and enroll in their load-management program, which means you get a break on off-hour usage. If you have an electric water heater, wash your clothes with cold water.

- **Heat:** Set your thermostat higher in the summer and lower in the winter. Close off vents in rooms that you seldom use. Add insulation in the attic. Clean the furnace filter once a month. Close the damper on your fireplace when you're not using it. Save up to 10 percent on your heating costs by plugging up air leaks around doors and windows. (Use inexpensive felt weather stripping available at all hardware stores.)

- **Hot water:** Lower the setting on your water heater — every ten degrees saves you about 7 percent of the total cost. You can also wrap the water heater in an insulating blanket.

- **Telephone service:** Compare long-distance rates, even if you spend an hour calling around before switching companies. Use e-mail and instant messaging as often as you can in place of long-distance calls. Do what a lot of single parents are doing: Cancel your long-distance carrier altogether and use your cell phone long-distance minutes instead. Another trick: Continually change long-distance companies whenever you receive a check in the mail from one of the companies. We know one parent who didn't have to pay anything for her long distance calls for an entire year because she kept switching companies and cashing their reward checks.

- **Water:** Take showers instead of baths. Install a low-flow showerhead. Only run your dishwasher when it's full. Turn the water off when you brush your teeth. Use a shut-off nozzle on the hose when you wash your car. Set your sprinkler system on a timer and run it in the middle of the night (if local rules permit) so you don't lose water to evaporation. (Or give up on watering the lawn and hope for rain.)

ANECDOTE

Finding a home in the 'burbs for half the cost

Frank is a single father of a 12-year-old son who plays soccer on the city-league team. During Saturday morning practices, Frank became friends with Gene, another single father of a boy on the team. Frank, Gene, and their kids became pretty good friends during the season, and after practices, the four usually went out for lunch. During these lunches, Frank and Gene compared notes on single parenthood. The biggest problem for each of them was maintaining their large four-bedroom family homes — financially *and* physically. They felt their homes were way too big for two people, but neither had a solution.

One day as Frank wrote out a check for his monumental mortgage payment, he had a thought. Maybe Gene and his son would consider moving in with him and Andy, not only to share the costs but also a few cooking and housekeeping duties. Frank sketched out a list of his expenses — the mortgage, utilities, maintenance expenses, and so on. He divided the total by two, decided the figure was reasonable, and gave Gene a call.

Gene jumped at the opportunity. It was a perfect solution to his strained budget. His home was way too large and expensive to maintain as a single parent, so he went along with the plan. He sold his home and paid off some bills with the profit, and he and his son moved in with Frank and Andy.

Fortunately the four personalities meshed, and the arrangement worked out pretty well. The solution wasn't perfect. Occasional disagreements arose over what to watch on the widescreen TV and what to fix for dinner. But, on the whole, the good far outweighed the bad: Each father's costs were cut in half; the boys were thrilled to be "brothers" living in the same house; the guys watched each other's kids when one of them was out of town on business or had a date; and the meals were a little more interesting than before with four people contributing to the cause.

Frank highly recommends this concept with one disclaimer: Be *sure* you know your potential housemate pretty well before suggesting the plan. In this case, everyone gets along real well, so Frank's experience is definitely a success story!

That's my deductible?!

The cost of insurance can suck up a hefty percentage of your spendable income, especially when you consider all the policies you're carrying. You can read more about this topic in *Insurance For Dummies,* by Jack Hungelmann (Wiley Publishing, Inc.), but for now, here are the basics:

- **Auto insurance:** Your first step is to shop around because auto insurance rates vary widely from one company to another. You may find lower rates if you're a nonsmoker, if you have a good driving record, if you drive less than 10,000 miles per year, or if you have an antitheft alarm on your car. Your premiums will also be lower if your car is older or if you own a dorky car that thieves wouldn't even think about stealing. Go for the highest deductibles you can tolerate, and if you own an older car that you've paid off, you may want to forget the collision and comprehensive coverage altogether and just keep the less-expensive liability coverage.

- **Disability insurance:** Disability insurance is usually pretty affordable, especially if it's part of your term life insurance policy. Group policies are often available through employers, unions, or professional organizations. Don't go for the moon — just sign up for enough to get you by in case you become disabled and unable to work.

- **Health insurance:** If you're in danger of losing your health-insurance coverage due to separation or divorce, a federal law called COBRA protects you. (COBRA stands for Consolidated Omnibus Budget Reconciliation Act of 1985, and that's why people usually don't spell it out.) This law mandates that you can continue your health-insurance coverage *at your expense* for a specific period of time. This is good news and bad news. It's good news because your coverage continues uninterrupted. It's bad news because your payments may total $400 or more per month for you and your children. Here are a few possible solutions to this mess:

  - **Negotiate with your ex to see if he or she will at least help out with the children's health-insurance premiums.**

  - **Find out if your children may be eligible for free Medicaid or Child Health Insurance Program (CHIP) health-insurance coverage.** If your children don't qualify for Medicaid because your income exceeds the threshold, they may qualify for CHIP, which offers insurance on a sliding scale. Parents who earn more money pay a higher portion of the premium. Parents living in many countries have subsidized health care.

  - **Look for a job with better benefits.** As much as you may love working for your current employer, if he or she doesn't offer health insurance, looking for a company that offers health-insurance benefits to its employees may be necessary. Many companies pay full health-insurance benefits for as little as 20 to 32 hours of work per week, and other companies share the costs on a percentage basis. If you have a company in mind, a discreet call to their human-resources office can provide the answers to your coverage questions.

- **Consider a less expensive type of coverage called *catastrophic* or *major medical* coverage.** These policies are regular health insurance policies, covering the same type of health problems as normal policies, but they are more affordable because they have a high annual deductible. The problem, of course, with one of these plans is that the deductible can be quite high.

- **Sign up for group coverage through a union or a professional organization you belong to.** Group policies offer lower premiums than individual health plans.

✔ **Homeowner's or renter's insurance:** Cut costs here by raising the deductibles as high as you can stand them, which may save you 10 percent or more, and installing a few bells and whistles that can also save you money. Smoke detectors, fire extinguishers, security alarms, and other safety features fit the bill.

✔ **Life insurance:** Shop around for the most reasonable *term life insurance policy* you can find; forget *whole life* and other options at this time in your life. All you need is enough coverage to pay off your major liabilities and provide a chunk of money to tide your children over until your ex or a relative takes guardianship. Term life policies (which some people refer to as *renting your insurance*) are very affordable.

One of the main differences between term life and whole life is that term life builds no value (you just make the monthly payments), but whole life does build value (a certain amount of your payments becomes a type of savings account). Another way of looking at it is to consider term life insurance as *temporary* and whole life as *permanent*.

Call several insurance companies to compare their premiums and get a hefty discount by consolidating all your insurance policies with one company. And be sure to avoid the three biggest insurance rip offs: mortgage life insurance, travel insurance, and credit disability insurance. Many financial advisors consider them rip offs because you pay a disproportionate amount of money for coverage that statistics show very few people ever need.

Sending the kids off to grandma's

Child care is a huge concern because you not only want quality care for your child, but you also need to be able to afford it. Many grandparents and extended family members provide child care for free. This is especially true when the single parent and her child are living in the relative's home.

Here are some of the most affordable choices for child care:

- **Grandparents:** Lots of grandparents are watching their grandbabies.

- **Other relatives:** Perhaps your sister, cousin, or aunt may be willing to babysit one or two days a week.

- **Non-relatives in the child's home:** A non-relative is anyone outside the family who cares for your child in your home. In other words, an all-day babysitter.

- **In-home day-care providers:** An in-home day-care provider takes care of children in her own home.

- **Day-care centers:** According to U.S. Census Bureau data, day-care centers take care of 12 percent of the 19.6 million preschoolers in the United States, at an average cost of about $83 per week.

- **Non-custodial parents:** Believe it or not, some terribly civilized divorced parents actually make this situation work. For example, if a babysitter is with your children for three or four hours, your ex may be able to relieve the sitter until you get home from work. This arrangement is great for the kids because they're in their own home, and they get to spend time with both parents throughout the day.

- **Employer-sponsored child care:** More and more employers are getting with the program and furnishing onsite child care for their employees' children. If you're looking for a new employer anyway, try to find one that provides this helpful service.

- **In-school child care:** If you're lucky, your school district provides before- and after-school programs at your child's school. These programs are quite affordable, but the key is to sign up early.

- **Recreation departments, city parks, and YMCAs:** Many folks don't think of the Y or the local recreation department when considering child-care alternatives, but these organizations often offer child-care services. A nearby YMCA may have an after-school child-care program, or your city recreation department may offer a day camp in the summer.

- **Church-sponsored programs:** Check out the churches in your area to see whether they offer child care or preschool programs, which are usually more affordable than the programs at for-profit care centers.

- **Teenage babysitters:** Hire a neighborhood teenager to be with your children between the time they get home from school and the time you arrive home from work. A teenager's hourly rate is usually quite a bit less than a professional care provider's fee, plus your children have the advantage of remaining in their own home.

- **Babysitting co-ops:** A babysitting co-op is made up of a group of moms and dads who take care of each other's children for free, based on the number of credits you have in the co-op's bank. If you work fulltime, you probably don't have time to create enough in-kind credits (by babysitting other kids) to cover your children's care for all the hours you're at work, but you can come up with enough credits to provide free after-school care for your school-age children. For a more detailed explanation of a babysitting co-op and how it works, take a look in Chapter 4.

Wheeling and dealing

You have to have some kind of wheels, but the total cost of your ride needs to fit into your budget. How much is your car costing you right now — including auto insurance, gas, oil, repairs, and depreciation? When you total it all up, you shouldn't be spending more than 11 percent of your total after-tax income.

You don't have to buy the biggest, newest, flashiest, fastest car ever created, despite the advice TV commercials give you. To keep your car budget on track, buy a used car that's two-years old or older. Look for a vehicle with low miles, a warranty, and a good maintenance record. Check with these sources when you get an idea of a few makes and models that you want to consider:

  ✔ *Consumer Reports:* Look for analysis of the car you have in mind. You need to go to back issues that correspond to the year the car came on the market. Take a look at their Web site at `www.consumerreports.org`.

  ✔ *Kelley Blue Book:* Find out the current value of the vehicle you're considering with this book or check it out online at `www.kbb.com`.

  ✔ **Your insurance agent:** He or she can give you the insurance rates for each car you're thinking about.

When you've located a particular car that may be a possibility, be a smart shopper:

  ✔ Ask to see the maintenance records.

  ✔ Spend the $100 or so to have it inspected by a reliable mechanic. You may hate to part with the money, but you absolutely *must* have the vehicle inspected before plunking down your money. Not doing so can cost you a lot more than $100 in the future when the engine blows up.

  ✔ Drive the car out on the freeway and examine the body carefully.

If anything about the car or the seller makes your skin crawl (or even makes you pause), don't buy the car. When the car is the right one, both you and your mechanic will feel good about it, so be *patient.*

Want to save some money on repair bills? Have your car repairs done through the auto-mechanic department of your local vocational school or technical college. The costs will be a fraction of those performed by an auto mechanic.

Cutting down on medical and dental expenses

Unexpected medical and dental expenses can absolutely kill your budget — we know because we've *definitely* been there and done that. So how do single parents save money on these necessary evils?

- **Get help:** Depending on your income, your children may be eligible to receive free medical care through government assistance programs like Medicaid or CHIP. Contact your local Department of Social Services office for details.

- **Use students:** Check out the closest dental school, which will usually cost 50 to 75 percent less than a private dentist. The work is supervised, so don't worry about a "Whoops" or an "Oh, darn."

- **Be medication savvy:** The following are a few of our favorite money-saving medication suggestions.

  - Buy generic prescriptions and over-the-counter drugs.

  - Have your prescriptions filled at your supermarket warehouse store or through mail-order programs.

  - Always ask your doctor for free samples before you drop the cash on a prescription. Often free samples have enough tablets to meet your needs at the moment.

  - Ask your doctor to prescribe your pills in larger dosage tablets that can be split in half.

  - Purchase prescriptions and over-the-counter drugs in Canada or Mexico, which is what a lot of seniors do because it's cheaper.

Cooking yummy vittles on a small budget

We're not talking possum stew here. But the food thing is a big deal for a single parent: You try to create irresistible meals on your meager budget *and* pull it all off with the little bit of energy you have left at the end of each day. We sympathize with you because we raised our children while working full-time, and we know shopping and cooking are a constant drag. No wonder a single parent tends to fall into one or more of these traps:

- You often shop when you're hungry on the way home from work, which is the very worst thing you can do. You're too hungry and tired to shop for bargains, and you tend to pick up more expensive convenience foods because they're quick and easy to prepare.

✔ You're a real softie when the kids beg for a Burger in a Bag Fun Meal on the drive home, so you pull in for fast food instead of preparing a healthy, economical meal at home.

Many single parents have escaped these traps, and you can too. Here are a few of their tips:

✔ **Shop once a month or once every two weeks:** Make out your menus and corresponding shopping lists, get a sitter for a Saturday morning, and buy everything you need. Take a look at Emily's success story in Chapter 4 for proof that the terms *grocery store* and *sanity* can coexist.

✔ **Use coupons and ad-matching offers:** *Ad matching* means that if you bring in ads from other grocery stores, the store matches the prices. A handy way to keep track of your ad-matched groceries while shopping is to place them in the bottom rack of your cart along with the ad. Then when checkout time arrives, you'll know which groceries need to be ad-matched, and you'll have the competitors' ads ready to go in case you need to show them to the clerk.

✔ **Watch for grocery stores offering double and triple coupons.** If the coupons are for items you buy and use regularly anyway, this can save a lot. Check out the weekly supermarket ads to see which stores are offering the best deal.

✔ **Buy in bulk:** Packaging costs money, so buy the large jars and cans of everything possible. You can always freeze what you don't use for a given recipe.

✔ **Shop at a discount food warehouse or membership club:** Visit these places instead of your local neighborhood supermarket. Be wary though: They do *not* have the lowest prices on *everything.* They're usually good on bulk grocery products, meat, frozen foods, and bakery goods.

✔ **Join a food cooperative:** You can purchase your food in bulk at a great discount. Check your yellow pages for *food cooperatives.* Members own a food co-op, so the food is bought wholesale and offered for sale at wholesale prices, plus the costs of running the co-op.

✔ **Buy produce straight off the farm:** This advice is particularly relevant for folks who live in rural settings. You can also visit farmers' markets, which are common just about everywhere from big cities to small towns.

✔ **Avoid fast-food restaurants:** Don't use them as a substitute for cooking at home. They may be fast, but they aren't necessarily affordable. You may be able to cook fast-food type meals at home for a third of the cost.

If your kids constantly beg for toys from kids' meals, let them indulge once a month. Or, if they just want the toy, pick up a kids' meal for your lunch and save the toy as a surprise. Cool idea, huh? We won't tell anyone that you eat a kids' meal for lunch once in a while.

✔ **Brown-bag your lunches for work:** Not only will you save money on your lunches, but you tend to eat healthier. You'll also save on gas because you won't need to drive to a restaurant. In some cases, employees take turns making lunches one day a week for the rest of the gang at work.

✔ **Puree your own baby food:** You want to save hundreds of dollars during your baby's first year? You'll need to buy a food processor or grinder, such as the Happy Baby Food Grinder, which is available at most baby stores for about $10. Making baby food is as easy as 1, 2, 3:

1. Prepare large amounts at a time.

2. Pour the goop into ice cube trays.

3. Pop out the frozen cubes and store them in freezer bags until you're ready to thaw them out.

✔ **Serve water instead of canned sodas:** Your doctor will love you for taking the natural route for meals and snacks. And forget the pricey bottled water — attach a water filter to your faucet and fill up from the tap.

✔ **Plan a couple meatless or near-meatless meals a week:** You can make these meals fun for the whole family by coming up with themes like Soup and Sandwich Night, Top the Potato Night, and Breakfast Dinner Night.

✔ **Locate a day-old bread store and stock up:** You can find some great bargains at these locations.

✔ **Avoid convenience foods:** Avoid the frozen-food aisles at the grocery store like the plague. An example: Frozen lasagna costs about four times more than homemade.

✔ **Have a Saturday cook day:** Prepare meals that can be frozen for the month, such as

- Meat loaf

- Spaghetti sauce

- Sloppy Joe mix

Keep your oven, stove, barbecue, and crock pot going all day long. Whipping up a bunch of grub can actually be a fun, creative way for you and your kids to spend a Saturday. (We discuss crock-pot cooking in Chapter 4 as well.)

✔ **Buy generic instead of name brands:** No-brainer, huh?

✔ **Substitute other forms of protein for expensive cuts of meat:** You want examples? Well we just so happen to have a few:

- 1 egg equals 6 grams of protein.

- 1 cup of dried beans equals 8 grams of protein.

- 1 cup of cooked brown rice equals 5 grams of protein.

- 1 cup of yogurt equals 8 grams of protein.

✔ **Cut down on junk foods:** You don't need the fat grams in your diet, and you certainly don't need the extra expense. Pop your own popcorn, prepare homemade dip, and mix up a few pitchers of lemonade.

✔ **Check out the free lunch program at school:** The school secretary is a good person to check with to see if your child qualifies.

✔ **Think vegetable garden:** Never had a vegetable garden? Don't worry; Mother Nature does most of the work. You don't have space for a garden? Even a square foot of space will do. (*Square Foot Gardening,* published by Rodale Press and written by Mel Bartholomew, is a great reference that tells you how to get the most from your space.)

Filling your leisure time for pennies a day

Leisure time includes all your entertainment and recreation expenses. If you've just gone from two incomes to one, the idea of *pennies a day* probably seems like science fiction. Maybe the story used to be a lot different: Your kids' favorite rock group came to town — no problem! You just got on the phone and reserved the tickets. Or, if you adore watching Olympic ice skaters perform in person, you probably didn't give a second thought to dropping $45 on each ticket. But what do you do if a pile o' cash isn't left over at the end of the month for concert tickets? Look for ways to have fun without the expense.

Here are just a few suggestions for you and your kids:

✔ **Rent a movie or better yet, borrow one from the library:** Have a few friends over for a movie night. Tell them that you'll provide the drinks if they bring a few snacks.

✔ **Plan a picnic:** Head to the beach or your favorite lakeside park.

✔ **Be a thrifty restaurant patron:** When you do eat out, look for meals that you can split, order an appetizer as the main dish, skip the dessert, and order water instead of a soft drink or iced tea. Keep an eye out for restaurant coupons that are in newspapers and flyers that come in the mail. And go out for lunch instead of dinner.

✔ **Take your kids to a cheap-o matinee movie:** Choose something you'll all enjoy (and maybe smuggle in your own popcorn or candy bars).

✔ **Hit a flea market or garage sale:** Scrounge around the house for spare change and bring it with you. Let the kids spend their allowances if they see something they can't do without.

✔ **Visit a local museum:** The art museum, natural-history museum, or whatever. Most museums are cheap or free (especially for the kids).

✔ **Make regular visits to your local library:** Call the library to find out when they schedule their story times for kids.

- **Go bargain hunting at a bookstore:** Bookstores have attractive children's departments, and they often schedule interesting speakers, musical performers, and story times for the little ones.

- **Search your newspaper:** Most newspapers have weekly inserts that list free and affordable upcoming events.

- **Find vacation savings:** Here are a few ways to save if you or your kids are planning a trip:

    - **Put frequent-flyer miles toward free airline tickets:** Traveling by air doesn't have to break the bank. Accumulate miles by purchasing everyday groceries, gasoline, and other goods using one of the many credit cards. The trick here is to *always* pay off your credit card in full each month.

    - **Use travel Web sites when making vacation plans:** Reserve your hotel room and rental car ahead of time through one of the discount travel Web sites such as Orbitz or Priceline.com.

    - **Save money while on vacation:** You can find bargains almost anywhere, from eating the complimentary continental breakfasts at your hotel to using public transportation instead of a taxi.

Getting cheap goodies

By goodies we mean all those goods and services you buy and use throughout the year, such as

- **Banking:** Shop around for a bank that doesn't charge fees for checking and savings accounts and, preferably, pays interest on these accounts. Many checking accounts are free if you have your paychecks deposited electronically, which is a time-saver for you anyway. And don't buy your checks through your bank.

- **Cigarettes:** Wouldn't this be a perfect time to quit?

- **Clothes:** Be careful how much you spend on clothes. This statement does *not* mean you and the kids have to dress like a nerd or misfit. You can still wear name brand clothes, if you really insist, but there *are* ways to spend less:

    - **Stay away from trendy fad styles, especially for your career wear.**

    - **You can find classic styles at upscale resale or consignment shops.** The name brands will blow you away, and you'll spend only a fraction of what these labels cost off the rack at your favorite department store. Resale shops are also great for kids' clothes.

- **Clothes for your baby or toddler don't need to be name brand.** If your teens insist on name brands, give them the budgeted money for their clothes and let them add their allowance, birthday, or Christmas money to it.

- **Don't buy clothes with the dreaded dry-clean-only tag.** If you already have a closet jam-packed with these duds, try a product that dry-cleans your garments in your home dryer.

- **Save money on panty hose.** Save a pair when one leg has a run; wait until a matching pair develops a run, then cut off each pair's injured leg at mid or high thigh and wear two pairs at once, each with one good leg. Who says we can't? The Panty Hose Police aren't out on patrol.

- **Buy inexpensive multi-packs of men's extra-large, white T-shirts to use as sleep shirts or beachwear for your kids.** If you're feeling artsy, you and the kids can do a little artwork on their shirts. The kids will love to wear them.

- **Catch the sewing bug.** Sewing can be a fun hobby and save you money. You can buy a portable sewing machine for about $200 and save that much or more with your first few creations.

✔ **Cosmetics:** Find a few drugstore cosmetics to substitute for those expensive cosmetics you've been buying at your department store; if you have one or two department-store favorites you just can't bear to give up, put them on Santa's Christmas list.

✔ **Entertaining:** Whether you host a kid's birthday bash or a dinner party, the tab can get crazy quickly. Take a look at *Great Parties on Small Budgets* by Diane Warner (Career Press), which contains hundreds of ways to host a warm, fun party on a small budget.

✔ **Furniture and appliances:** Buy used items. Classified ads, estate sales, and bulletin-board ads at upscale retirement communities are great places to check.

✔ **Greeting cards:** We don't know about you, but we think that the price of greeting cards has gotten out of hand. Create your own cards, purchase cards in bulk, or write your own notes on a blank card.

✔ **Haircuts:** Try visiting a beauty college or discount hair salon.

✔ **Photo developing:** Don't get in the habit of dropping your film off at your local drugstore. You can save money by having it developed at your warehouse club.

✔ **Sports equipment:** Look for used equipment in the classified ads. You can also visit used-sporting-goods stores where merchandise costs 30 to 50 percent less than retail, plus you can trade in your old sports equipment for credit toward your purchases.

Bartering for stuff

Have you ever heard of bartering? No? Well, *bartering* is a concept where individuals or families exchange services, which means that the service is free as far as *real* money goes. This idea was part of everyday life way back when, and it's pure gold for the single parent in today's society.

You can get into the bartering thing in a couple ways:

✔ **Barter with family and friends:** You can casually exchange services with family and friends in a number of ways. Here are a few ideas:

   • Mothers-of-the-bride save thousands of dollars on their daughters' weddings by preparing and serving the food for each other's wedding receptions.

   • One single mother needed a computer tutor, while the other needed help sewing and hanging curtains. They exchanged their services and saved the big bucks.

   • An aerobics instructor offered to teach one class each week for free membership in her favorite health club.

✔ **Join a barter club:** Look in your yellow pages under *barter, exchange clubs,* and *reciprocal trade groups.* You can also check out the Internet. Let your favorite search engine hunt for barter organizations. However, please access the sites at your own risk.

Barter clubs usually charge a membership fee. Formal bartering often uses the same concept of credits and debits as a babysitting co-op (as we describe in Chapter 4), except that the credits and debits are in *dollars* instead of *hours.*

Check that a club is legit before you join, especially if it's a national network. Look for a club that's at least five years old and talk to other members before signing up.

We wish we had room to fill you in on all the ways you can save money, but that would take an entire book. Fortunately, Deborah Taylor-Hough has written that book. Pick up a copy of *Frugal Living For Dummies* (Wiley Publishing, Inc.).

Knowing When to Seek Help

If your money crisis is beyond *severe* — so discouraging that no amount of cheap haircuts, bulk groceries, or thrift-shop wardrobes will make a dent — you need to find some help.

Getting on your case

When you apply for a federal or state program through your local Department of Social Services office, you'll be randomly assigned to a caseworker. Not all caseworkers are created equal, however, so you hope you'll be assigned to one who's kind and compassionate. If not, don't give up if you're casually dismissed from the start because the caseworker decides you won't be eligible for whichever program you're applying for. If this happens to you and you're pretty sure you *will* qualify, be persistent and fight for your rights. When you meet with your caseworker, take notes, ask questions, and if you're denied on the spot, ask for the correct spelling of your caseworker's name and *insist* on having the denial in *writing*. This reaction will usually shake things up a little, because if your caseworker isn't *sure* that you'll be denied, he or she won't put it in writing. This gives you another chance to present your case and to receive a denial in *writing*. If your request *is* finally denied in writing, ask for an official appeal through a hearing office. You'd be surprised how many people are finally approved after going through the appeal process.

Consider a typical single parent scenario: Even after the *equitable* divorce settlement, you still owe $21,000 in credit-card debt, your mortgage payment sucks up half of your take-home pay, and the child-support payments have become fodder for a fairy tale. If your finances are this messed up (or worse), don't simply accept the situation. No! You *must* get some help or you'll never survive the year.

Taking advantage of government assistance

Why do federal, state, and local government agencies offer assistance to single parents and their children? Because you may need a little help until you get on your feet. Don't be embarrassed or ashamed to accept this help.

Here are a few programs that may be available to you, depending on your income:

- **Children's Health Insurance Program (CHIP):** Every state in the United States offers this free or low-cost health insurance to infants, children, and teens. For little or no cost, this insurance pays for doctor visits, prescription medicines, hospitalizations, and more.

- **Extended Opportunities for Programs and Services (EOPS):** These programs provide help to qualified students attending college, including counseling, seminars, tutoring, grants, loans, work study, and help with child care and transportation. These programs and services are administered by each state; however, you apply for them through the Financial Aid Office at the college or university your child plans to attend.

✔ **Food stamps:** This federal program serves as the first line of defense against hunger. It enables low-income families to buy nutritious food with coupons and Electronic Benefits Transfer (EBT) cards.

✔ **Medicaid:** This is a jointly funded federal/state health insurance program for low-income and needy people, including children. It is an income-qualifying program and may be called something other than "Medicaid" in your state.

✔ **Subsidized child care:** The federal government provides child-care assistance to single parents who are at risk of losing their jobs because they can't afford to pay for their children's care.

✔ **Supplemental Security Income (SSI):** This federal supplement program helps people who have little or no income by providing cash to meet the basic needs for food, clothing, and shelter.

✔ **Surplus foods:** The government distributes food items, such as canned meats, flour, cornmeal, and cheese, at designated locations on certain dates according to your zip code. You must register ahead of time to participate in this give-away program.

✔ **Welfare:** Also known as Aid to Families with Dependent Children (AFCD), this program, financed jointly from federal and state funds, provides transitional financial assistance to needy families. Eligibility is based on each state's standard of need.

✔ **Welfare to Work:** This program is designed for single parents with low incomes who want to complete their education.

✔ **Women, Infants, and Children (WIC):** The mission is to safeguard the health of low-income women, infants, and children (up to age 6) who are at nutritional risk. The program provides nutritious foods to supplement diets, information on healthy living, and referrals to health care.

To find out more about these programs and whether you may qualify, start by contacting a Department of Social Services (DSS) office. Look for a telephone number in the government section of your telephone book or go to www-libraries.colorado.edu/ps/gov/us/federal.htm.

Collecting child support

Sadly, only about 50 percent of child-support payments are received in full, and a high percentage of this support arrives late. Isn't there some way to go after these deadbeat dads and moms? (Yes mom owes dad child support a good part of the time.)

The Uniform Reciprocal Enforcement of Support Act (URESA) makes collecting delinquent payments a bit easier than it used to be. You can even have support payments withheld from the non-custodial parent's wages, but first you have to track the deadbeat down.

1. **Contact your local IV-D agency.**

   Your local Department of Social Services office has the contact info. The federal government requires IV-D (a federally funded agency named after Title IV-D of the Social Security Act) to help you collect delinquent child-support payments. After you locate this agency, provide them with the parent's full name and social security number and let them go to work.

2. **If IV-D is unsuccessful, call one of these organizations:**

   - State Parent Locator Service (SPLS) for searches within your home state

   - Federal Parent Locator Service (FPLS) for out-of-state searches

   These searches include departments of motor vehicles, the unemployment insurance office, income tax records, and criminal justice files.

   No luck? Follow these last-resort steps.

3. **Call businesses, utility companies, and telephone companies to see whether the parent left a forwarding address.**

4. **Call your ex's past employers, friends, relatives, coworkers, or anyone who knew him or her.**

   You may luck out and find someone else who is as angry as you are and will give you just the break you need.

5. **If you're pretty sure you know which city and state your ex is living in, contact companies he or she may work for.**

   For example, if your ex was a car salesman, call car dealerships and ask if he or she works there. If your ex's profession requires membership in a union or a professional organization, check them out as well.

   If your ex is working for a certain employer, don't ask to speak to him: Turn this information over to your local Department of Social Services office. Don't go to the place of business and confront your ex personally!

6. **Consider a private collection agency.**

   The bad news is that fees (sometimes a percentage of any recovered payments) are involved at this point in the search. But a lot of single parents go this route because a percentage of something is better than 100 percent of nothing. To locate one of these agencies, look under "Child Support Recovery Services" in the yellow pages or use your favorite search engine on the Web.

Watch out for unscrupulous collection agencies. Ask for references, check with the Better Business Bureau, or insist on an agency that's a member of the American Child Support Collection Association.

Accepting help from a credit counselor

If you're having weird nightmares where credit-card police chase you down dark alleys waving axes and snapping whips, you're probably ready to see a *credit counselor,* a professional who specializes in helping people deal with their debts. One of these counselors may be able to contact your creditors and arrange for a restructured payment plan, including reduced interest rates and payments.

Try to find a non-profit organization like the Consumer Credit Counseling Service (CCCS), which has hundreds of offices in the United States. (Look in the yellow pages under "Credit and Debit Counseling.") This organization can help you negotiate lower interest rates and extended payments, stop collections, and avoid repossession or foreclosure. These fine folks can also help you set up a budget and avoid the spending habits that got you into trouble in the first place. If you don't live in the United States, look in your phone book under Credit Counselors to find a similar type of professional organization.

Be wary of for-profit companies (many of which have names similar to the CCCS) whose main goal is to loan you money so you can consolidate all your loans into one. However, by the time these companies add their application fees and other charges, the total payment may actually be higher than all your original payments put together.

Check with the three major national credit agencies to take a look at your credit record. If you've been denied credit recently or you suspect credit-card fraud, these reports may be free. Here are the toll-free numbers:

- ✔ **Equifax:** 888-511-1992
- ✔ **Experian:** 866-200-2313
- ✔ **TransUnion:** 800-680-7289

Applying a financial advisor's advice

You may be overwhelmed with the financial decisions you're being forced to make. If you're facing really depressing stuff, such as past-due rent, threats of having your car repossessed, or the prospect of a business going bankrupt, you may feel like a capsized sailor going down for the third time.

What you need is a level head — someone who has the answers and can help you without putting you down or making you feel even worse than you already do. Search out an amateur or professional *financial advisor,* someone who won't try to sell you anything like stocks or other investments, but will take a look at your entire financial picture and help you decide what is best, including decisions about your estate, taxes, and investments. Find someone who can help you get on your feet — with no strings attached.

If you're really buried in debt but have assets that can possibly be *liquidated* (sold for cash) to pay off your debt, your financial advisor can evaluate these assets. By assets we mean such things as

- Automobiles, boats, campers, or other vehicles
- Certificates of deposit
- Coin or stamp collections
- Life insurance policies that have cash value
- Money market funds
- Pensions, IRAs, or Keough accounts
- Real estate
- Stocks, bonds, or mutual funds
- Furniture, antiques, or valuable tools

Ask around and you may find someone who will give you free advice. These kind people often supply their services through a church. Or you may even have a non-biased friend who's knowledgeable and has the time to sit down with you some evening to sort things out.

If you can't locate a free advisor, find a professional financial advisor (also known as a *financial planner*). The key is to find a *fee-based* financial planner, which means that the planner is paid a fee to help you, as opposed to making money from commissions on products he or she sells. For example, many insurance agents, stockbrokers, and commodity traders call themselves financial planners, but in fact, their income depends on the commissions they receive from selling you policies and investments. We're not saying that these people are dishonest or unethical; it's just that a conflict of interest may exist when a salesman tries to give you financial advice.

So, where do you find a fee-based financial counselor you can trust? Start by asking for referrals from your religious advisor, your friends, or your attorney. You can also call the Institute of Certified Financial Planners (Phone: 800-282-7526). This organization can refer you to a financial planner in your area who has satisfied certain educational requirements. If your financial planner gives you tax advice (and he or she undoubtedly will), the cost of the planning services may be tax deductible. Ask your tax attorney or accountant, and while you're at it, find out what the tax implications are for child support or alimony. This may help you decide what type of support to pursue in your divorce/child-support agreements.

Going from welfare to work

Tracy became a mother at age 19. The baby's father wasn't supportive, so she was on her own. Fortunately, Tracy's parents and the baby's paternal grandmother were as supportive as they could be. Tracy lived with her parents and had a minimum-wage job. Things went along pretty smoothly for a while — until Tracy's father became seriously ill. She didn't want to remain a burden to her parents, but what could she do?

First, she phoned the local Department of Social Services to schedule an interview. This step was difficult, but her drive for independence overruled her reluctance. Fortunately, she connected with a social worker (caseworker) who helped her through the maze of paperwork. The social worker told Tracy about all the services available to her. At that time, Tracy had no assets and made $800 per month. The caseworker encouraged Tracy to apply for healthcare and housing assistance right away.

Tracy qualified for free Medicaid, which provided her and her son free healthcare, because her total assets were less than $2,000. She also applied for public-assistance housing (also known as Section 8 housing). After several months on a waiting list, Tracy was able to move into a two-bedroom apartment within walking distance of where she worked.

Settling in her own place with her son was a turning point for Tracy. For the first time, she began to think about her future. She knew that she didn't want to get by on a low-paying, unrewarding job at a discount store. She longed to go back to school and pursue a career that would allow her a few luxuries.

Tracy visited the financial-aid office at a local junior college and was pleasantly surprised to find that she could apply for several financial-aid programs. She enrolled in classes (a real morale booster) and filled out the Free Application for Federal Student Aid (FAFSA) paperwork.

A counselor at the college told her about the Welfare-to-Work program designed specifically for single parents with low incomes and a desire for education. Much to her amazement, she would receive $1,800 per month if she enrolled in 12 units each semester. And Tracy was walking on air when her employer agreed to rearrange her work schedule to accommodate her class schedule. Her sister and both grandmothers agreed to help with babysitting. Because she was attending school fulltime and working part time, her total income went up to $2,400 per month. Now she knew she could do it.

While attending school, she heard about another awesome program — Extended Opportunities for Programs and Services (EOPS) — that provides counseling, tutoring, vouchers for textbooks, and free child care during her classes and study time.

Tracy has utilized the public-assistance program (welfare services) as it's intended to be used — to help her become financially independent. Her goal is to become a radiology technician. In the meantime, she and her son are doing well, and they have a close relationship with (but are no longer dependent on) her family.

In the ideal world your ex will pay what is owed in "child support" until the child is grown. In the real world, that often is not the case. Do not make the mistake of counting on regular child support. If it does arrive on time, then you can rejoice. Learn to live on what you have control over.

Part II
Keeping Close to Your Kids

The 5th Wave   By Rich Tennant

"Please try not to be late dropping her off from ballet class again. It's just hard for her to keep up on the soccer field wearing ballet slippers and a tutu."

In this part . . .

As a single parent you're overwhelmed with responsibilities involving your job, your home, and your kids' activities. This doesn't leave much time or energy for developing relationships with your kids. This part's chapters talk about ways you can stay close to your kids and be the kind of parent you long to be.

All kinds of obstacles present themselves as you strive to accomplish this feat. Each of your children is unique and needs to be handled a little differently, depending on his age, quirks, and stages. Then add the gender issue, which means you need to understand why raising a son is different than raising a daughter, and what you can do to make the job a little easier. You also learn a lot by listening to your kids' point of view. It may be a revelation when you realize how your child is suffering from the loss of his other parent, how he's longing to have time with you alone, and how he needs reassurance that he's safe and loved.

Chapter 6

Weighing in with Both Parents

. . . .

In This Chapter

▶ Treating your kids as individuals

▶ Listening with a purpose

▶ Adjusting your schedule

▶ Letting loose with the whole family

. . . .

*I*sn't it fun to be a single parent? Just think, every day is an exciting new adventure! You get home from work, and instead of collapsing in your recliner chair and reading the morning paper — that you never got to because your morning was a disaster — you get to fix dinner for all your kiddies. Now, that sounds like a blast! Then, of course, dinner is never boring, between Joshua pushing the peas around his plate, Marcie accidentally spilling her milk *again,* and Michael describing in great detail how *gross* it was when Christopher ate his boogers at preschool!

Such a deal — raising your kids alone! In this chapter we talk about some of the issues you're facing: Dealing with your kids' ages, stages, and personality quirks, explaining about the birds and the bees, encouraging happy talk in your home, and adjusting your schedule so you can break loose and have fun with your kids once in a while.

Single parenting is an enormous challenge and we admire your perseverance! We hope this chapter will help you understand your kids a little better so you'll enjoy this special time of your life.

Dealing with Ages and Stages

Is your toddler going through that stage where he's afraid of scary things? Does your teenage son seem to be ignoring you lately? How about your teenage daughter? Does she need a lot of encouragement at this awkward stage of her life? You want to meet the needs of your children at whatever age or stage they're at, but doing so can become a little overwhelming at times.

In the following sections, we provide some helpful tips for being the best parent you can possibly be to your kids, because by understanding your kids' ages and stages, you'll know how to react and deal with each one.

Parenting by the numbers

Life would be so much smoother for parents if children came with an instruction manual with precise answers for every problem (and preferably a hefty "Troubleshooting" section). Unfortunately, we all have to wing it while raising kids in this complex and sometimes frightening world. Although we're not writing the definitive instruction manual here, we can offer you a few basic guidelines to supplement your existing knowledge for these general age groups:

Babies

If you're trying to raise a baby, life probably isn't always a walk in the park right now. A baby's needs and moods change daily, and what worked yesterday may not work today. A baby takes a lot of patience. Even when he's screaming his head off, you have to keep a cool head and try to figure out what's wrong this time. Maybe he's hungry. He might be tired. Of course, he could be sick. You can always try checking the diaper. Or maybe it's just gas.

All single parents face the challenge of playing baby detective on a regular basis. But, if you're a single dad, your biggest problem will be the bonding thing. Most moms form a natural bond with their babies, especially if they nurse them from birth, so you may need to put in some extra work. Spend a lot of time holding and cuddling your baby until the two of you bond.

Toddlers

If you think a break is in order after bringing up baby, just wait. You have your work cut out for you now. Raising a toddler is a fulltime job. A child, by the way, is a *toddler* from the time he begins to walk until he reaches about 3 years old. A toddler runs all over the house, opens cupboards, finds bottles of dangerous stuff, falls off steps, closes herself in closets, tries to crawl inside the dishwasher, and performs all kinds of other scary antics.

And we haven't even mentioned potty training. You'll probably lose ten pounds when you and the little one get to this point. Constantly picking her up, carrying her into the bathroom, stripping off her training pants, and plopping her down on the potty chair can be a workout. Then, after she's done her thing, you get to help her put a pee-pee or poo-poo sticker on her potty seat as a reward for doing such an *awesome* job. The aerobics also come into play getting her re-dressed and back to the kitchen just in time for her to cry out, "Daddy, Daddy, now I have to go *big* poo-poo!" Oh, joy. Don't worry though: In a few months, she'll be able to toddle into the bathroom, pull down her pants, and take care of things pretty well all by herself. (*Potty Training For Dummies,* by Diane Stafford and Jennifer Shoquist, published by Wiley Publishing, Inc., can help you if you're starting from scratch here.)

You'll probably buy a bottle of champagne to celebrate. But hold that thought because your toddler could regress. (You can read more about regression in Table 6-2. While you're there, take a look at another interesting stage — the tantrum stage. You know, the one where your toddler screams, kicks the floor, and occasionally holds her breath?)

Middlers

If you have a child in the 5-to-12-year-old bracket, you're facing a different problem every week. One week your 8-year-old may suddenly become afraid of the dark, bullies at the bus stop, or his mean teacher, and the next week, your lovely, mature daughter may decide to throw a tantrum at the mall. (Check out Table 6-2 for info on both the fearful and tantrum stages.)

When your children reach the age of 10 or so, sit them down and have a frank discussion about drugs and alcohol. Many parents think that they can wait until their kids become teenagers to tackle these subjects, but that's not the case. Kids are introduced to drugs and alcohol in elementary school and junior high, so you need to face this head on.

Teenagers

By the time your kids get to be teens, you may have strong relationships with them. Hopefully, you face problems head on and talk them out before they build up. You're also ahead of the game if your discipline techniques work. If you could use a little advice on disciplining your children, take a look at Chapter 9. Meanwhile, if you have teenagers in the house, you need to be ready for the rebellious stage, another test of your true grit! Table 6-2 offers information about this dreaded stage.

Birth order of your children can also make a big difference in their behavior. Be aware of your kids' tendencies and be ready to step in when one of them is suffering due to his birth order. Table 6-1 has a few basic birth-order characteristics and explains what you can do to help each of your children.

Table 6-1	Birth Order and Resulting Behavior	
Birth Order	*Personality Tendencies*	*What You Can Do*
First born	Tends to be a leader and a high achiever; however, she also tends to be a perfectionist.	Don't be too demanding. Offer specific praise instead of open-ended praise. If your child builds a great birdhouse don't say, "That's the best bird-house I've ever seen." Instead say, "I really like the colors. I bet they'll attract a lot of birds." Tip: The single biggest gift a parent can give their "perfectionist" child is to *not* model perfectionism.
Second born	Tends to be more easy-going, creative, and playful than his older sibling, which are great traits. However, he also wants to outdo his older sibling if he can, especially if you're constantly praising your first-born child.	Give him as much praise as possible, encourage him to talk about his feelings, stop praising your first-born child in front of him, and show him you love him every way you can.
Middle child	This kid is wedged between an older and younger child, so she tends to be both a leader and a follower, which may cause her to feel left out and insecure. This child may feel compelled to serve as mediator between the other children.	Make her feel special and cherished. One way to do this is to spend one-on-one time with her each day listening to her, praising her, hugging her, and telling her how much you love her
Baby of the family	Your youngest is probably creative, outgoing, and affectionate, which is good. However, because the older kids tend to take over and do things for him, he may become dependent on others. The older kids may be a little jealous of your youngest, which can result in bullying.	Stifle any bullying and build confidence and independence in your youngest child by assigning him responsbilities and then praising him for doing a good job.

Staging a parenting exhibition

Children exhibit behavior patterns that aren't always triggered by their age or gender. These behavior patterns may have more to do with other factors within a single-parent household. In Table 6-2, we outline these behavior patterns and offer some solutions.

Table 6-2		Behavior Patterns Your Kids May Exhibit
Behavior Pattern	**What's Happening**	**What You Can Do**
Regressive	When a child is traumatized by divorce or the death of his parent, regression to an earlier behavior pattern isn't unusual. For example, you may have your 2-year-old potty trained and weaned off the bottle. After the separation, he may wake up one morning and say to himself, "Today I think I'll have a yummy ba-ba and make a great big poop in my nice comfy diaper!"	Give him more physical affection.He needs reassurance, so hold him, kiss him, hug him, and spend more time with him for a while until he recovers.
Fearful	Your kids may pass in and out of this behavior pattern, suddenly becoming fearful of the dark or, because his other parent is nolonger living with him, he may be afraid that he's longer safe.	Take the fears seriously; never disregard them as insignificant. Sympathize with the child and offer a way out. For example, if your 7-year-old is afraid now of the dark, take him with you to purchase a night light. If your toddler is afraid to go to bed alone, let her sleep with you for a while — it won't matter ten years from now anyway.
Tantrum	Toddlers are often the tantrum-throwing culprits, but older children sometimes throw them, too. Don't you wish that you could throw one every once in a while? By the way, this isn't only a single parent problem:	* For toddlers: Build a *tantrum tent* in your toddler's bedroom by throwing sheets or blankets over a couple of chairs.When your daughter throws a tantrum, pick her up, place her in her tantrum tent,

(Continued)

Table 6-2 *(Continued)*

Behavior Pattern	What's Happening	What You Can Do
Tantrum	Most parents have to face this behavior pattern sometime along the way.	and say, "We don't enjoy watching your tantrums, Ashley. When you're all done, you may come back into the kitchen to eat your dinner." Then close the door to her bedroom and leave her there to thrash around as long as she wants. * For older kids: Take him to his room and shut the door. Then, when he's worn out, suggest that the two of you have a talk. Ask him what upset him, *listen* to his response, and talk about productive ways to solve the problem in the future.
Rebellious	Rebellion can strike at any age, but teenagers seem to master the art, especially around age 16. You may have an I-know-everything-and-you're-an-old-fashioned-dorky-mother-type teen on your hands. Another form of rebellion is when your teen doesn't want to spend time with you and his brothers and sisters, but prefers to spend all his time with his friends. Another common form of rebellion in a single parent home is when your teen announces that he or she wants to go live with the other parent. When your teenager is acting obnoxious and seems to be trying to hurt you, take the actions as a cry for help.	Love, praise, and communication are the key. Your child is acting out because he 15 or needs your sympathy and understanding. Try to get your child talking about *why* she's feeling so rebellious. If necessary, seek out a family therapist.

If you see your children moving into the fearful stage, they may be picking up on your fears and anxieties. Be careful what you say or how you react to situations in front of your kids. For example, since your ex moved out you may have become afraid of someone breaking into your home at night and you may panic if you hear a noise in the backyard after dark. Try to stay calm and call the police if you think it's necessary. The key is to stay as calm as you can so you don't transfer your fear to your kids.

You Want What on Your Sandwich? Coping with Kids' Quirks

Each of your children is a unique, one-of-a-kind person. (In some cases, *unique* may be an understatement.) Don't make the mistake of lumping them into a one-size-fits-all relationship. You need to handle each child's idiosyncrasies a little differently. Your young daughter may burst into tears when you casually reprimand her for not cleaning her room, but your older daughter may respond in good humor with, "Hey, Dad, chill out. I'll have my room ready for inspection in 30 minutes, and you'll be *sooo* proud of me!" The sooner you catch on to the differences in your children's personalities, the better your relationships will be, especially as you learn the importance of *really* listening to your children and practicing positive talk.

Opening your ears

Listening to your child is one of the greatest ways you can demonstrate your love. (We're talking about *really* listening here, not uncomprehendingly nodding and grunting as you stuff their wriggling feet into their boots. Yes, we know that parental sanity does call for the use of mental autopilot at times — but not all the time.) Why is listening so important? Because it's the only way you can find out what your child is thinking, how he might be hurting, and what makes him angry. How can you help him if you don't know what's on his mind?

Wouldn't it be a perfect world if your kids *always* told you what's bothering them, and you could *always* be there for them with a solution? Well, the world isn't perfect, but you can still try as hard as possible to get inside your kids' heads.

A single mother we know shared this helpful word of advice with us: If you want to have a heart-to-heart chat with your child and get him talking, wait until bedtime. Turn off the light and sit on the edge of his bed. After he starts talking, he'll want to keep you there. Spending time with you in this cozy setting is an easy, relaxed way for your child to share his thoughts and feelings.

If you get your child to open up, here's a sampling of what you may hear:

- ✔ "Why do you promise me that Dad will pick me up when you know he won't show?"
- ✔ "I think it's totally stupid to have to share a bedroom with Trisha! How many boys my age have to share a bedroom with their sister?"
- ✔ "Why can't we go fishing anymore? When Mom lived with us, we used to go down to the canal and catch catfish all the time."

To be a good listener, you need to figure out what your child is *really* saying. Try this four-step process out:

1. Restate the problem.
2. Ask if you correctly understand the problem.
3. Ask your child for her solution to the problem.
4. Offer your own solution, if there is one.

    If you can't come up with a solution on the spot, tell your child that you should both think about the problem and talk it over later. Assure your child that you *will* work it out.

While you go through these steps, keep a few other things in mind:

- ✔ Look your child in the eye.
- ✔ Show genuine concern.
- ✔ Never pass off the problem as being insignificant.

In the following bullets, we take a look at each of the issues from the earlier sample questions your child may come up with and suggestions for possible solutions.

- ✔ Dad doesn't show up as promised.
    - **Restate the complaint:** "You're upset with me because I promise you that Dad will pick you up, and when he doesn't, you're angry because you think I lied to you, is this correct?"
    - **Offer a solution:** "When I tell you that Dad is coming to pick you up, I'm passing on *his* promise to you, but I'm so sorry he lets you down. I'm also sorry I make promises that aren't kept because I don't like broken promises any more than you do. Let's talk to Dad about this the next time we see him. We'll let him know how he disappoints you when he doesn't do what he promises."

✔ Junior has to share a bedroom with his sister.

  • **Restate the complaint:** "You feel insulted because you have to share a bedroom with your sister, which means you don't have private space of your own, is that it?"

  • **Offer a solution:** "I'm sorry you have to share a bedroom with Trisha. I know that's not cool at all. We can't move to a larger apartment for a while, but maybe we can figure something out. What if we divide the room in half by taking the tall bookcase in the living room and making it into a room divider? We could also move your dresser so it seems like a little wall when you first walk in. Would that help?"

✔ Fishing time with Mom has dramatically diminished.

  • **Restate the complaint:** "You miss doing things with your Mom, right?"

  • **Offer a solution:** "Listen, I'm a heck of a fisherman. Let's grab the fishing gear and catch some catfish next Sunday, how does that sound? We'll bring the portable barbecue, and we can cook a few of the fish on the spot, just like you and Mom used to do. And I'll make the beans that you like to bring along."

If carving out some quiet time to listen to each of your kids each day is difficult, here's an idea: Make an appointment with each child for a private chat, and don't let *anything* interfere with this appointment. You may have to take the phone off the hook, but these daily appointments will build relationships. And remember that the length of time you meet with each child isn't the important part. The quality of your time together and how well you listen is what really counts.

Encouraging positive talk

If you're a single parent because of divorce or the death of your spouse, falling into the victim trap may be easy. If you feel like the victim of your tragic circumstances, you may accidentally slip into a pattern of negative talk. Negative talk includes the following:

✔ **Dumping your problems on your kids:** Do you complain to your children about the difficulties in your life or your gloomy outlook? If you've fallen into this pattern of negativity around the house, stop! You're frightening your kids and taking advantage of them. Your children aren't small adults, and using them as free in-house therapists isn't fair.

✔ **Badmouthing the other parent:** In spite of what your ex has done to you and the kids, in spite of the selfishness and irresponsibility, and yes, in spite of the immoral habits, keep your mouth shut. Remember the old saying: *If you can't say something nice, don't say anything at all.* Divorced parents *must* protect their kids' images of each other. The other parent is a hero and caregiver in the children's eyes (even though he or she may not deserve to be). So think of something upbeat to say once in a while like "You're a natural athlete, just like your father" or "You really have your mother's talent for math." Remember this: To criticize or attack your child's other parent is to criticize or attack your child's DNA!

✔ **Mucking around in your grief:** If your spouse died and your heart is still heavy, don't rain on your kids' parade day after day. Smile and praise their mother or father's wonderful qualities. Get in the habit of talking about your husband or wife and all the fun stuff you did as a family. At the same time, look to the future and all the good times you and the kids have to look forward to.

If you're having trouble dealing with your grief, if you're angry with your spouse for dying and leaving you to raise the kids alone, or if you just can't seem to get over your depression, take a look at Chapter 12 for practical, healing advice. You may also need professional therapy. Take a look at Chapter 14 for a list of signs that you may need help.

A positive attitude, as well as positive talk, is uplifting and healing — not only mentally, but emotionally and physically. Here are a few upbeat ways to bring positive talk into your home:

✔ **Try hard to lighten up a little:** Look for the humor in your single-parent routine.

✔ **Practice smiling:** A smile can heal and lift everyone's heart, including your own.

✔ **Think up positive talk ahead of time:** At the end of the day, be ready to praise your daughter for getting an A on her spelling test and compliment your son on all the rebounds he pulled down in his basketball game.

Adjusting Your Schedule

You're a single parent, and you have a complicated, difficult, busy life. We know all about your frantic schedule and trying to keep up with a job, a home, and all the activities that accompany childhood. It's a wonder you get any sleep at all.

Maybe it's time for you to sit down and think this thing through. Can you adjust your schedule to free up a little more time for your kids? Chapter 4 has some great advice (if we do say so ourselves) and tips for lightening your load in a number of areas of your life. For now, here's a brief outline (check out Chapter 4 for all the details):

✔ **Your career:** Is your job wringing you dry? Are you totally spent at the end of each workday? Is your commute beyond ridiculous? If your answer is *yes* to any of these questions, you may want to investigate this area of your life further.

✔ **Your extracurricular activities:** You may be involved in more activities than you can handle right now, especially if you became a single parent quite recently. Practice saying *no.*

✔ **Your children's activities:** In addition to school and church, your kids may be involved in too many extracurricular activities right now. Cut back, Jack.

If you've adjusted your schedule as much as you can and your children still arrive home before you do, here's some soon-to-be-award-winning advice:

✔ Always have your children call you at work or on your cell phone when they get home from school.

✔ Keep your cell and work phone numbers taped to all phones in the house. This list can also include emergency numbers and alternate contacts (dad, grandpa, Mrs. Jones from across the street, and so on). (See the Cheat Sheet in the front of this book.)

✔ Set up strict rules for the kids to follow until you get home, such as no cooking on the stove, no having friends over to play, no swimming in the pool, no wrestling in the living room, and so on.

✔ Teach your children what to do in case of emergencies.

  • Have fire drills so they know the escape plan.

  • Teach them how to use the first-aid kit.

  • Arrange for an adult neighbor to be on call in case of an emergency.

✔ Warn your kids about strangers who may come to the door or call on the phone; rehearse what they're to do and say.

✔ Keep a signed and notarized authorization form handy in case one of the children needs emergency medical care. Most doctors and hospital staff require one of these permission forms before they will treat your child. Figure 6-1 shows an example form.

RELEASE FORM

_____ has my permission to authorize
Fill in the complete name of your sitter

medical treatment to my child(ren) _____ in case
List the names of your child(ren)

of a medical emergency. This is effective from _____ forward.
date

Signed,

_____   _____
Sign your complete name   *date*

Figure 6-1:
You can
copy this
form to give
to anyone
you feel
comfy giving
medical
authority to.

Making Your Time Together Fun

When we talk about *fun,* we don't mean watching TV with your kids on the weekend. We mention watching TV in particular because this activity is as much fun as a lot of single parents have with their children all week. At times, you really do need to kick back at the end of the day and watch a little television, but the kind of quality fun we're talking about includes activities that build relationships with your kids — things you do together that feature interaction with your children.

You don't need to whip out the weekend super-dad or super-mom bit. And, if you're a non-custodial parent, you may have to fight the urge to put on a super-parent cape even more. Your kids just want your time and your love, and you can fill these requests with affordable fun that fits easily into your busy schedule. Here's the point: Your time and your love mean more to your kids than new dolls, video games, or trips to theme parks.

You have literally hundreds of ways at your disposal to spend quality time with your kids during the week, on weekends, and over summer vacation. Ask your children what sounds like fun to them, but have a few suggestions ready, such as these ideas submitted by single dads:

✔ Shoot Saturday morning hoops with your kids in your driveway or at the school playground.

✔ Teach your kids how to fly fish.

✔ Spend an afternoon at the county fair.

✔ Go on a weekend camping trip together.

✔ Take scavenger-hunt nature hikes and look for things along the trail.

✔ Attend a baseball game.

✔ Challenge the kids to a game of miniature golf.

✔ Take up a hobby together like photography, stamp collecting, or ant-farm maintenance.

✔ Ask your kids to help you with a project you're working on. This will teach them that work can be fun. Of course, your project may take twice as long to complete with them helping you — but that's okay.

✔ Plan regular family fun nights:

 • Let every child (even the 3-year-old) help prepare dinner.

 • Turn the TV and telephone off for the evening (let the answering machine do its job).

 • Play board games (and if you could care less whether you land on Park Place or not, fake it — just for an hour or so).

 • Pop popcorn or roast marshmallows over the coals in your fire-place or outdoor barbecue.

These ideas give you a place to start, but your kids may suggest something that's way out of your comfort zone, such as doing a little inline skating in the park. Are you ready for the challenge? If so, get your children totally involved in every part of the activity — from buying the blades to signing up for beginner lessons.

The key is to spend time with your kids, treat them with respect, and tell them that you love them every day. And finally, during your precious family time together, sprinkle them with praise. Children thrive on praise, so do everything you can to make them feel loved, cherished, and admired. For general parenting advice, pick up a copy of *Parenting For Dummies,* 2nd Edition (Wiley Publishing, Inc.).

ANECDOTE

Lee, the networking single mom

Lee is a single mother of two daughters. When she and her husband divorced, he moved out of state. This left Lee alone with her daughters, but she did have her mother nearby, who was not only supportive, but also involved with her granddaughters. One day a friend invited Lee to join a single mother support group sponsored by a local church. A couple of the women invited Lee to go with them on a singles-only Mexican Riviera cruise. Lee was a little shy and reluctant to do anything socially, especially since her divorce, but she needed a vacation, so she decided to sign up for the cruise. She explained to her friends that she was on vacation. She definitely did *not* want to get into the dating scene.

During the cruise, Lee kept to herself. While her friends visited various ports-of-call, Lee hunkered down beside the ship's pool and read. That's where she met a man who had the same idea — also to avoid the dating scene. They had dinner together that night and soon were enjoying each other's company.

When the cruise was over and they were home, they talked on the phone a lot. He encouraged her to participate in a community outreach program sponsored by a singles group he belonged to. It was an outreach to juvenile hall where the members brought pizza to the teenagers who lived there, then spent time talking with the kids. Lee went with him and enjoyed it very much.

Then Bill invited Lee and her two daughters to a barbecue he was sponsoring as a fundraiser.

She accepted his invitation and during the get-together Bill's son and Lee's daughter, who were about the same age, really hit it off.

Lee and Bill and their kids do a lot of things together now, including hiking and biking. Not only is the socializing fun for Lee and Bill, but their joint activities also provide a female role model for Bill's boys and a male role model for Lee's girls. And their relationship allows their kids to see that adults *can* get along without conflict, something none of the children had seen before. Lee helped Bill with a redecorating project and Bill spent a weekend helping her rebuild her deck.

In the meantime, Lee got involved in another single parent family group that met weekly. This was a co-ed group where she discovered how other parents were handling some of the same issues she was dealing with. This group had outings for the children and her daughters loved to play T-ball with the co-ed tem.

Slowly, but surely, Lee healed from her disappointing marriage and found a new strength within. She's pleased that she know handles a lot of things her husband used to take care of, and she's especially pleased that through her networking in various support groups, she has an active social life and her children have been provided with male role models.

Lee's still dating Bill, but the kicker of the story is that Lee's Mom is dating Bill's Dad!

Chapter 7

Talking Trucks and Tutus: Gender Issues

In This Chapter

▶ Appreciating parents

▶ Finding out about gender issues

▶ Breaking the gender mold

▶ Looking at some major mistakes

▶ Giving your kids someone to look up to

"**H**ey, did you hear that Jan and Ted had their baby last night?" What's the first thing you ask? How much the baby weighed? When the baby was born? How long Jan was in labor? Of course, not. The first thing is, "Was it a boy or a girl?" Why is this the first question everyone asks? Because it matters!

There is a difference between the two. That's why in this chapter we talk about trucks and tutus and the problems single dads and moms face as they raise their sons and daughters. We also take a look at unique gender differences, how to provide male and female role models for your kids, and how to avoid the biggest mistakes made by single moms and dads.

Digging On Dads

Well, Dad, here you are. It's just you and the kids now, and as you've probably already discovered, you're required to wear many hats as a single father.

When you're in the kitchen trying to put something healthy together for your kids, you don your chef hat. When you're up in the middle of the night with your sick daughter, you need your nurse hat. Of course, when you attend your son's Little League games, you wear your cheerleader hat or your referee hat, depending on your disposition. Or, you might need to wear two hats at once, like one father we know who became an instant paramedic and disciplinarian when he discovered his 16-year-old daughter bleeding profusely from her belly button. She was using a safety pin to pierce her belly button so she could wear a belly ring like the rest of her friends.

Oh, the joys of fatherhood! But take heart, you're not alone. Other single dads have not only survived, but also thrived, as they developed satisfying, lasting relationships with their kids.

Marveling at Moms

Hey, Mom, are you having fun yet? Or is having fun the least of your worries these days? If you're like most single mothers, you're just trying to survive. We know you have gobs of high-stress stuff going on, including your complex budget, your demanding boss, the leaky dishwasher, and your baby's baboon-bottom diaper rash!

Dad and his teenage daughter

Sean was 34 when his daughter Beth moved in with him fulltime. It was a great relief to him because he didn't have to worry about her as much. However, he didn't have a clue about how to coexist with a teenage girl. Spending weekends and vacations together had always been great. Living together on a daily basis was a different story altogether.

To begin with, they didn't know how to talk to each other. Sean had been a bachelor for the past ten years. He was very meticulous and liked things a certain way. But Beth had never had any structure or rules in her life and didn't appreciate being told what to do. When Beth moved in with her dad she had to get used to a new school in the ninth grade. She had no friends and felt painfully shy. Her father was concerned about her, but covered it up with a list of chores she needed to do before and after school. They drove to school each morning in silence. Sean didn't ask her about school and she didn't offer any information.

Fortunately for them, they had a confidante in Beth's grandmother. When either of them was fed up with the other, Grandma got a phone call. Before long, Grandma realized that she was in the middle of the conflict, so she did everything to try to get them to talk and work things out. The school counselor suggested that Beth and her dad see a family therapist. Sean refused to go after the first session, but agreed to pay for Beth to see the therapist every other week.

Sean's girlfriend tried to help Beth communicate with her father about some of her needs. They included Beth in some of their activities, like going to movies or out to dinner. However, when Sean and his girlfriend broke up, Sean blamed it on Beth. In fact, he was so hurt and angry that he ordered Beth out of the house.

This is the point where Beth's grandmother went to the therapist and insisted on her son going too. Hurray for Grandma! After meeting with the therapist for a time, Sean and his daughter were able to face their crisis together. They eventually began to see things from another point of view and were able to forgive one another for their failure to get along, to talk, and to deal with their conflicts.

Sean began to meet with the therapist alone, but also in joint sessions with Beth. On the recommendation of the therapist, he started to attend a class for parents of teens and Beth attended Al-Anon meetings, to be able to deal more effectively with her mother, who was an alcoholic.

Family help also came from another source. Sean's cousin was a warm motherly type and she and her husband took a particular liking to Beth. They had two younger boys and asked Beth to babysit occasionally. On weekends they invited Sean and Beth to go camping and water-skiing. Somehow father and daughter were able to relax and laugh at themselves on these fun weekends. The cousins convinced Dad that Beth was responsible enough to get her driving permit and Dad actually enjoyed teaching her how to drive.

When Grandma's health deteriorated, Sean and Beth spent as much time with her as they could. During a prolonged hospitalization, Beth and her father became closer and their own struggles faded in light of Grandma's serious illness. They realized how important they were to each other. Slowly Beth's grades improved and they were able to agree on household chores and an allowance. Sean encouraged Beth to invite friends over and he began to date again.

Today they are getting along pretty well and you can see them walking their dog together and tooling around on Sean's new motorcycle. They were strangers when they started living together, but three years later they both agree they are no longer lonely and are a bonded family of two.

In this chapter we show you some helpful, practical solutions to your problems. First of all, discover ways to let go of the super mom thing — you can't be everything to your kids every minute of every day, or you go bonkers!

Mothers and Sons, Dads and Daughters

Gender can make a difference in your relationships with your children. Raising a girl is different than raising a boy in many ways. All things being equal, a child tends to get along better with the same sex parent, plus, girls in a divorced household tend to adjust better than boys, not only at home, but in social skills and school grades. A girl adjusts better because she matures faster than a boy in every way.

You may find that communicating with your son and daughter is quite different.

✔ Your son may tend to think in terms of logic and problem solving, because a male has a more active left brain.

✔ Your daughter may tend to focus on relationships and feelings, because she has a more active right brain.

Although your son and daughter may exhibit these inherent tendencies, it's possible to consciously decide to *step over* from one side of the brain to the other. For example, if you're a single mother, try to think with the left side of your brain when you're listening to your son. If you're a single dad, try to think with the right side of your brain as you listen to your daughter.

Single dad raising his . . .

As a single dad, you need to listen and relate to your daughter and son in different ways. This is not a difficult concept to grasp. It's simply a matter of understanding that boys and girls think and express themselves differently.

Son

Raising a son may be a little easier for you than raising a daughter, especially if you and your son have a lot in common. Here are some of the advantages of a father/son home:

✔ You tend to roughhouse with your boys from an early age, which is good because it teaches them self-control and fair play. This can result in a close relationship between you and your son.

✔ Your boys see that it's okay for a man to cook, clean, shop, and do laundry, which helps them grow up to be great parents themselves.

Yes, a father/son home has many advantages; however, you may still have a tendency toward one of the problems presented in Table 7-1.

Table 7-1	Ah, Puberty: Boy Stages	
Problem	*What's Happening*	*What You Can Do*
You may unconsciously model and encourage your son to hide his feelings.	This makes a close, trusting relationship with your son more difficult.	Don't be afraid to open up with your son and let your feelings show.

Problem	What's Happening	What You Can Do
Your son may go through a difficult time during elementary school and junior high when he feels inferior to the girls in his classes.	He feels scrawny.	Tell your son that girls mature faster than boys. Get your son involved in an activity where he *can* excel, whether it's a sport, academic pursuit, or extracurricular activity. This is the time to pump him up and make him feel good about himself in every way you can.
Your son may feel shy around girls and confused about the sexual stuff.	Your son has the same questions as your daughter when it comes to sex and reproduction.	Beat your son's friends to the punch: Be the *first* to talk to your son about wet dreams, reproduction, and the dangers of unprotected sex, including all the gory details about sexually transmitted diseases and pregnancy.

Daughter

Sure, you may find it a little bit more difficult raising your daughter than raising a son, but you also find a few advantages to a father/daughter home:

- It's okay to roughhouse with your daughter as she's growing up because you teach her assertiveness. So, don't treat her like a china doll — she needs the physical play.

- As you cook, shop, and do the housework, you're showing your daughter that it's okay for a man to break the stereotypical mold that only a woman does this sort of work. When your daughter helps you with the housework, she discovers teamwork. Dusting with Dad is fun!

- When you model a warm, loving relationship with lots of praise, you're showing your daughter what to expect from the men in her life when she grows up.

It will be more difficult for you, as a father, to raise your daughter than your son. Here are some reasons why:

✔ **You and your daughter may have very different interests:** It's only natural for you to interact more easily with your son, because you and your son are the same gender and probably have more interests in common than you do with your daughter. So, make a conscious effort to allow equal talking and listening time with your daughter.

✔ **Your teenage daughter may idolize and want to please you and help around the house.** She may do this because she thinks she needs to fill the role of nurturer to you and caregiver to the younger children. In other words, she feels compelled to become the "woman of the house." Watch for these tendencies and if she goes overboard, explain to her that you love her just the way she is and that she doesn't need to take care of you or do all the housework. Encourage her to enjoy her years as a teenager. By the way, a girl being raised by a single mother doesn't have these tendencies, because her mother is already fulfilling these roles.

✔ **You may tend to baby your daughter:** This can result in a dependent, non-assertive young woman. It can also set her up to expect the same thing from her husband some day. So, try not to be overly protective of your daughter. Cut her some slack, but don't hesitate to assign her responsibilities.

Extra effort may also be required as she's going through the typical stages listed in Table 7-2.

Table 7-2	Ah, Puberty: Girl Stages	
Problem	*What's Happening*	*What You Can Do*
Because you are a male and tend to hold your emotions in check, you may unconsciously encourage your daughter to hide her feelings.	This may prevent you from forming a close relationship with your daughter, because she'll tend to hide her feelings from you as well.	Try to see things from your daughter's point view. A girl needs to express her emotions and feelings and it's up to you, as her dad, to encourage this.
Feeling awkward.	Until your daughter reaches high school, she may be stronger and taller than most of the boys in her class, which can give her a feeling of being a misfit. She perceives herself as being a freak: too tall and gangly.	Praise her beautiful features and her academic and sports achievements, hug her, and tell her you love her. It may also help if you explain that girls develop earlier than boys in every way, including their height and academic achiement.

Problem	What's Happening	What You Can Do
Feeling fat and pimply.	When your daughter reaches puberty, she may go through mood changes, plus she may struggle with complexion problems and feeling fat.	Be a good listener and show your daughter love, sympathy, and support. A visit to her pediatrician may be in order.
Feeling dumb about sexual stuff.	Don't let your daughter find out about menstruation, reproduction, and the dangers of premarital sex from her friends.	Bring up the subject so she knows you're willing to talk with her about it. Let her know that you're not only available now, but any time she has questions in the future. Provide literature from helpful sources, such as Planned Parenthood. If you sense that your daughter would feel more comfortable talking with a female, ask a female friend or relative to talk to your daughter about everything from the menstrual cycle to pregnancy to sexually transmitted diseases.

Single mom raising her . . .

A single mom faces unique challenges as she raises a son or a daughter due to male and female gender traits. You relate to your daughter more easily than your son because you're the same sex. Raising a son, on the other hand, will be the greater challenge. Your son may not open up and expose his feelings and emotions in the same way as your daughter.

Daughter

If you're lucky, your daughter looks to you as a role model and a friend who can help her with her problems and decisions. What a privilege! What a challenge! Here are a few advantages to a mother/daughter home:

- ✔ You and your daughter are the same gender, so it's only natural for you to interact more easily with her than with your son.

- ✔ Your daughter will consciously and subconsciously emulate you, as you run the household and juggle time between your job and your children.

- ✔ She will also model you as you praise others and express your feelings and emotions.

- ✔ Your daughter will learn from watching you that it's okay to break away from the stereotypical mold that only a man fixes the plumbing, changes a tire, or helps build a doghouse.

Son

Raising her son can be a little bit trickier for a woman than raising her daughter, especially if she doesn't have many common interests with her son. You'll find, however, that there are some advantages to a mother/son home:

- ✔ If your son has close contact with his non-custodial dad, he will probably get along with you quite well. This is because he uses his father as a role model, which will build his self-esteem.

- ✔ Your son observes you in your role as mother, housekeeper, nurturer, and friend, which serves as a positive model as to what he wants and expects from his wife some day.

Here are a few problems you may encounter with your son in a mother/son home:

- ✔ **A son tends to take a divorce harder** than a daughter does, especially when the father has left the home. In fact, in a recent seminar attended by single mothers of teenage kids, most of the moms felt it was much more difficult raising a teenage son than a daughter.

- ✔ **Feeling in love with Mommy:** Don't be surprised if your son goes through a stage where he wants to marry you when he grows up. This is the old Oedipus complex, but it needn't become a problem. Explain to your son that even though you love him, you can't marry him because a mommy loves her son in a different way than a grown-up man and lady love each other. However, be sure to explain that he can marry someone just like you when he grows up.

- ✔ **Feeling like the substitute father and husband:** If you have a teenage boy, especially if he's the oldest of your children, he may feel compelled to take on the responsibilities of the man of the house. He feels he needs to make the younger children behave and to provide you with a social life. Watch for this tendency in your son and if you see it beginning to develop, have a talk and explain that he doesn't need to take on this heavy burden. Tell him that you love him just the way he is and that he doesn't need to try to be a husband to you or a father to his brothers and sisters. Encourage him to enjoy his life as a teenager.

Don't ever let your son bad-mouth you or put you down. If you do, you're giving him permission to treat his wife the same way some day.

Talking about sex, no matter the gender

If one of your kids comes home from school one day and tells you the health teacher said he would be giving out "condominiums," pay attention! USA Today recently reported that by age 14, 19 percent of boys and 21 percent of girls have had intercourse. A 14-year-old is a high school freshman. So, this may be the time to talk to your child about sex. If you're not sure how to go about it, check out www.parentsoup.com, a Web site for parents. Click the Expert Advice link, which takes you to Talking to Kids About Sex.

Many children view oral sex as safe sex or not "really" sexual at all. Explain that oral sex is not only a sexual act, but an act that spreads sexually transmitted diseases, including syphilis, gonorrhea, and herpes.

Every family and culture is different, so the following guidelines are only guidelines for you to consider and modify as you see fit. You can also take a look at these guidelines:

✔ **Under 8 years old:** Your child doesn't need to know the details of sexual relationships until 9-years-old or older. At this younger age your son or daughter isn't emotionally able to understand about sexual intercourse. Your child may ask basic questions, such as "Where do babies come from?" or "What do a man and lady do to make a baby?" You can answer with a question of your own, such as "What do you think?" or "What made you bring that up?" Be prepared for a hilarious answer. You might explain simply by saying that a baby grows in the mommy's tummy, and then when the baby is born he gets bigger and bigger every day. Tell him about how excited you were when he was born. Then, leave it at that.

✔ **Preadolescence:** Kids between 9 and 12 may be at the ideal age to hear a more detailed explanation of sex — depending on each child's maturity, of course. The preadolescent is at that stage where he or she is curious. Start at the beginning, explaining how a man and a woman love each other very much and want to hold each other real close. When they love each other very, very much, they make love, which is sometimes called intercourse. Then explain the mechanics of having intercourse in any way that's most comfortable for you.

From this point on, you're home free because it's pretty easy to talk about mommy's egg and daddy's sperm and how they join inside mommy's womb to form a new life. Show your child pictures of how the egg and sperm join and the stages of growth within the womb. After the show and tell, encourage your daughter or son to ask questions — tell them they can ask you anything!

✔ **Teenage years:** Even though you have probably discussed this subject with your son and daughter when they were younger, it's time for another talk when they become teenagers. Be sure to use the correct terminology for body parts, which your child probably already knows by age 13. When a kid is this age you also need to talk about pregnancy, the sacredness of sex, how to say "no" to sexual advances, how to handle sexual feelings, and give a detailed description of the sexually transmitted diseases, including HIV, AIDS, syphilis, herpes, and so on. Come to this meeting prepared with visual aids!

Your son or daughter may have been through a sex education class at school and learned a lot of the basics. But having a personal chat with the kid is the only way to get into the moral and spiritual side of the sexuality and let your kid know what you believe is right and wrong. And remember that the more open you are on the subject, the less your children need to experiment to find out for themselves.

Avoiding Stereotypical Behavior

Stereotypical behavior is usually, though not always, characteristic of a male or female. For example, some people might associate men with overhauling engines, re-roofing a home, or becoming a professional boxer. Others may think of women as those who bake cupcakes, iron the clothes, and take ballet lessons. Of course, in reality women can overhaul engines, roof homes, and do, in fact, become professional boxers. Likewise, men bake, iron, and become ballet dancers. It's good to break through your own gender's stereotypical roles because you provide your children with examples of how they can cope with their own gender tendencies.

In spite of the occasional role reversals, for simplicity's sake, we assume here that a great deal of stereotyping still occurs.

Macho, macho man

As a single dad, you're forced into traditionally female roles in order to survive in your home, and this is a good thing. Why? Because, you're demonstrating to your children that it's okay to break the stereotypical molds.

Here are some healthy ways you can do this:

✔ **Hone your cooking skills:** Hint, hint: Look at the backs of those packaged mixes near the spice shelf in your grocery store. You find everything you need to know for putting together a meat loaf, tacos, spaghetti sauce, French dip sandwiches, or fajitas. Really! It's so simple — that's how the rest of us started out, and our kids love our cooking.

✔ **Be willing to put a Halloween costume together from scratch — without Grandma's help!** Glue, felt, and scissors can work wonders toward this end.

✔ **Sit down on the floor with your 3-year-old daughter and play dolls or trucks with her:** Do this for more than five minutes.

✔ **Take your teenage daughter to a department store cosmetic counter for a makeover:** Then take her to a nice restaurant for lunch if she wants to show off. If your daughter's a bookworm, take her to a bookstore. If she loves horseback riding, go with her to pick out a new riding outfit. The important thing is to be sensitive to her interests and willing to spend time with her pursuing something that's important to her.

✔ **Don't be embarrassed to kiss your child's boo-boo, bandage him up, and give him a healing hug:** Same goes for crying, laughing, and expressing the emotions most people feel. Even if it's not easy for you, encourage your children to express their feelings.

✔ **Get the vacuum out and clean that carpet with gusto:** Pretend you're really enjoying it! Do laundry like a champ. Study all about those alien bottles and boxes on the shelf in the laundry room, such as fabric softener, all-fabric bleach, and anti-static dryer sheets, and read the manuals that came with your washer and dryer. Water temperature and mysterious things like "gentle cycle" do make a difference!

✔ **Don't be embarrassed to take in a few "female-oriented" activities with your kids:** Take your daughter to a "chick-flick." Get a massage with your kids, or take your daughter to a fashion show.

✔ **Adopt a female pet:** This may sound silly, but if you're thinking of adopting a pet, look for a female.

Saving yourself from the castle: Women

As a single mom, you're forced to take on a lot of Dad's duties. What you may not know is that this is positive role modeling for your kids because it encourages them to step out of their own gender roles.

For example, here are some ways you can break through stereotypical barriers for your children:

✔ **Be assertive in your career, asking for a raise or going after a promotion.** Take charge by going back to school to train for a more prestigious, better paying position.

✔ **Take control of your finances.** Get in the habit of paying your bills as soon as they arrive in your mailbox; keep a record of bills paid, and balance your checkbook every month!

✔ **Go to Home Depot for a few free lessons on home maintenance.** They teach everything from repairing your plumbing, to re-wiring a room, to stripping and refinishing your kitchen cabinets.

✔ **How about a tool belt?** Have you seen one sitting around the garage? Take a look at the screwdrivers, wrenches, pliers, and hammers — interesting, huh? It can be a lot of fun to discover how to use these gizmos — give them a try!

✔ **Master car maintenance basics.** You can check the fluids and tire pressure, and lube and change oil. Your car needs a little attention once in a while.

✔ **Don't be embarrassed to take up a few "male-oriented" activities with your kids.** Take the kids fly-fishing, camping, or out on the lake in a motorboat. Don't shy away from taking your son to see the latest action flick. Get tickets to his favorite sport and drag your daughters along too.

Having sole — Custody, that is: Dads

Whether you became a sole-custody father through death, divorce, or by choice, it may comfort you to know that, according to the latest U.S. Census Bureau data, there are over 2 million of you in the United States, an increase of over 62 percent in the last ten years alone. This means that almost 23 percent of the total 9.8 million single-parent households in the United States are parented by sole-custody fathers. Census Bureau reports show that the bulk of single custodial fathers, 46 percent, are divorced, while 34 percent of you have never married.

You're not the lone duck, but a member of a large fraternity, each seeking answers to these difficult questions:

✔ How can I balance my career with being a good dad?

✔ Can I carve out more quality time with my kids?

✔ Will I be able to continue dating? How can I find the time?

✔ How do I handle each child's individual personality?

✔ How can I get my kids to tell me what they're worried about?

✔ What do my kids need from me?

Thousands of single dads have not only resolved these questions, but also found great joy in the process. In fact, research shows that single fathers can nurture and parent their kids just as well as single mothers. So, don't take your influence lightly — you are *very* important in the lives of your children.

Bill and Melinda — it takes a village

Bill became an instant sole-custody parent of a 20-month-old baby girl. He had dated the girl's mother, who became pregnant with his baby. After Melinda was born, the baby lived with the mother until the mother realized she wasn't able to cope with raising a child, so she gave full custody to Bill, who loved his child very much. Bill was a bachelor, new to the area, with very few friends. His family lived several states away. He had no crib, no diapers, no baby food, no anything — except for one very important thing: He had unconditional love for his baby girl.

Bill's first reaction was to take a week's emergency leave from work to convert his bachelor pad into a suitable home for Melinda. His next reaction was to turn to his neighbors for help, even though he barely knew them.

Guess what? Bill and Melinda became the darlings of the apartment complex — everyone wanted to help out, the women with their maternal instincts, and the men, in fear and amazement, rallied to the cause as well. The neighbors helped Bill screen day-care centers and even volunteered as fill-in babysitters. What had seemed to be an unfriendly neighborhood became a source of warmth, fun, and support, with spontaneous gatherings and potluck barbecues.

Then, even more good stuff happened to Bill:

- He met with his boss and arranged to transfer to a job that didn't require overtime.

- He began to feel competent and pleased with his ability to soothe and play with Melinda.

- He loved to read to his baby as she drifted off to sleep to the sound of his voice.

Throwing off your cape: The super mom myth

We've all heard the term *super mom*. What is a super mom? She's someone who's compelled to try to be everything to her child at all times. However, as much as you *want* to be super mom, and as much as you *try* to be super mom, and as much as you may *believe* you *are* super mom, you need to realize that you're taking on an impossible task! You're a single mother and you just can't do it all. If you insist on trying, you only make yourself sick.

What's the answer? Take an honest look at what you're trying to accomplish with your kids. If you're overdoing it, cut back a little. See whether anything on this list rings a bell. Understand that it's only natural for you to be doing one or two things at a time. It's when you try to take them all on at once that you're facing the impossible:

- **Super mom shops at Toys 'R Us.** Super mom buys a soft, huggable book with colorful padded pages to help her baby learn his colors while playing in his crib, and a junior-size laptop computer for her 5-year-old, so she can learn how to use a computer before she goes into kindergarten.

- **Super mom always prepares healthy, well-balanced meals for her kids.** She scrubs all the fresh fruits and vegetables with anti-bacterial soap and scalding hot water.

- **Super mom purchases a pattern, fabric, and accessories so she can make a customized angel costume for her daughter on Halloween.** She takes two Saturdays to get it right.

- **Super mom bakes special holiday treats for her daughter's preschool class.** She spells out each child's name with frosting.

- **Super mom makes sure her daughter practices the piano every day from 4:10 p.m. to 4:55 p.m.** She sets a timer.

- **Super mom plays educational videos for her 1-year-old to watch while he sits in his high chair.** And she feeds him baby food she has pureed herself.

- **Super mom plays learn-to-speak Spanish CDs in the car when she and the kids are on a trip.** Her 5-year-old has learned twenty-seven verbs so far.

- **Super mom stands watch in the bathroom to be sure her daughter brushes until the green light flashes on the electric toothbrush.** She gives the brush an alcohol rinse before putting it back in its slot.

Exhausting, huh? Super mom needs to give more thought to the value of down time with her kids — time to kick back, act a little silly, and enjoy each other — which might even free up a little time to actually communicate with her children.

Fouling up: Avoiding the Biggest Mistakes

You're a single parent trying to do the best job possible raising your kids. In the process, it's only natural to make a few mistakes. Single parents often make these common mistakes. Forewarned is forearmed!

- Pressing your child to heap more and more onto his plate.

- Encouraging your kids to be your private detectives.

- ✔ Labeling your kids.

- ✔ Denying yourself a social life.

- ✔ Allowing your kids' traits to ring your bell.

- ✔ Getting sucked into power plays.

- ✔ Being a poor role model.

- ✔ Expecting your children to deliver messages to your ex.

- ✔ Allowing your kids to con you into buying things for them.

- ✔ Failing to establish boundaries in your children's behavior.

- ✔ Refusing to consider professional therapy for yourself or your children.

If any of these mistakes ring a bell, take a look in Chapter 9 where we talk about each of these mistakes in more detail, and reveal ways to avoid them.

Raising kids is an art — not a science — so try not to overreact to every little crisis. If you do, you wear yourself out physically and emotionally. Here's a great word of advice: Choose your battles wisely! That way you have energy left over for the things that really matter. And here's a word of encouragement: Messing up once in a while isn't fatal. You can learn from mistakes and go on from there.

If you do bungle the job at all, you probably make these mistakes.

Living vicariously through your kids: Dads

Although single moms occasionally fall into this trap, too, it's quite common for a sole-custody single father to consciously, or subconsciously, push his children into lifestyles and careers of the father's choice.

If you're a super jock yourself, it's only natural for you to get your children involved in sports activities, starting with T-ball when they're young and progressing to summer soccer league, Pop Warner football, basketball, swim team, or gymnastics, depending on your interests. If you excelled in gymnastics, for example, you may hire a private gymnastics coach for your son and eventually press your son into competing in gymnastics tournaments. But what if your son would rather get involved in computer programming or theater arts? Can you handle that?

And what about your children's future careers? Do you find yourself talking up law school to your daughter, either because you're an attorney, or because that's the career you always wanted to pursue, but your daughter wants to be a kindergarten teacher instead?

As a single dad, you need to take a good hard look at which activities and academic pursuits you may be expecting your children to love as much as you do. Take a step back and give them some room to breathe! Then, get them talking about what really interests them and help them fulfill their dreams.

Babying your children: Moms

As a single mom, you worry about your kids, you strive to protect them, and you want desperately to make everything better. Your call to nurture is fine and good until you start babying your children.

This is a typical single mother mistake and it's easy to see how it happens. If you've survived death or divorce, you've been through a lot of painful struggles, and because they've been so painful, you do whatever it takes to protect your kids from this kind of pain. You walk ahead of them every step of the way, smoothing the path so they don't stumble, fall, or get lost. You pull up every thorny bush, kick away the sharp rocks, and fill all the potholes before you let your kids out of bed in the morning!

The problem with your plan is that you're keeping your kids too safe, which means that as they grow up, they don't find out how to solve their problems and move the roadblocks along the way. If everything is done for them and life is easy, they're living in a fairy tale world — or a fairy tale jail — that they never have the strength to break out of as they grow older. So, even though your loving single mother heart is well intentioned, please don't baby your kids — you're just creating emotional midgets who never mature and can't fend for themselves when you're not around. They whine their way through their adult lives, expecting others to pick up the pieces, fix things, and make their lives better.

Avoiding the warm, fuzzy stuff

Don't be afraid to demonstrate warmth and affection, and don't bury your feelings. Be emotionally expressive, nurturing, and huggable with your kids. Studies show that what really matters most to a child is feeling loved.

In fact, a child luxuriates in feeling your love and a child who feels treasured develops a positive image of himself. He perceives himself as being a lovable person, which is the beginning of self-esteem. The key is to make your child feel accepted and prized for who he is, not only for what he *does*. A child who grows up with a parent who shows his affection has a greater chance of growing up to be an interesting, emotionally sound, happily married adult.

Not every parent is big on kissing and hugging, and if you fit that category, show your affection in ways that are comfortable for you. Here's one sure-fire way to get your feelings across: Say, "I love you" to each of your children every day.

Striving to become your teen's best buddy

Sure, you want to be a friend to your children, a playmate, a fun person, a sympathetic listener, and a concerned parent, but you can't be your child's best friend and maintain your authority as a parent.

One of the biggest mistakes is when the single mother of a teenage daughter decides to become her daughter's closest pal. In an effort to emulate her daughter, Mom dresses like her, styles her hair into something chic, and copies the latest in teen makeup. Then, when she's finally lookin' good, she chases around town with her daughter, shopping, stylin' around the mall, attending rock concerts, and generally hanging out with her daughter and her friends. She enjoys the way she fits in with the crowd.

This is an easy pattern to fall into, mainly because you think this is the way to stay close to your teenagers, but also because you enjoy the satisfaction of looking and acting younger than you are. The you-know-what hits the fan, however, the first time one of your kids commits a major no-no and you need to don your disciplinarian hat. You feel really silly, standing there in your Britney Spears get-up, laying down the law on what happens when your son takes your car without your permission!

Feeling guilty when you're working

Recognize this tendency and try not to feel guilty when you're at work. You're a nurturer, so it isn't easy, but even when you're required to work overtime, realize that you're working because you must work to provide a decent standard of living for your family.

Expecting your child to make your life better

Here's a sticky trap: expecting your child to nurture you, comfort you, and make things all better again! If you're extremely needy, it's easy to let your kids try to soothe and smooth out your life.

Your children are only children, after all, and they can't be expected to fill the hole left in your heart. Don't expect your child to serve as your counselor or therapist. Don't expect your kids to provide you with a social life. And don't expect them to cater to you because you're feeling down and depressed.

If you're really hurting and you're expecting your kids to fix you up, you need to find people to help you other than your children. Join a parent support group, where you can unload your problems and get practical advice, call your pastor, your crisis hotline, or enlist the services of a private practice family therapist. If you receive the help you need, you can get over the victim syndrome and be able to be there for your children — they need you!

Providing Role Models

A *role model* is a positive example of a particular type of behavior or social role that you would like your child to emulate. In other words, you want your kids to hang out with adults they can look up to and who provide inspiration and guidance for their lives.

Female

Your children need to be around feminine role models, especially if they have little or no contact with their mother.

- **Daughter.** She especially needs this influence because she doesn't know what's expected of her as a wife and mother unless she observes women in these roles. Strive to find strong, successful women. Of course, just because a woman is strong and successful doesn't mean she's a perfect person; the more models you provide, the easier it will be for her to compare and be impressed with those who do have stellar qualities. You can also take your daughter to see movies that are based on true life stories of admirable women and provide her with autobiographies of women who have achieved greatness, such as Amelia Earhart and Eleanor Roosevelt.

- **Son.** He needs the influence of positive female role models not only because this exposes him to women who express their emotions more easily than many men, but teaches your son what to expect from a wife and mother. A positive female role model can bolster his self-esteem in small ways, such as complimenting him on his new hairstyle or clothing. Depending on the circumstances, a boy being raised by a single father may also feel that his mother didn't want him, and in this kind of circumstance, a positive female role model can be invaluable to his self-esteem.

Male

Your children don't have to have Daddy around as a role model, but they sure need some type of male influence.

- ✔ **Son.** He needs a positive role model because research shows that if he doesn't have one, he tends to act out his anger and be more physically aggressive and difficult with friends and teachers. By watching a mature older male he finds out what's expected of him when he finds himself in one of the roles of husband and father.

- ✔ **Daughter.** She needs a positive male influence in her life, especially when she starts to date boys. A girl growing up in a single-mother household, with little or no contact with her dad, may have the mistaken idea that her father deserted her because she's unattractive or undesirable. She needs the influence of a strong male figure who makes her feel good about herself. It's also a good idea to provide a male role model who challenges her to be the best she can be.

Here are a few ways to provide role models for your kids:

- ✔ **Join single-parent organizations:** Get involved in a single-parent organization that has regular social activities involving single moms, dads, and their kids. Parents Without Partners, for example, has just about equal numbers of single mothers and fathers, so their get-togethers provide a way for your kids to soak up the positive influence provided by the single dads. Sign up for a camping trip or an afternoon at a professional baseball game.

- ✔ **Contact Big Brothers/Big Sisters International:** Get in touch with your local Big Brothers organization for a male role model to mentor your son on a regular basis. Many teachers also get involved pairing up a student with a big brother, so chat with your child's teacher.

- ✔ **Request certain coaches and teachers:** Always request opposite-sex coaches and teachers for your kids, if they are available.

- ✔ **Hang out with two-parent families in your circle of friends:** When friends invite you and your kids to join them for a trip to Disneyland, a day water-skiing on the lake, or a weekend hiking and camping trip, say, "Yes." Sometimes a single parent feels like the lone duck on one of these outings with two-parent families, but get over it! Your kids need the influence.

- ✔ **Encourage sleepovers at friends' homes:** If your son or daughter is invited to spend the night at the two-parent home of a friend, do everything you can to see that it happens. Even a simple sleepover once in a while gives your kids a chance to be around a male role model.

Check things out ahead of time so that you feel assured that your child is in a safe environment when spending time with role models — especially when sleeping over at friends' homes.

✔ **Entertain at home:** Ask a few single moms and dads and their kids over for a potluck dinner, a movie night, or a just-for-the-fun-of-it party. That way, your kids have a chance to interact with single dads.

✔ **Find a surrogate:** Find a friend who is willing to serve as a surrogate Daddy or Mommy, someone whom your child can confide in, when she doesn't want to talk to Mom or Dad.

✔ **Look into loving relatives:** Your family is probably full of uncles, aunts, grandpas, grandmas, and older cousins who may be honored to fill in occasionally as role models. You might have to toss a few subtle suggestions out from time to time, such as, "Michael would sure love to go to a hockey game with you and Jim once in a while," or "Would you like to come watch Trisha play in the state basketball playoffs next week?"

Chapter 8

Considering Your Kid's Point of View

In This Chapter

▶ Needing to feel safe and loved

▶ Craving your attention and affection

▶ Crying out for answers about the split

▶ Coming to you to talk

▶ Warning signs that your child needs professional counseling

Three single mothers sit on a park bench and savor mugs of hot coffee while they watch their sons play. An onlooker would never guess that two of the boys have recently lost their dads, or that the other boy is adopted. The three kids laugh and joke as they leap off the ramps on their skateboards — they seem like normal, happy kids who don't have a care in the world.

Stephanie adopted her 11-year-old son through the Foster Child program when he was 7. Donna is recently divorced with a 12-year-old, and Melanie's husband died in a boating accident, leaving her with a 10-year-old son. The three families have formed an informal support group.

Stephanie comments to Donna, "Jason's really doing well, isn't he? He seems so happy and well-adjusted, even though your divorce was a rough one."

Donna replies, "He seems fine to me — it's as if the divorce never even happened. He's doing well in school, too."

What many parents may not realize is that a divorce almost always wounds the heart of a child, even though the child may not show it outwardly. Often a child shuts down after a divorce, which is a way of protecting himself from the anger, sadness, and confusion he's feeling. The same thing can happen when a parent dies. Unless the child is encouraged to talk about her feelings, the wounds may fester for years and never heal over completely. Even those fortunate children who have been adopted by a single parent may have unspoken questions and concerns that they never mention to anyone.

In this chapter, we hope to help you relate to your child's point of view, her hurts, her needs, and the longings of her heart. When you look closely, you can see that your kids are going through a difficult time right now, especially if you've become a single parent quite suddenly. So even though you may be having a tough time yourself, the kids still need to be number one in your life as you face your future together. They need you now more than ever before.

Loving Them Up So They Feel Safe

If your child has recently lost his parent, he's probably feeling pretty crushed — much like Humpty Dumpty who fell off his wall. The kid feels his parent has deserted him. His happy life has crumbled and he wants his security blanket back! At the moment he may even feel like he's been tossed out with the trash. Obviously, you've got your work cut out for you!

One of the saddest things about divorce is that kids realize it's possible to stop loving someone. When your child realizes his parents don't love each other anymore, he may fear you'll stop loving him, too. This may seem crazy when you're trying your hardest to reassure your child that he is precious, adored, and the most important thing in your life, but a child is fragile and he may be afraid that you'll turn against him, too.

A divorce affects children differently, depending on their ages at the time of the divorce. We thought you might be interested in a breakdown by age group.

Birth to age 2

You may think that children in this age group don't understand what's going on, but they feel trouble through their sensory system. For example, your child responds to the feel of your touch, the sound of your voice, and your body language. Take a look in Chapter 6 for ways to deal with tantrums and regression.

Symptoms:

- **Your child senses that one of his parents is missing from his life.** This absence makes him feel very insecure, which is why he gloms onto his remaining parent.
- **She misses the smell and the voice of the absent parent.**
- **He also senses your distress, so try to remain calm as you feed him, hold him, and care for him.** Your child will let you know when he's reacting to your stress by crying more than usual.

✔ **Your 2-year-old may begin to throw tantrums and she may regress to previous behavior, such as thumb sucking or wanting her pacifier.**

✔ **Your child may refuse to sleep in his own bed and insist on sleeping with you.**

✔ **She may become afraid of strangers.**

✔ **Your child may become possessive of his toys, not wanting them to be moved or shared.**

Here are ways to help him:

✔ **Spend more time with your child than you ever did before, holding him, cuddling him, reading to him, and playing with him.** Chapter 4 has great suggestions for ways to free up the extra time you need to be spending with your child.

✔ **Give her more hugs and kisses than usual.**

✔ **Smile a lot — kids can't help smiling back and smiling helps you, too.**

✔ **Experts say that it won't harm your young child one bit to sleep with her parent.** The gain in his security is well worth the little elbow and knee jabs. Besides, how often do you get to sleep with a real, live Easter bunny in his fluffy blue Dr. Denton's?

Ages 2 to 5

By the time your child reaches this age bracket, he's becoming more aware of your feelings and the effects of his environment.

Symptoms:

✔ **Your child feels stressed and confused by the changes in his world.** His daily routine has been interrupted, making him feel insecure and frightened.

✔ **She may become clingy and tearful, especially when you have to drop her off at day care or leave her with a sitter.** She doesn't want you to leave, which is also known as *separation anxiety.*

✔ **Your child may become a whiner.**

✔ **He may insist on taking his favorite toy, stuffed animal, or security blanket with him everywhere!**

✔ **You may begin to see a few tantrums, if you haven't before.**

Here are ways you can help your child:

- ✔ **Try to establish a consistent, predictable routine in his life.**

- ✔ **Maintain the same standards of discipline that were in place before.** See Chapter 9 for ways to maintain continuity in your child's life and consistent standards of discipline.

- ✔ **Encourage your child to talk about her feelings.** Have paper and felt-tip markers available as you and your child talk, and encourage her to draw a picture that shows you what she's feeling. For example, one child drew a stick figure of a girl with tears coming down her face. A boy drew a face with huge teeth and large, dark eyes. The first picture depicts sadness and the second shows anger.

- ✔ **Take a tip from professional child psychologists by providing sand tray therapy in your kitchen.** Make a waterproof sandbox, preferably on foldable legs. Provide plenty of miniature toys that depict family life and nature. As your child arranges the miniatures in the super-fine sand, just observe — no analysis is needed. We know a family that keeps a sand tray going all the time. Hint, hint: Grownups can benefit from it just as much as the kids!

- ✔ **Spend more time with your child than you did before, playing with him, reading to him, and cuddling him.**

- ✔ **Go along with her need to haul Bucky, her huge stuffed pony, with her everywhere you go.** We know a single mom whose 3-year-old daughter insists on bringing her favorite doll with her when they eat out in a restaurant. When they get there, the little girl insists that the waiter brings a high chair for her doll to sit in during the meal. What a cute sight that would be!

All kids have problems

Don't beat yourself up by assuming your kid's problems are caused from being raised in a single-parent home. Two-parent families have similar problems with their kids because many of the problems just come naturally as a child grows and matures.

Here's something that should cheer you up: Mental health professionals have found that a child from a divorced home is usually better adjusted than a child from a two-parent home with constant conflict. And according to several studies, 70 percent of girls and 60 percent of boys are beginning to function reasonably well within two years after the divorce. In fact, two things that children of divorce seem to develop in spades are independence and resilience.

Ages 6 to 12

The average age of a child in a divorce is 8-years-old.

Symptoms:

- **He may worry about what will happen to him because of the divorce, such as where he'll live and who'll take care of him.** These worries may affect his physical health, his concentration, and his ability to do his schoolwork.

- **She may experience stomachaches and headaches.**

- **He may have nightmares or even walk and talk in his sleep.**

- **She may develop a nervous tic or start biting her nails.**

- **He wants desperately for you and your ex to get back together again, so he may come up with ingenious ways to accomplish this!** A common plan is for a child to misbehave in such a way that he knows you will both have to get involved. Other clever ploys are imaginary illnesses and threats to run away.

- **Your child may become angry with you because she blames you for causing the divorce.**

- **He may be embarrassed or ashamed to tell his friends about your breakup.** He may also be teased at school about being from a bad or broken family.

- **She may tend to side with the parent she feels has been wronged, trying to make that parent's life happier.**

Here are a few helpful ways to cope with your 6- to 12-year-old:

- **When it comes to dealing with your child's anger, take a look at our suggestions later in this chapter.**

- **Be a good listener.**

- **Tell him and show him that you love him.**

- **Never talk to someone about your child in *front* of her.**

- **Watch for ways to praise him.** For example, thank him for being quiet while you were on the phone, or thank him for helping his sister with her homework.

- **Establish a strong support network for your child.** Enlist the help of her teacher, her friends' parents, and your child's relatives, including her non-custodial parent.

✔ **Reassure your child that a divorce is nothing to be embarrassed about and that it's not a freak occurrence.** In fact, over half the kids in the United States are from divorced homes. Let him know that it takes two people to have a marriage and that you and your ex were equally to blame for not being able to fix it. In fact, you can reassure him that you both made the decision to divorce.

✔ **Try to involve your child in a few extracurricular activities, including a hobby, a sport, or a club, such as Boy Scouts or Girl Scouts.**

✔ **Be consistent with your discipline and don't give in to her begging for expensive toys or entertainment.**

Teenagers

Many experts say that if your teen seems moody and difficult at home, but is doing well in school, worry a little. However, if your teen is doing pretty well at home, but is having trouble in school, worry a lot!

Symptoms:

✔ **A teenager already lives an unpredictable up-and-down existence, straining to break free from his parents' control one minute, and feeling confused and insecure the next.** In fact, his development task during his teen years is to try to figure out who he is and to begin to break away from the family. However, his parent's divorce adds even more uncertainty to his life. One day he may be bopping around the house to his favorite CD, and the next he may blow up because he can't find his other tennis shoe.

✔ **A teenager tends to grieve deeply over the loss of his parent, which can lead to bouts of moodiness, irritability, and depression as she hides away in her room for hours at a time.**

✔ **Your teenager may be angry with you because he thinks you're selfish and the divorce is your fault.**

✔ **She may lose his concentration and her grades may drop.**

✔ **Your teenager may develop an eating disorder.**

✔ **Your teen may abandon his old friends and take up with a bad crowd (be on the lookout for butt cracks, spiked Mohawks, and pierced cheeks!).**

✔ **She may become sullen and not want to participate in family fun.** You know the drill: You ask her to come with you to play miniature golf and she rolls her eyes and says, "Oh, yeah, Mom — DUH! Like that's supposed to be fun!"

 ✔ **Your teenager may feel so stressed that he turns to drugs, alcohol, or sex for relief.**

Wow! Like you weren't already having problems with your teenager, now you have all this to look forward to! Well, here are a few helpful ways to cope with your unhappy teen:

 ✔ **It's very important for you to maintain the same standards of discipline that were in place before the divorce.** At the same time, cut your child a little slack if she's just having a bad day. See Chapter 9 for practical ways to maintain a consistent pattern of discipline in your child's life.

 ✔ **Encourage your child to maintain his relationships with his old friends.**

 ✔ **With your teen's help, establish a structure and a consistent routine in your daily lives.** Structure helps re-establish a sense of stability in his life.

 ✔ **Schedule one-on-one time with your child, and be a good listener.**

 ✔ **If you think your child is showing signs of an eating disorder, take quick action.**

 ✔ **Treat your teenager with respect, honesty, and understanding.**

 ✔ **Look for ways to praise your teen.** If she gives the dog a bath without being asked, thank her. If she takes out the trash without complaining, tell her you really appreciate the way she helps you around the house. Or, if she excels in anything — at school, in sports, or in any extracurricular activities, praise her. If her accomplishments warrant it, celebrate with a decorated cake after dinner, with tickets to a live concert, or even dinner in her honor at a nice restaurant. Make a huge deal out of the stuff she does right and a miniscule deal out of her mistakes!

 ✔ **Stay involved in your teen's life — know what he's up to!**

 ✔ **Know what your teen is doing on the Internet — don't assume everything must be okay because it's so nice and quiet in there!**

 ✔ **Get involved in your teen's school — meet her teachers, attend her games, and keep tabs on whom she's with and what she's doing after school.** Never give in to a hands-off policy just because it's an easy out!

 ✔ **Don't hand your child money every time he asks for it.** Depending on the need, make him earn some of it.

 ✔ **No matter what she yells at you, no matter what she does to you, and no matter how hard she tries to rile you up, never give up on her.** When she's acting out, she's actually reaching out! Your child is hurting, and she needs your love now more than ever. Give her gobs of approval and tell her you love her every day.

Children often wind up taking care of their parents during and after a difficult life transition. They seem strong as they support their parents. Supporting an adult is not their job and doing so can damage them emotionally. You need to find support from other adults, so your children can remain children and do what they need to do.

Rebuilding physical security

When a child loses a parent, she no longer believes in happily ever after. Her security blanket has been snatched away and it may take a long time to regain trust and rebuild a sense of physical security.

Physical security is feeling that everything is in its place and that all is right with the world. Even parents need this. Changes in living arrangements, moving to a new apartment, even moving into a different bed, can temporarily take away the familiarity that breeds contentment. Transitional objects can help adjust to new surroundings. For example, encourage your kids to take a favorite stuffed animal or security blanket to bed with them.

You need to work on rebuilding your child's sense of physical security day after day until she finally feels secure when you tuck her into bed at night. Or, when she walks to school on her own from now on, she may not feel safe, because her missing parent always dropped her off on his way to work. So, your job is to assure her that you're there for her, to take care of her, to watch out for her, and to make sure nothing bad happens!

You may need to enlist the help of a neighbor or relative to fill in for you until your child feels more secure. Your children will feel more secure if they know they can reach you by phone at any time. They also need to know that the school has your phone number, plus the name of a third party who can help out in case of an emergency.

In your child's world, security is very important. His feelings of self worth depend on the familiarity and security of his home and his room, along with the presence of his brothers, sisters, and parents. His home and family have always been there for him — he's depended on you all these years. So, it's understandable that when his physical environment is messed with, he feels unstable and needs mega-doses of your love and reassurance.

Here are ways you can make your child feel safer:

✔ **Tell him over and over again how much you love him — never assume that he already knows.**

✔ **Explain that he will be taken care of and provided for — that he will always have a room and a bed and a place to live.**

> ✔ **Tell him that he shouldn't worry about anything — that everything is going to be all right.** With the help of willing grandparents, godparents, aunts, uncles, and other relatives, your child will always have the help he needs — he _will_ be all right.
>
> ✔ **Try to stay upbeat, smile, and keep your sense of humor.** This will reassure your child that you aren't always sad and upset. If you're able to laugh, joke, and tease, your child will think everything is okay after all! At the same time, let your child know that it's okay to feel sad or to cry sometimes too. Tell him how you cry and feel sad yourself, and don't hide your tears from your child — he needs your permission to cry.

As you watch your children struggle with the aftermath of your divorce, you may have doubts about whether the divorce was the right choice. You may wonder if you should have just sucked it up and stuck with the marriage if you were in a difficult marriage, perhaps suffering verbal or physical abuse, or the humiliation of an addictive or unfaithful spouse. Remind yourself that being part of a marriage where you have to suck it up for the kids' sake is no way to live. So, by breaking out of a difficult or unhappy marriage, you're role modeling self-caring and self-respect, which your children need to see. Remember that your kids learn how to be husbands and wives by watching their parents.

Rebuilding emotional security

When a child loses his parent, his emotions are in turmoil. One day he may be lashing out in anger, and the next he may be curled up in his room, feeling sad and unloved. Both are signs of depression.

If your child's symptoms don't clear up, you need to take action by seeking out a therapist or a counselor who can help him. If you ignore the symptoms, they may get worse, so deal with them the best you can and if you don't see improvement, get some professional help.

Dealing with angerrrrrr

Your child's anger may show up in various ways:

✔ **Your child gets into fights at school, something he never did before the divorce.**

✔ **Your child complains loud and long about such things as his "turd-brained teacher" or the "crappy food" they serve in the cafeteria.**

✔ **Your child becomes belligerent at home, talks back to you, and generally acts out.** Then, he runs to his room, slams the door, and sulks the rest of the evening.

ANECDOTE

Man of the house

Ron knew that his parents argued, but he and his sister were completely shocked when their mother announced they were moving out and she was getting a divorce. Ron and his stepfather had become very close over the years, yet he wouldn't even talk to Ron about what was happening.

At first Ron and his sister saw their stepdad fairly regularly, but after a few months he just seemed to drift away. Ron remembers how sad the first Christmas was without his stepfather and his stepfather's family.

Looking back, Ron realizes that his sister and mother got along pretty well, doing female-type stuff together, like shopping and cooking. He felt left out and he had no male influence. He finally decided to take up wresting, and that made a big difference. One of his coaches became a mentor and confidant to him. His team went to the national competitions and came in eighth. Ron heard that his stepfather was proud of him, but he didn't come to any of Ron's meets.

When Ron got into trouble with a gang and ended up in jail, his mother asked her ex for help. He refused, saying that Ron had to "take it like a man." She was finally able to raise bail. Ron says his mother was always there for him and taught him what a parent should be like. One of Ron's goals is to become the best parent he can possibly be.

Meanwhile, Ron has broken an engagement because he's having trouble making commitments. He realizes that what's holding him back is his fear of being hurt and abandoned. He has become a big brother for a high school kid and is getting couple's counseling with his ex fiancée.

Of course, he's not really angry with his teacher, or the cafeteria food, or his friends at school. He's angry with you for getting a divorce, he's angry because his life is messed up, and he's angry because he's afraid.

So, how can you help your child get over his angry feelings? Here are a few suggestions:

- ✔ **Try to have a heart-to-heart talk with your child.** See if you can coax him into verbalizing his feelings. Until you get his feelings out in the open, it will be difficult for you to address them. Never interrupt your child when he's talking to you. When he's made his point, it may help for you to repeat what he's said, to be sure you understand what he's trying to get across and to assure him that you're really listening. The key is to assure your child that anger is a normal reaction to what he's been through and that you understand because you feel angry sometimes, too. See Chapter 6 for ways to be sure you're listening to your child.

- ✔ **Encourage your child to get involved in any type of physical exercise, such as karate lessons, playing tennis, shooting hoops in the driveway, swimming, or something as simple as brisk nightly walks around the block.**

✔ **Distract your child with humor.** You can even have a laughing contest. See which one of you can laugh the hardest and the longest.

✔ **Encourage your child to write a story about a child whose parents are divorced, including all the hateful feelings the child feels toward his parents.** Explain to your child that he doesn't have to show the story to anyone unless he wants to — it's a private story just for himself.

✔ **Go to the art store and buy a supply of felt-tip markers and drawing paper.** Ask your child to draw pictures of what he's feeling — this may be a shocking revelation for you, so buckle up for the ride!

✔ **Ask a friend, coach, relative, or one of his playmate's parents to talk to him.** See if that person can get your child to open up and talk about how angry he is.

✔ **You are your child's primary role model.** If you can find ways to appreciate each day, find humor in little things, and not be overly reactive, you'll set a good example. If you do blow up, apologize. If your child blows up, try not to take it too personally.

If none of these ideas seem to be working, and your child's anger is getting worse, it's probably time to meet with a professional therapist, preferably one who works with children and families. The school counselor may be able to help out or you can hire a professional therapist or psychologist.

Dealing with grief

Whether your child lost his parent through death or divorce, she grieves the loss. If only we could speed up the healing process, wouldn't that be a miracle? But studies show that it can take up to three years to heal from the loss of a parent.

When your child's other parent died, especially if it was a sudden death, you may see these tendencies:

✔ **Your child may ask you questions about death, what it means and what made his parent die.** Answering your child's questions about death is a difficult challenge — ranking right up there with talking to your child about sex. Here is helpful advice from child psychologists:

  • **Explain the death in simple terms.** In other words, don't use mysterious phrases like, "Your daddy expired" or "Mommy passed on." Your child needs to hear the *real* answer. For example, you might say, "Daddy had a real bad heart attack and died" or "Mommy had a very serious kind of cancer and she died."

  • **When your child asks what it means when someone's *dead*, explain that when someone's dead that person can't breathe or move or think.** Show your child how you can blink your eyes, hop around the room, and wave your arms — then explain that some-one who's dead can't do any of those things. The person's body doesn't function anymore because it is *dead*.

- **When your child asks what happens to someone when they die, your answer will depend on your religious beliefs.** If you feel your child's parent is in heaven, tell him that. If you're not sure how you feel, but you think that a person's spirit lives on after he's dead, tell your child that. If death is a mysterious thing for you, don't be afraid to tell him that you don't know what happens. Be as honest as you can, then let your child come to his own conclusion.

- **Don't use confusing explanations like, "God reached down and took Mommy because He loves her so much," or "Daddy has gone on a long, long trip" or "Mommy just went to sleep," and so on.** You don't want your child to think that Daddy has gone on a trip, because your child will think he's coming back. And you sure don't want your child to think that Mommy's just sleeping, because your child will think that sleep is a scary thing that causes some-one to die.

✔ **Your child may feel very insecure about being left at day care or with a babysitter because he's afraid you might never come back.** He may cry and cling to you, not wanting to let go.

✔ **If you happen to be a little late picking up your child after school, don't be surprised to see him standing there with his teacher's arm around his shoulders.** When you ask what's wrong, you may discover that your child panicked because you were late.

✔ **Your child may not show up at the dinner table.** When you look for him, you may find him curled up on his bed sobbing his heart out.

✔ **When you tuck your child into bed at night, he may panic when you leave the room because he's afraid that when he wakes up in the morning you'll be gone, too.**

What a sad, sad thing! If only you could kiss him and make it all better, like you've always done with his scraped knees and skinned elbows! But grief takes a long time to heal and you need a lot of patience. Here are ways to help him heal:

✔ **Spend a lot of time with your child, trying to get him to open up and talk about his feelings.** Your older son may be more likely to open up and talk to you about his feelings while he's involved in some physical activity, such as shooting hoops or washing the family truck.

✔ **Grief doesn't have a quick fix — it's a long, slow process that requires patience.**

✔ **One of the very best things you can do for your child is to tell him about your own feelings of grief.** Explain how sad you are because Daddy's dead or how much you miss him. Then, if you feel like crying, go right ahead. Shedding tears in front of your child is a very healthy thing to do, because it shows your child that it's okay to cry and show your feelings. The more honest you are with him, the more honest he can be with you.

✔ **Reassure your children that their parent loved them and remind them of the happy times you had together as a family before your spouse died.** Keep plenty of photos and mementos around so you can share them with your kids and get them talking about the good times.

✔ **Encourage your kids to talk to their missing parent.** Speculate together on what Mom might think or say about the day's events. For example, maybe she'd laugh if she knew what you fixed for dinner tonight or how you never sort the laundry before you toss it into the washer.

✔ **Establish a steady, dependable daily routine in your lives, with as few interruptions as possible.** Sit down with your child and let him help you draw up a weekly or monthly schedule in writing. Doing so helps him realize that your plans are concrete, not abstract.

Take some time to talk about contingency plans, in case emergencies do pop up. For example, if you're ever going to be late picking him up from school, tell him you'll call to let him know, that he is not to panic, and then decide where he is to wait for you. Some parents provide their child with a two-way radio receiver or a cell phone. Then they call their kids directly to let them know plans have changed, and a child can also call them if he's beginning to panic.

✔ **Work with your child to create a memory or photo book about the parent who died.**

✔ **Understand the six stages your child may face as he grieves for his parent.** Chapter 12 talks about those stages in depth.

- **Denial:** Your child's first reaction will be that he doesn't believe his parent is dead. This stage can last for several months, so be very patient with him during this time. It will take a while for him to accept the death. Let him know that this is normal and that you, too, have had wishful thoughts that it was all a mistake, or that Mom will suddenly return. Reassure him that some people even think they see or hear their parent and that this, too, is a normal part of getting used to the idea that she is gone. Then explain to your child that the way we can really keep Mom or Dad with us is in our hearts and our memories, which can never be taken away.

- **Anger:** As difficult as it is to understand, a child may become enraged with her parent for dying and abandoning her. As your child vents, your heart will break to hear her rage against her parent. During this stage it's important for you to cut her a little slack — she needs to express her anger or she'll bottle it up inside.

- **Sadness:** After your child has passed through the anger stage, he is left with a pathetic sadness. Comfort him as much as you can, and if you're having problems coping with your own grief, ask a friend or relative to spend time with your child, holding him and comforting him as he cries or talks about how sad he feels. You can also take advantage of bereavement groups for children offered by your local hospice or the social services department of your local hospital.

- **Depression:** Depression is a common stage in the grieving process. Your child doesn't want to eat, he doesn't want to play with his friends, and he may have trouble sleeping. Generally, he mopes around the house, everything seems to irritate him, and nothing seems to cheer him up. His restlessness and lack of cooperation may even make you wonder if he's had a complete personality change! If ever it's time to baby your child, it's now — buy him a few new toys, take him to the circus or a movie and basically get out of the house as much as you can. If you've never had a pet, this might be a good time to visit the animal shelter. Not only will a new puppy or kitten provide a few laughs around the place, but they can also become treasured friends and sources of comfort.

- **Guilt:** Your child may think the reason his parent died is because the child did something really bad, and he's being punished. This is a normal reaction and how you handle it will depend on the child's age. How you handle it isn't as important, however, as the fact that it *does* get handled. We know one intuitive father who asked his 9-year-old daughter whether she thought that Mom died because he argued with her too much, or because he didn't let her get the new car she wanted. His daughter immediately reassured him that nothing he did or said could have caused Mom's accident. By reassuring her dad, this child resolved her own guilty feelings. What a smart daddy! Maybe the same idea will work for you.

- **Fear:** Your child may be afraid that you will die or that he will die. He may develop *separation anxiety* — which means he panics when you leave him with a babysitter or drop him off at school. The key is to coax your child into talking about his fears so you can reassure him that you aren't going to die and neither is he. We know a 12-year-old boy who was afraid that his remaining parent would also die, so he asked his dad what would happen if his dad died, too. This opened up a dialogue between them that was very reassuring to the boy. His dad talked about the pros and cons of his son living with his grandparents, godparents, aunts and uncles, or various friends. After a candid discussion, his son decided that his first choice would be to live with his Uncle John and Aunt Carol, and his second choice would be his maternal grandparents. You can imagine how honored Carol and John were when they were asked to become legal guardians in the event of the dad's death.

Hang in there! Although it may seem like it's taking forever, healing is taking place every day.

Divorcing your spouse, not your kids

Children, being children, sometimes feel that they are being divorced too, and that the parent who is moving out of the home doesn't love them anymore. When Mommy or Daddy moves away, especially when it's a major move to another city or state, the children feel like they're being abandoned. It's no wonder they lose their childlike joy and spontaneity — their world has become a sad, sad place.

When the non-custodial parent moves out, encourage your children to stay close to that parent in one or more of these ways:

- **Encourage your kids to stay in touch via e-mails.** Or, if you don't exactly have a computer fund stashed away at the moment, you can buy a MailStation from Earthlink that runs from about $50 to $150. A MailStation is a way to have e-mail–only service — no computer required — for a monthly fee of about $10 per month for unlimited, toll-free minutes. All you need is a phone jack.

- **Letter writing might be just the thing for your child, depending on his personality.** Encourage him to write to his dad every single day, if that's what he wants to do, and tell him you'll be happy to provide plenty of stamps and envelopes. Take photos of your kids around the house or participating in their extracurricular activities, then have double copies made so your children can enclose the extras in their letters to Dad.

- **Long-distance phone calls are the best way to maintain a warm relationship between your child and your ex.** Perhaps your ex will subscribe to a personal 800 number so your children can call her whenever they want to talk to her. Otherwise, your best bet may be to sign up for a cell phone service that includes 3,000 or 4,000 long distance minutes per month at a flat rate.

- **Send cassette tapes back and forth.** Depending on your children's personalities, they may really get into the fun of creating cassette tapes for their dad or mom. A tape provides opportunities for your kids to ham it up. One might play his trombone, another might read a story she wrote for school, or one can walk around the house interviewing members of the family, just like a real talk-show host. After they get the hang of it, they'll love making tapes for their parent and, hopefully, your ex will reply by making tapes of his own.

✔ **An inexpensive fax machine might be worth the investment, too.** One single dad who was away a lot on business bought his children an affordable fax machine so they can stay in touch. Dad and his kids send letters, copies of report cards, drawings, and cartoons to each other almost every day. In fact, as soon as the kids get home from school, they run to their fax machine to see whether Dad sent them anything. What a great idea!

✔ **If you own a video camera, here's a chance for your kids to really shine!** Let them record each other at play, during their sports events, or other outside activities, such as an afternoon at the bowling alley or a day hiking your favorite trail. Your ex can pop the tape into his VCR and enjoy his kids while he eats dinner.

Psychotherapists who counsel children feel that kids are actually more resilient than we think — if they're told the truth. So, be as compassionately honest with your kids as you possibly can, considering their ages, and have faith that they'll bounce back! Note that children who have the hardest time bouncing back are those whose parents remain hostile towards each other!

Showing an Appetite: Craving Attention

When a child loses a parent, he becomes a little self-centered, so he resents it when you don't pay as much attention to him as you did before. He also bristles when he's asked to help out more around the house. You see, a child doesn't understand that you're going through hell and just barely hanging in there. In his mind, everyone has turned against him and he feels deprived and craves more attention and affection.

Feeling deprived

Even though you may be giving your child more attention than ever before, your child may still feel deprived because his other parent moved out. Your dear child was used to coming home to all the normal two-parent stuff — Daddy's or Mommy's favorite chair and the missing parent's clothes and other personal stuff strewn here and there around the place. You may be pretty well adjusted to the void left when your ex moved out, and for some of you, you may even be singing, "Hallelujah!"

Your child, however, may see the missing items as holes in his heart — all those things that gave him the assurance of both parents' love. Divorce is a devastating blow to your child, whether he's a toddler or a teenager.

Your child feels deprived of the other parent's presence and, although he may not say so out loud, he's feeling very lonely. He feels lonely when he sits down to dinner and peers longingly at the empty chair. She feels lonely when she shoots baskets in the driveway without Dad. Or, your child may feel lonely when she brings home an excellent report card and wants to show it off to both of her parents.

Let your child know that you're aware of his lonely, empty feelings. Arrange for him to spend a little extra time with his other parent. If this isn't possible, phone calls and e-mails may help fill the void.

Needing more of your time

Not only does your child miss his absent parent, he's also feeling the pinch of your schedule. If you're like most single parents, you're working longer hours just to keep things together financially, and you've taken on many of your spouse's old duties, too.

So, aren't you in another fine mess? Just when your child needs more of your time, you have less time to give. Of course, try explaining this to a 2-year-old, or even your teenager. They need you to fill the gap created when your spouse died or you got a divorce, right when you haven't anything left of yourself to give! Our hearts go out to you — it's not easy, and we know that! Chapter 4 gives you detailed information that can help you find (or make) more time.

Some parents become obsessed with their exciting careers or a new person in their lives, to the point where they don't pay attention to their kids. This type of person, known as *narcissistic/self-fulfilling,* is usually his or her child's primary caretaker. If you think you might have this tendency, seek professional therapy. If you don't, your kids may grow up to be very poorly adjusted adults.

Longing for time alone with you

Here's a tough one! Not only does your child need more attention and affection, but he also wants time with you alone! None of those pesky brothers or sisters horning in! Butting in on your conversation! Climbing up on your lap! Showing you what they made at school today!

So, how do you carve out private time to spend with each child every day?

Here are a few suggestions that will help you carve out daily one-on-one time for each child. Give them a try. If they don't work for you, plan one activity with each child each week, something each child can look forward to doing alone with you.

- ✔ **You need to make an appointment, even if it's only for ten minutes.** As soon as you get home and start dinner, set up your schedule: 7:30 with Ronnie, 7:45 with Lindsey.

- ✔ **After you have your appointments set up, decide on a quiet, private spot for your chat.** An obvious choice for your little talk is your child's bedroom. If the door has a lock, lock it! Otherwise, hang a clever sign on the door that says something like: "Do Not Disturb — VERY Important Meeting in Progress!"

- ✔ **While you're meeting with your child, turn off the phone — let the calls go to your answering machine — and give firm instructions to your other children that you're not to be disturbed unless someone's bleeding!** Then, assure them that each one will have his private time with you.

- ✔ **If your evenings are usually pretty chaotic, or you're involved with one of your kid's extracurricular activities almost every night, save the chat until bedtime.** Bedtime is a natural for warm, cozy talks!

- ✔ **Another way to have private time with one child at a time is to drop one child off at a scheduled activity.** Then instead of hanging out with the other parents until practice is over, use that time to take your son for a special treat. If your son loves ice cream, make a quick trip to the local ice cream shop during your daughter's practice and sit down together and see if you can get him talking about his day.

If you've been so buried in your own grief and despair that you really haven't taken time to spend a little one-on-one time with each child each day, it doesn't hurt to apologize. They've been hurting, too, so they'll understand. Then, assure them that your goal is to be a better listener from now on because you really want to be there for them.

Throwing a Fit About the Split?

If you've divorced just recently, your kid is probably pretty unhappy with you. You see, from your child's viewpoint, you're a very selfish person! Kids want both parents to live in the same house just like they always did. In other words, they want things to go back to the way they were. It's interesting that even adult kids in their 30s and 40s are so devastated when their parents split that they sometimes resort to trickery to get them back together.

The problem is that most kids don't know how things really are between their parents before the divorce. Most parents on the verge of splitting up shelter their children from the arguments, tears, and hurts that lead up to the divorce. It's impossible for these kids to understand why their parents split. In a child's mind, it's a no-brainer! Just kiss and make up, stupid! After all, isn't that what they always do on those TV sitcoms?

Or a lot of kids suffer as they watch their parents yell and argue, maybe slam out of the house and squeal the car down the block in a fit of temper. Scenes like these hurt your children tremendously. But even in these conditions, many kids hope for a kiss and make up solution to the very worst conflicts between their parents.

Your poor kids — they're really caught in the middle and confused, so who can blame them for crying out for answers to questions.

What's a divorce?

First of all, we need to say that if you're willing to answer this question, you're in the elite 20 percent. Amazingly, 80 percent of divorced parents never discuss their divorce with their children. Maybe they don't know how to go about it and they don't want to stir up the whole can of worms again — getting into the painful reasons for the divorce. Or, their biggest reason for avoiding the subject may be that they're scared to death of their kids' reaction.

So, as you discuss your divorce with your child, we commend you!

Start out by explaining that the word *divorce* means that Mommy and Daddy won't be married to each other anymore. You can go on to tell them that divorce doesn't mean you won't still be their parents — nothing can ever change that! Then explain how sometimes a mommy and daddy decide they would be happier if they didn't live together anymore, and that sometimes there is a *separation* first, which means that they live in different houses, but aren't actually divorced yet.

Go into as much detail as you think your child can handle about your own situation, which may have included a *trial separation* that eventually led to a final divorce. Be as gentle as you can, using phrases such as, "Sometimes a man and a woman make a mistake when they get married, then they find out later they don't get along with each other and they decide they don't want to be married anymore." Or, "Your mommy and I will always be good friends, and we'll always be a family, because we love you so much, but we won't live in the same house anymore."

Some children are more knowledgeable than others when it comes to the court system, the judge's decision, and so on. In cases like these, explain the procedure in user-friendly language, always pausing to ask your child if she understands, or if she has any questions.

Why can't you still be married?

Your child doesn't want his world to be turned upside down, and you don't want that either, but it can't be helped. You can only try your hardest to right his world. No child has a perfect parent or a perfect childhood. Your children learn a valuable lesson when they see you go through a hard time, so make the best of the situation. Try new ways of doing things and laugh at your own mistakes. This will help your child realize that life *does* go on. New beginnings *are* possible, and when your child sees that both parents are happier, that will be his best reassurance.

Don't hold out any false hopes for reconciliation. Explain to your child that you will not be getting back together again. Then, try to comfort your child, sympathize with his hurts, and continually reassure him of your love.

Why do you hate Daddy/Mommy?

If you've recently divorced, your child may think you're mean and hateful, which fills him with rage. As if you don't have enough to deal with right now, you need to explain to your kids that you do not hate their other parent. Tell them that their non-custodial parent loves them and always will. Then, reassure them by hugging them, cuddling them, and telling them how much you love them, too. You can also add something like: "It may sound corny, but it's true — the best thing about our marriage was having you!"

I'm to blame, huh?

You would have never gotten a divorce if it weren't for me! But if you'll get back together, I promise to be good! I'll make my bed every morning, and I'll always take out the trash as soon as you ask, and I promise to get better grades! Really, I promise!

First of all, don't be taken aback when your child thinks she's to blame! It's quite common for a child to blame himself for a divorce, or even for the death of his parent. Reassure your child that he is not to blame — that he's one of the best kids ever, and that it had absolutely nothing to do with him. Then, talk about your child's wonderful qualities, all the things you and your ex love about him, and how nothing your child could do would ever cause a divorce. Be very specific as you list your child's accomplishments and all those things that have made you so proud of him through the years. Tell your child that you love him just the way he is — you don't want him to change in any way.

If your child blames himself for causing the divorce or the death of his parent, he may also feel responsible for the pain you're experiencing. If he sees that you're crying or feeling sad, he may feel that it's his responsibility to parent you, because he thinks he's caused your sadness. You may notice your child giving up something special he had planned with his friends so he can spend time with you, to "make it all better." If you see this type of pattern developing, you need to reassure your child that the death or divorce was not his fault and that you want him to enjoy being a kid. Also, you might take a look at the way you're handling your own grief or loss. Have you been using your child as a sounding board? If so, look elsewhere for someone to lean on — a close friend, a member of your support group, or a professional therapist.

Why did you divorce Daddy/Mommy anyway? He/she didn't do anything wrong

Right now is the time to name every good quality you can think of about your ex — even if it curdles your stomach! Then, as carefully as you can, explain that you and Daddy had a lot of differences and just couldn't get along together. Reassure your child that Daddy loves him and that you will all still be friends.

The most important thing to get across is that you and Daddy are not going to get back together, which is probably the underlying reason for your child's question in the first place. He wants you to admit that his Daddy really didn't do anything wrong at all and you should take him back right away, so you can all be a happy family again.

Your teenager wants to know the details about your divorce — what caused it and why you couldn't work things out. Your younger children may be okay with "sometimes a mommy and daddy don't get along with each other any more . . ." but you can't hand your teenagers a pat answer. Take their questions seriously and answer them as truthfully and completely as you can, going into more detail than you would with your younger children without revealing any intimate personal aspects or anything that would hurt them. If you aren't truthful with your teenagers, you may never be able to have close personal relationships with them in the years to come.

Are you going to stop loving me, too?

Wow! This one will hit you in the gut! Who would ever imagine that your child would think such a thing? But it's a common fear for children of divorced parents. When they see how seemingly easy it was for you to stop loving Mommy, they think it can be just as easy for you to stop loving them.

You need to look your child in the eye and tell him that you have always loved him, you love him now, and that you'll never stop loving him. Explain that a parent loves a child with a very special kind of love, so special, in fact, that nothing can ever change it. Also, reassure your child that no matter how bad she is, no matter what rotten thing she does, and no matter how upset you are with her at the moment, you will never, never, never stop loving her.

Finally, ask your child, "Will you ever stop loving me?" He'll say, "No, of course not!" Then you should say, "Well, I love you the same way you love me, and nothing can ever come between us."

What's going to happen to me now?

Who's going to take care of me? Where am I going to live?

Obviously, the situation has caused your child to feel insecure. He's not only feeling insecure about your love, but about his future. Now is the time to sit down and have a long talk, because there are important details your kid needs to know about the custody agreement, your living arrangements, and how often the child can see his other parent.

Start at the beginning and go slow. Tell her about custody, and what that word means. Tell her which parent she'll be living with. Then, ask whether she has any questions. Go on to the living arrangements, which hopefully will provide as much continuity in your child's life as possible. Reassure her — if this is the case — that she can still attend the same school, have the same friends, and attend the same church camp with the same bunch of kids. Again, ask whether he understands or has any questions.

If you aren't sure there will be continuity, be honest and tell him so. Reassure him that you'll give a heads up about any changes as soon as you know. Let him know that you are in this together and that the goal for everyone in the family is to be happier in the long run.

Finally — and this is really important — explain to him that even though you and your ex are no longer husband and wife, you are still his parents and always will be. Nothing can take that away from him. Now is also a good time to reassure him that his relationships with his grandparents, aunts, uncles, cousins, and other relatives will stay the same as always.

Can I go live with Daddy/Mommy?

Don't be too upset when your child asks whether he can live with his other parent, it's a common question. If your young child asks this question, you can say something simple like, "No, not for now. You and I live together and we're going to have a fun time." If an older child asks this same question, the key is to give him hope, even though that's about as likely to happen as money falling out of the sky. However, you can always say, "Maybe when you're older, but for the time being you live here with me. Your dad and I don't plan to change that arrangement any time soon."

Why do you cry all the time? Do I make you cry?

How sad that your child thinks he's the reason you cry! Tell him that he is not the cause for your tears and that you just feel sad because things can't be the way they used to be. Your child has these same feelings, so it helps to tell him that you feel that way, too. Then, explain how something sad makes you cry sometimes, but that doesn't mean things won't be okay. Tell him he shouldn't worry about you and that he is definitely not the reason you're crying. Give him a huge hug and assure him that he could never make you cry because you love him so much!

If you feel helpless, hopeless, and unable to control your tears at work or in front of your kids, you may be clinically depressed. In that case, you need to get some professional therapy. If you don't begin to feel more in control, your psychotherapist may suggest you see your physician or a psychiatrist about taking antidepressant medication for a short time.

Encourage your child to ask questions — whatever is on his mind. Don't be misled into thinking that a silent child is a happy child. When your child is wrestling with questions and problems, those questions won't just go away. Encourage your child to get everything out in the open so you can talk together. This will help your child heal and eventually feel stable again. *Dinosaurs Divorce,* by Laurie Krasney and Marc Brown (Little Brown & Co.), is a good resource for children ages 4 to 12.

Wanting to Talk About Stuff

Your child has a lot of questions he needs to talk over with you. He may be feeling put upon because you've been leaning on him lately, needing him to be there for you. Or, he may be worried over how everything is going to work out.

When you're up to your elbows in housework or you have 20 things to do before leaving for work, if your child comes up with a question out of the blue, stop what you're doing, sit down, look him in the eye, and give him your best answer. It's okay if the housework doesn't get done — and you've probably been late to work before — so keep your priorities straight and take your kid's questions seriously.

Feeling put upon

You don't need us to tell you how your life has changed since you became a single parent. Your schedule is twice as full as before, and your children have to help you out around the house or you'll never get everything done. So all those extra hours you used to spend teasing, laughing, and cuddling your kids have been replaced with the drudgery of never-ending chores, tight schedules, and a generally testy attitude.

Do your kids take these changes in stride? Probably not. You see, they think they're being punished because Dad or Mom is no longer around. What a sad misconception, but you may not even realize they feel this way.

So, what's going on inside your son's precious little head? Here are just a few questions he may be asking:

How come you make me do all the extra chores now?

Explain to your child in simple terms that you have twice as much to do as before and you need his help. Thank your child for all the extra things he's been doing for you lately, and then always end the conversation on an up note by reminding him of something fun coming up soon. This will turn a negative into a positive and give him something to hope for.

For example, if you know you'll be spending the day with your sister and her family a week from Saturday, talk it up! Try to get your child excited about seeing the newborn colt or feeding the ducks, or whatever your family enjoys about your sister's little farm. Then, of course, hug your child and tell him you love him — that's what he's really worried about anyway.

Why don't we get to eat good stuff like when Mom lived with us?

It may not have occurred to you that your children notice the little things, like the change in menu! If you're a single dad, this may be the first time in your life you've tried to cook anything but a hamburger or a frozen pizza in the microwave. So, it's no wonder your children are complaining. Or, if you're a single mom, you may be fixing more prepared foods because of your time crunch, or you may be giving in to fast foods, just for the convenience of not having to cook big meals. However, what may seem to be a huge relief to you —

picking up pizza from the deli after work, bringing home sub sandwiches to eat around the TV, or boiling up a quick hot dog before you rush out the door for your kids' school conferences, is just another blow to your children's stable world. The best way to handle this problem is to sit down and have a family meeting — talk about your menus, why you opt for the quickie meal once in a while, then make a list of the types of foods your kids have been missing.

How come you're always dumping on me about Dad (or Mom)?

Your children are such convenient little therapists, always available and willing to listen as you vent about your ex. But are they really that willing? We don't think so! Remember that your ex is a beloved parent who can do no wrong — he's their hero, a precious person in their lives, so it's really unfair of you to assume they want to hear all the obnoxious things your ex said or did lately.

ANECDOTE

Emily's story

Emily was an only child who lived with her parents in a middle-class neighborhood in Detroit. She adored her mother and father and thought her life was pretty wonderful. Then, one day when Emily was 6-years-old, her mom told her that she and Emily were going to Seattle to visit her mom's relatives. A few weeks after their arrival, Emily was enrolled in school, which seemed a little strange to Emily, because she thought they were only there for a short visit. Finally, a couple months after that, Emily's uncle told her, "Well, Emily, you're old enough now for us to tell you something. You see, your mom and dad have gotten a divorce and you won't be going back to Detroit to live."

Never going back? Emily was devastated. What did he mean? How could that be? All her stuff was there — her toys, her dog, and everything in her room. And what about her dad? Would she ever see him again? Emily's mother refused to answer any of Emily's questions and told Emily that she should never speak of it again. Emily was in shock, but she was a well-behaved child who was always eager to please. So she retreated inside of herself and never asked about

it again. The tragedy, of course, was that no one knew or cared that her heart was broken. In fact, everyone thought she had adjusted well to the divorce and was just a normal, happy child.

Long after Emily had grown up, her husband encouraged her to fly back to Detroit to look for her father. He knew that she needed to see for herself that her father wasn't some sort of wicked monster.

Emily flew to Detroit, checked into a motel and called her father's home number, which was listed in the phone book. He was astounded and thrilled to know she was in Detroit. The first thing he said was, "Oh, baby, honey, where are you? Please don't move. Promise me you won't move — I'll be right there." Emily and her dad had a joyous seven days together. He explained that when her mom took Emily to Seattle, he threatened to find them and kidnap Emily. No wonder her mother was so protective through the years! Emily was overjoyed to find that her dad was a handsome, successful businessman and that, after all those years, he loved her after all.

If your divorce has just recently become final, it's easy to get into the habit of using your children as sounding boards at the end of a rough day at work, or when you're worried about the budget or the car breaking down again. But remember they're just kids, after all, so let them enjoy being kids and tell your troubles to a friend, a relative, your pastor, or someone in your support group. Don't dump on your children! It really isn't fair.

Don't encourage your child to choose between you and your ex by competing for your child's love with gifts and expensive entertainment. Your child has the right to love each of you equally.

Feeling confused about the details

When your child's world has been turned upside down, panic often sets in. Especially when it comes to the little things, like what happens to all his stuff if you have to move, why is Mom's name going to be different now, when will he get to have visits with his other parent, and will there be enough money to buy food and clothes and birthday gifts?

When we move, what happens to all my stuff?

Children feel secure in their rooms surrounded by all their personal treasures, and it's upsetting for them if they think they have to give any of it up. If you're moving to a new residence, you need to reassure your kids that their new rooms will be just as nice as their current rooms and that they can take all their stuff with them! Then you need to throw in a few perks for them to look forward to, such as a new bulletin board for all their photos and mementos. If you'll be purchasing new bedding, tell him he'll get to pick it out, and so on. The important thing is to turn what he perceives to be a negative into a positive.

How come you're changing your last name? Don't you want your name to be the same as mine?

If you've decided to change your last name after the divorce is final, you need to have a chat with your children, explaining why this is important to you and why their last names will probably stay the same for now. Reassure them that you're still a family and you love them just like always.

If your children are strongly against you changing your name, you might want to reconsider your decision. Your kids have enough going on in their lives right now without worrying over something like this. If you feel this will be a major upheaval for them, you can always put off the name change for the time being.

When do I get to see Daddy? Will he come to see me?

Be as honest with your child as you can possibly be. If the custody agreement allows Daddy to spend every other weekend with his kids, don't promise your kids this will happen. Explain to them that they'll probably be able to see their dad a couple weekends a month, but keep it a little vague in case it doesn't work out that way. Your kids need to know they can believe what you tell them. Be as honest as you can and hope Daddy cares enough to spend time with his children as he promised.

Does this mean we won't have enough money to buy what we need?

Money is a huge issue for children. Unless they're under 4 years old, they've pretty much figured out what money can buy: lunch at Jack in the Box after the games on Saturdays; new tennies when the old ones wear out; and good presents on Christmas morning. If your total income will be about the same as before, explain this to your kids and reassure them that nothing will change.

However, if that's not the case, don't make the mistake of telling your kids you have plenty of money when you know you don't. Take a look in Chapter 5 for some of our cost-cutting suggestions. Then go over some of these ideas with your kids so they understand the situation and are willing to shop at discount stores or consignment shops once in a while.

I don't want you to date anybody but Daddy (or Mommy)!

Wow! Nothing like getting things out in the open from the start! You probably haven't even given a thought to dating again, especially if you've just recently become a single parent. But your child may bring it up from the get-go!

If you know you'll be dating someone soon, this would be a good time to break the news to your children as gently as you can. You can say something like, "Mommy isn't married anymore, Tracy, so she might go out on a date with someone someday. Don't worry about it now — we're going to be doing lots of fun stuff together as a family." Or, if you're adamant against ever dating anyone, especially after what you've just been through, reassure your children by telling them that, for the time being anyway, you have no plans to date.

Calling for Help: Needing Professional Counseling

If you're doing everything you can to help your child recover and get back to her normal self, but you know in your loving, single-parent heart that nothing is working — or that she's developing distressing new habits that seem to persist or become daily behaviors — it may be time for your child to see a professional therapist. It's normal for teens to have fluctuating moods. Persistent mood, behavior, or personality changes are clues that you need to get some outside help.

Here are signs that your child may need professional counseling:

- ✔ He has extreme mood swings, happy one minute and holed-up in his room the next.

- ✔ She has a short fuse and everything seems to bother her. She is so irritable that her friends have given up on her.

- ✔ If your child has always been active and talkative, be wary if he suddenly becomes inactive and quiet.

- ✔ Your child stops associating with her long-time friends and either becomes a loner or starts hanging out with a bad crowd.

- ✔ He withdraws from normal family fun, such as playing games. If your child won't even go to Pizza Galore with the family, you know you're in big trouble!

- ✔ She has problems at school, such as cutting class, getting into fights, or grades dropping.

- ✔ He seems to be sleeping much more or less than he used to.

- ✔ She walks and talks in her sleep, or she begins to wet the bed during the night.

- ✔ He complains frequently about headaches, stomachaches, or feeling tired.

- ✔ His facial expression is flat and he has no enthusiasm — even for a good fight with his sister.

- ✔ She seems depressed for weeks at a time.

- ✔ He takes unnecessary risks and does self-harming gestures, such as scratching his arms with a razor blade. (This is called *self injury, SI,* or *cutting* and you can find out more about it at www.self-injury.net/.)

- ✔ She displays uncharacteristic signs of anger, rebellion, violent behavior, or running away.

If your teenager shows any signs the he may be considering taking his own life, call this emergency hot line immediately: National suicide hotline: (800) SUICIDE. Here are danger signs to watch for in your teenager:

- ✔ Your teen talks about suicide.

- ✔ He starts giving away his possessions.

- ✔ Your teen has been deeply depressed for a long period of time, but one day appears to be magically better.

- ✔ He seems overly tired most of the time, sleeping during the day on weekends and going to bed early on weeknights.

- ✔ Your child won't tolerate any kind of praise or rewards.

- ✔ You child has become a loner — won't communicate or take part in family activities.

Getting dumped

We know a single mother who was always tired by the end of the week and needed a treat, so she thought her 14-year-old son would be happy to go to dinner with her every Friday night. Wrong! After three straight weeks at Mr. Steak, her son said, "Mom, I love you, but we can't go steady any more." It's common for a child to try to take the place of the missing parent. Chapter 7 talks more about this problem and how you can help prevent and solve it.

Part III

Challenging Your Maturity: Co-Parenting

The 5th Wave   By Rich Tennant

"You get an allowance? Is that like child support?"

In this part . . .

This part addresses the most serious problems single parents face as they raise their kids. In these chapters you learn how to compromise as you develop a workable co-parenting plan, coexist peacefully with your ex and all the other parents in your children's lives, and keep your cool as you resolve serious co-parenting problems that may pop up now and then. We tell you how to cut your ex a little slack for the sake of your children, cope with holidays and other family celebrations, ease transition anxiety, and deal with the truly frightening problems that sometimes rear their ugly heads. You also find out how to get help in the case of parental abuse, kidnapping, and other custodial interference.

Chapter 9

Compromising: Knowing When to Fold 'Em

In This Chapter

▶ Designing a co-parenting plan that works

▶ Making the plan work well

▶ Avoiding the biggest mistakes made by single parents

▶ Creating a bill of rights for the kids

*W*hen you and your spouse get divorced, you're given a choice. You can choose to take the High Road, which is a tough, steep climb, or you can opt for the Low Road, the path of least resistance. The High Road leads to Victory Mountain, with some fascinating stops along the way:

⤶ City of Sweet Relationships

⤶ Village of Rich Rewards

⤶ Township of Well-Adjusted Children

The Low Road, on the other hand, is a slippery path that seems easy at first but offers few rewards and many sorrows. It dead-ends at Quicksand Gulch, with stops at:

⤶ Oh-So-Sorry Swamp

⤶ Wasn't-There-For-Them Marsh

⤶ Bayou of Broken Promises

The High Road we're talking about here is also known as successful *co-parenting*. Here's our definition of a successful co-parenting relationship: Sharing parenting responsibilities with your child's best interests at heart.

For the sake of your children, you need to work out an arrangement that provides your kids with love, stability, and continuity in their lives to help them become well-adjusted, happy adults. If this is your mission, you've chosen the High Road.

As you walk this challenging path, turn to the helpful, practical co-parenting advice in this chapter. We tell you how to design a co-parenting plan that works, how to achieve harmony in your relationships with your child's other parent, and how to avoid the biggest mistakes made by single parents. We admire the love and concern you have for your children and we're happy to give you a leg up in this chapter as we consider the do's and don'ts of co-parenting.

Avoiding a Leaning Tower of Co-Parenting: Designing a Sound Plan

What is a co-parenting plan exactly? Why is it important? And how do you go about putting one together?

A *co-parenting plan* is a written agreement between parents who have joint custody of their children. This doesn't mean each parent must share equal time with the children, but they do each have certain responsibilities for care and nurturing.

A co-parenting plan is important because it forces you and the other parent to discuss and agree on responsibilities and joint goals. Joint goals may include such things as providing continuity in the children's lives, agreeing on discipline policies, and saving toward college expenses. Such a plan makes you think about where your kids live, who pays for what, and how much time each parent spends with the children.

A divorced couple in agreement on a co-parenting plan is usually in contrast to a couple in an adversarial relationship whose conflicts may eventually have to be resolved by a court-appointed mediator. However, if the two people can't agree on the terms of the co-parenting plan but want to resolve the situation, they can hire a private mediator.

As your co-parenting plan goes into effect, you may be encouraged to know that five positives can result from your children dividing their time between parents. If everything's working out well

✔ **Your children are rescued from the tension of living in your conflict-ridden, dysfunctional, pre-divorce home.**

✔ **Your relationship with your ex after your divorce may be much better than before your divorce.**

✔ **Your relationships with your children can be much sweeter and richer after the divorce.** Not only because you're able to spend more one-on-one time with each of them, but also because you're no longer obsessed with your problem marriage.

✔ **Studies have shown that children raised in two-home families mature in several ways.** Because kids of divorce must adapt to their parents' individual homes, lifestyles, and differences, they tend to have highly developed skills in problem solving and getting along with different types of people.

✔ **Because you're sharing the custody and care of your children, you are relieved of the responsibilities of being a fulltime parent.** So you're free to pursue your own interests during your off time without the expense of paying for babysitters or day care.

Putting pen to paper: What to include

Every plan is a little different, especially if it has been custom-designed without the help of an attorney. However, most co-parenting plans should

✔ **Be put together in an unemotional, businesslike, mature manner.**

✔ **Either be filed with the court or be a private agreement that's binding between parents.** If filed with the court, it's legally binding. You can also split the agreement into two parts: one that is filed with the court and one that is a private agreement.

✔ **Include the parents' rules of conduct and communication, including**

- **Each parent's right to be involved in the children's lives as situations pop up.** You want to make sure it's okay for both parents to attend a piano recital, a sports activity, or graduations.

- **Neither parent bad-mouths the other in front of the kids.**

- **Each parent has the right to see the children's school records, meet with their teachers, and be involved in parent-teacher conferences.**

- **The parents always let each other know how they can be located if they are out of town or away from home for a long period of time.**

- **Each parent promises to be accessible to his children by telephone, e-mail, regular mail, fax machine, or pager.**

- **The parents agree to share important information about their children, including problems they may be having, their progress**

in school, and their achievements in their extracurricular activities. Some parents agree to have a *family meeting* once a month, in person or over the telephone, to share information and deal with any problems that have come up during the month, such as disagreements over discipline techniques.

- **The parents will be cooperative and accommodating if their child begs to spend more or less time with one of his parents.** This is an issue that will need additional, open discussion when it arises.

✔ **Contain conditions for the children's medical and dental care.** Indicate which parent pays for their health insurance and which one is responsible for setting the appointments and providing transportation to the appointments.

✔ **Spell out child-care conditions. Include which parent provides and pays for the children's care, or how the expenses and responsibilities are split between the two parents.**

✔ **Include a detailed schedule that spells out which parent has custody of which child during the school year, during school vacations, and over holidays or other special family get-togethers.** If you plan to file your agreement with the court, the schedule needs to be very detailed, including specific times for pick-up and drop-off as the children transition from one home to the other.

✔ **Address who provides transportation for the children between the parents' residences.** Can Mom deliver the kids to Dad's home for weekends, then can Dad bring them back to Mom's home on Sunday nights?

✔ **Spell out what type of religious training the children receive.** Which church do you want them to attend? What will they be taught at home, if anything?

✔ **State educational goals for the children.** Do you want your children to follow the college track during high school? What type of college or university do you want the kids to attend? Who pays for their college education?

✔ **Talk about what happens if one of the parents doesn't follow through on taking the children during designated weekends or vacation days.** Failing to take your kids as scheduled may cause a financial hardship for the other parent who must pay for a sitter or day care during that time. Many agreements contain a clause that requires an increase in child support or trading compensating like days in the future. *Like* days mean even trades: vacation days for vacation days, or weekends for weekends, and so on.

> ✔ **Explain conditions for future catastrophes, such as loss of income, serious illness, or death of one of the parents.**

> ✔ **Explain specific conditions in case one of you moves out of town or out of state in the future.**

> ✔ **Specify the duration of your agreement and what happens if you want to renegotiate its terms in the future.** It's a good idea to spell out the steps to take in case of disagreements when renegotiating. For example, you can specify a certain number of days to resolve things on your own before presenting your disagreement before a trained mediator, and so on.

ANECDOTE

Bird nesting

Andy and Chris are very fortunate little boys because they have two parents who love them unconditionally. Their parents, Paul and Liz, were determined to do everything in their power to make their separation and divorce as pain free as possible for their sons. At the time of the split, Andy was beginning first grade and Chris was in a great day-care situation, so Paul and Liz wanted to maintain continuity in their kids' lives by keeping them in the same school district and in touch with their same friends.

Paul and Liz's mission was to remain friends after the divorce and be totally cooperative with each other for the sake of their children. In other words, they wanted the best co-parenting arrangement possible. Their first idea was for the boys to change residences on alternate weeks, one week at Dad's new apartment and one week with Mom. This seemed like a workable idea, so Liz helped Paul find a place that was large enough for the boys to each have their own bedrooms during their weeks with Dad. Unfortunately, the cost of renting a large apartment turned out to be prohibitive, so Paul and Liz came up with a novel idea.

They decided to find a smaller apartment for Paul and also purchase a condo in the same general area, and practice a concept called *bird nesting,* a plan where divorced parents each have their own residences, plus a third residence — called a bird nest — in which their children live fulltime. They found a very nice bird nest, a condo only five blocks from Liz's home. Paul and Liz pooled their money and purchased it together. They also joined forces to furnish the nest with familiar things from the children's original family home, plus they bought furniture from a consignment store. Finally, they both pitched in to help decorate the place. The children now live in the condo full-time and Paul and Liz alternate weeks.

The arrangement has worked well for them. First of all, they're able to pool their financial resources to share the nest's living expenses, according to their individual incomes. Also, the plan avoided the problem of the non-custodial parent having to pay large amounts of child support, despite only seeing her kids every other weekend, as is the case with so many divorced families. Paul and Liz are to be commended for their innovative plan. They are very pleased with the way it's working out, especially the fact that they have every other week off, which gives them privacy and less housework. And here's the very best thing of all — Andy and Chris get to sleep in their own beds every single night!

If you plan to have your co-parenting agreement filed with the court, which makes it legally binding, we advise you to hire the services of a family law attorney to check the terminology you have used in your agreement and to suggest clauses required by your state's laws.

If you and the other parent are having trouble agreeing on certain clauses in your co-parenting plan, you can hire the services of an attorney or a professional mediator to work as a liaison between you to resolve your differences.

Sampling a plan

We wanted to include a sample co-parenting agreement for you to look over before coming up with your own unique plan.

This is only an example of the clauses included by a hypothetical couple. Your agreement may be entirely different, contain more or less detail, include important clauses or verbiage recommended by a family law attorney, and it should be in keeping with the laws of your state. The agreement may also refer to the specific terms of any existing custody, child support, or spousal support agreement, and it may be attached to and filed with any of these agreements as a legal addendum.

Putting the Plan to Work

Designing a co-parenting plan is one thing — making it work is something else altogether. You can have the best intentions, but if you're a little fuzzy on how to follow through, you're in for a struggle. So we thought we'd give you a few helpful hints when it comes to successful, cooperative co-parenting:

Agreeing on workable schedules

Every family is different, and your custody schedule will be customized to suit your children's ages and your own work and vacation schedules, the main factors involved in setting up a workable schedule.

Ages may affect the schedule

The younger your children, the more difficult it is for them to adjust to the two-home-shuffle. You know your own kids, but here are a few general ideas of what to expect for different ages:

✔ **Birth to age 2:** It's pretty common for the primary caregiver to be clos-est to the baby, especially if the primary caregiver is a mother and still nursing her child. The other parent's custody may be limited to an hour or two here and there, babysitting, so to speak, so Mommy can have an occasional break from her fulltime parenting responsibilities. As the child gets closer to 2 years old, Daddy can take his child on an occasional outing to Grandma's house, or to the park to kick a ball or feed the ducks. It's very unlikely Daddy will have a child this age overnight, not because he doesn't want to, but because it's difficult for the child to adjust to a two-home shuffle that includes overnight stays. Of course, many single fathers have sole custody and manage very well, but in the case of joint custody, the mother usually spends the most time with the child.

✔ **Ages 2 to 4:** A child in this age bracket will spend all overnights with the primary caregiver and have visits to the co-parent's home ranging from an hour to half a day, depending on the child's age.

✔ **Ages 5 to 7:** This is the age where you can begin to share overnights between the co-parents. Start out slow with one overnight away from the primary caregiver, increasing to two or three nights a week, depending on how well the child adjusts.

✔ **Ages 8 to 10:** If your child is in this age group, he can probably handle half a week with each parent. He's not quite ready, however, for alternat-ing weeks — one week with Daddy and one week with Mommy.

✔ **Ages 11 to 18:** Finally, your child is ready for any schedule that works out best for her and for you as co-parents. You can divvy up your child's company in many ways, with half a week spent with you and half with the other parent, or the two of you can alternate weeks. Or come up with your own schedule — as long as you, your co-parent, and your chil-dren are satisfied with it, it works.

Taking a look at sample schedules

Here are a few sample co-parenting schedules for you to consider. Remember, you can be as creative as you like, taking your kids' ages into consideration.

✔ **Alternating weeks:** Your kids spend one week with you and the next week with your ex.

✔ **Weekends plus:** Your kids alternate weekends, with added weekdays tacked on. For example, your weekend with the kids may include Monday and Tuesday overnights. Then, your ex's weekend with the kids may include Wednesday, Thursday, and Friday overnights.

✔ **Long weekends:** One parent has the children from Monday afternoon after school through Thursday morning when they're dropped off at school. The other parent picks the kids up Thursday after school and drops them off at school Monday morning.

✔ **Split months:** You may have custody of your children from the first to the fifteenth of each month and your ex may have them from the sixteenth through the last day of the month.

It's a good idea to divide up the transportation duties so that one parent isn't stuck with picking up and returning the kids all the time. By dividing up the pick-ups and deliveries, you not only lighten the driving load, but you also eliminate the problem of one of you seeming to be the heavy. By the *heavy,* we mean that if you're the one who always provides transportation, your children may perceive you to be the meanie who takes them away from the other parent.

When you first put your schedule into effect, don't be surprised if your kids seem a little confused for a while. You may also notice that one of your kids really seems to be missing the other parent and may be a little down while he's with you. If that's the case, encourage contact with your ex by suggesting your child call your ex as often as necessary to get over his blue feelings.

Maintaining continuity

If you think the divorce has been tough for the two of you, you ain't seen nothin' yet! Your kids feel like they've been in a train wreck — their emotions are all over the place. (Chapter 8 can give you more insight to how your kids are feeling.) Being a kid in a happy, well-balanced traditional home is struggle enough — your son is worrying about the bully at the bus stop, whether he makes the team at tryouts tomorrow, and who can help him put his science project together by next Friday. When you add a divorce to that mix, things get even more complicated. It's not easy being a kid!

So, here you come along with huge changes for his life — Mommy or Daddy moving to another house, spending part of the time with one parent and part with the other, adjusting to yet another after-school babysitter, and wondering what will happen to his new puppy! Wow! No wonder his world is upside down.

As you strive to make your residence a real home for your kids when they're with you, make your mealtimes a family bonding time where you dine together in peace. No standing at the counter as you eat, no gulping the food down because you're in a hurry, and no slop-it-on-to-the-table to get it over with attitude. Remember: Animals eat, but human beings dine. So, make your evening meal a dining experience that's mellow and relaxed, with pleasant, upbeat conversation about the day's events. Now, that's a real home! Of course, we all know about the *bad hair days,* when everything seems to go wrong and you're lucky to cook up something to eat at all, much less *dine* on it! However, at least strive for a calm, peaceful dinner hour, even if it doesn't turn out that way all the time.

We're talking about the High Road, however, so it's up to you to make these transitions as smooth as a puddle of freshly churned cream. Here are ways to maintain continuity in your kids' lives as you divide up your household, divvy up child rearing responsibilities, and make new arrangements for after-school child care, transportation, and other changes in his life:

Keeping major changes to a minimum

Even though your kids are living with both of you part of the time, try your best to keep everything else the same if you can, at least for the first two years after the divorce. Keep the same school, the same church, the same day-care provider or babysitters, and the same clubs and extracurricular activities. Continuity may not be convenient for you, but it's important for your kids.

Establishing two real homes

If your kids are living with you part of the time and with your ex the rest of the time, they need to build a nest in each home. In other words, each child needs his own private space, hopefully in his own private bedroom. If he shares a bedroom with a sibling, he still needs as much privacy as possible. He also needs a decent place to keep his clothes, plus a shelf or two to display some of his favorite mementos. If your children have a pet, you need to decide whether the pet will live at only one home or at both homes, traveling back and forth with your children. If you want to transport the pet with the kids, you need a dog bed in both houses, two dog runs in two backyards, two dishes, and so on.

Ideally, your kids need to be so comfortable and feel so at home in both residences that they only need a small overnight bag when they travel between them. To accomplish this feat, you need to have duplicates of several things:

- ✔ Plenty of clothes: all staples, and don't forget hats, coats, rain gear, all types of shoes (tennies, boots, sandals), and pajamas.

- ✔ Swimsuit, beach towel, sun tan lotion, beach bag.

- ✔ Umbrella.

- ✔ Personal items: toothbrush, comb, hairbrush, deodorant, and so on. (Single dads with daughters age 10 or older should keep a supply of sanitary pads on hand. Your daughter may feel uncomfortable asking you to buy them for her. When she arrives for her visit, tell her where they are stashed.)

- ✔ A supply of the child's prescription drugs.

- ✔ An extra pair of glasses, if applicable.

- ✔ Favorite toys: stuffed animals, puzzles, games, including video games.

- ✔ Bedding that the child has chosen himself: including comforter, pillow shams, sheets, and so on.

- ✔ Cassette or CD players.

- ✔ Desk or table for his school things: including his own set of accessories, such as pens, paper, tape dispenser, stapler, scissors, paper clips, pocket calculator, glue, clock, and so on.

- ✔ Bulletin board, white board, or cork board: for displaying photos, report cards, schedules, reminders, and mementos.

- ✔ Sports equipment: if applicable, such as a basketball for shooting hoops with Dad or a tennis racquet for playing tennis with Mom.

Duplication like this may be impractical, especially due to the expense. It can be expensive to have video games or a basketball hoop at each residence. As you take a look at the recommendations, apply them only if they seem practical and affordable for you.

Staying in contact with old friends, making new friends

Your child needs to stay connected with his childhood friends, whether friends from the neighborhood, his school, church, or kids he knows through his extracurricular activities. If your child is shuffling between two residences, it may help if he can bring a friend home with him once in a while. In other words, ask a childhood friend to spend the weekend with him when he goes to Dad's place for the weekend. This is such a simple gesture, but it goes a long way toward maintaining continuity in your child's life.

Another smart idea is to take the extra effort to locate a few new friends for your kids to play with when they're with you. Maybe you meet kids the same age when you're down at the swimming pool, or it doesn't hurt to take a walk around the neighborhood once in a while. Who knows? You may find a great friend your kid's age just two doors away!

Encouraging open communication between you and your kids

Do everything you can to create settings where your child feels free and comfortable to talk about the stuff going on his life. Here are ideas that have worked for other single parents:

- ✔ **Mealtime chats:** Make it a rule that you all sit down to eat together — around the table, not on TV trays in front of the you-know-what! Create a little ambiance — what can it hurt? You know — turn off the TV, turn off the telephone (let your calls go to the answering machine), turn off your cell phone, turn off the overhead lights, and eat by candlelight, if that doesn't seem too far from your comfort zone!

✔ **Casual conversations** during a joint activity: Dad, you might find that your son opens up more easily when you're pitching golf balls onto the practice green together at your favorite golf course. Or, your daughter may talk her head off while she's helping you wash the car some Saturday afternoon. The "key" to get them talking is for you to listen with real interest in what they are sharing.

Encouraging communication between your children and your ex

When your kids are with you, encourage them to give their other parent a call, to check in, to see whether the rain storm flooded the back yard again, or just to chat about nothing at all. Telephone calls are a great way for your child to stay connected to his other home, which also helps maintain continuity in his life. If you have access to e-mail, encourage your kids to stay in touch that way, or by using Instant Messaging, which serves as an inexpensive way for them to chat with your ex during their stay with you. Then, encourage your children to stay in touch with you the same way when they're at Mom's house. Your goal is to establish a seamless continuity in your children's lives.

Make a deal with your ex that you won't believe half of what the kids tell you about her if she won't believe half of what they tell her about you! In most cases, the child will eventually tell each parent what they think that parent wants to hear.

Smoothing your child's physical transition between homes

Here are five ways to achieve a seamless move from one home to the other each week:

✔ **Call him the day before he's scheduled to come to your home.** Chat with him a while, ask how things are going, and tell him you're looking forward to seeing him tomorrow.

✔ **Ask your child to save some of his school work or an art project to bring with him to your house.** Tell him you want to display it on the refrigerator!

✔ **Tell him about the activities you have planned to do together while he's with you.** Include anything exciting you can think to say, such as, "I bet you get a hole-in-one at mini golf," or "I can't wait to see that movie — it's supposed to be really funny."

✔ **Go over a list of what he's supposed to bring with him in his suitcase.**

✔ **When you pick up your children to bring them back to your home for their stay, start out the visit with something fun, to loosen things up and avoid any awkwardness caused by not seeing them for a few days or weeks.** You might stop for ice cream on the drive home, or bring along a bag of popped corn to feed the ducks in the park. Also, as you're driving along, talk up any fun stuff you have in mind for the weekend and ask them all about what happened at school during the week, or any other interesting tales they may have to tell.

Younger children need a transitional object to keep with them as they travel from one home to another. A *transitional object* can be a comforting blanket, a favorite toy, a doll, or a stuffed animal.

You may reap many personal rewards by being cooperative toward and complimentary and supportive of your ex. For example, if you don't grouse over having the kids on Saturday morning — his morning to have them — because your ex must attend a required training conference, he may be agreeable one of these days when you need him to bend a little to accommodate your schedule. Cooperating with your ex not only benefits your children — it can also benefit you. Of course, cooperation needs to go both ways. If you feel you're the one making all the compromises, take some time to have a thoughtful, adult discussion with your ex — when the kids aren't around.

Parents 1, Kids 0: Presenting a united front

You want your co-parenting venture to be successful, right? This is why you chose the High Road in the first place. So, as you honor your co-parenting agreement, sharing the discipline of your children and trying to maintain continuity in your kids' lives, here's a concept to keep in mind: It's important to present a united front.

Don't be wishy-washy or vacillate on your co-parenting agreement, your discipline plan, or your schedules. Be rock solid in your commitment to your children.

Here are ways you can present a united front to your kids:

✔ **Family meetings:** Get together for a family meeting once a month or so to go over scheduling conflicts, decisions that need to be made regarding the children's activities, school, or discipline problems, or anything else you need to be in cahoots about. We call this a family meeting because everyone is in attendance, including your ex. It's especially important for the kids to attend so they can see that both parents are on the same page. Your children soon realize that they can't play one of you against the other.

A good example might be a mother who refuses to allow her 16-year-old daughter — who just got her driver's license by the way — to use Mom's car to tool around town after dark with a few of her friends. However, when daughter is at Daddy's house, she begs until he gives in and lets her run a few errands after dark in his SUV. When Mom finds out, she's livid — not only with her daughter, but with her ex. This is where the family meeting comes in! Mom makes it clear to her ex and her daughter that she doesn't approve of a 16-year-old bopping around after dark, no matter whose car she drives. Bottom line: Both parents unite, in front of their daughter, and lay down the law. Their daughter may not drive either car after dark until she's a little older.

On the positive side, a family meeting can also promote family unity by giving everyone a chance to present their side of a question. Listen attentively as your children speak — with no interruptions. In fact, plan these family meetings over a meal or in a quiet setting, with no television, no telephone (let the calls go to your answering machine), no pagers, and no cell phones! These meetings are really crucial to the success of your co-parenting efforts. *Note:* In the case of a serious discipline problem that needs resolving during the family meeting, it's a good idea for the co-parents to talk privately beforehand.

What if a standoff occurs? Agree to disagree for now. Let the children know that you are deferring the decision until you can discuss it at length. Assure them that they will be told what the conclusion is. Your children will see that you can handle disagreements in a civilized and constructive manner — great role modeling. If the question is very complex, consider getting an objective opinion from a parenting expert, your pastoral counselor, or a family therapist.

If you can barely stand to be in the same room with your ex, just suck it up for the time it takes to get through these meetings. Sure, you may be seething because just this morning you saw your ex at the post office with this cute young thing — the one who caused the split in the first place! But, remember, that's old stuff now and the most important thing is to be the best Mom and Dad you can be to your kids. So, take an antacid table, plaster on a smile, and go to the family meeting with the best attitude you can muster. You can survive anything for an hour!

✔ **Show your ex that you appreciate his or her efforts:** If your ex is sincerely trying to make this co-parenting thing work, it won't kill you to let him know you appreciate his efforts. The non-custodial parent often feels he's on the giving end and never on the receiving end of things. Encourage your older kids to bake a batch of cookies to take to Dad, along with a thank-you note: "Thanks for taking the kids to Funtastics — they had a great time!" Or, "I really appreciate the way you've been helping Mark with his algebra — he's catching on now, I think. Thanks a lot."

When you deliver a word of praise now and then, be sure your kids know all about it. That way they see that their parents are trying their best to make the post-divorce routine work.

✔ **Give clear, consistent feedback that you and your ex aren't getting back together:** Kids of all ages often hold the wish that their parents will reconcile.

✔ **Back up your ex's decisions:** If your kids return from Mom's house and complain that her rules are way too strict, back her up! They might complain that she doesn't let them watch R-rated movies. Whatever you do, don't side with your kids because that shows that their parents don't support each other's decisions on major issues.

By the way, it doesn't hurt to keep your lines of communication open between you and your ex via e-mail or voice mail. In the case of the R-rated movie, for example, you can zip off an e-mail that says something like, "I'm with you on the R-rated movie thing — I'm monitoring what they watch here, too. Keep up the good work!"

When parents have joint custody of their children, a dangerous pattern can develop called *parallel parenting.* Parallel parenting seems to be a good thing at first glance, but at second glance we see that it's heart wrenching and unfair for the kids. The good of it is that both parents are interested and involved in their kids' lives, attending their games, parent-teacher conferences, and dance recitals. The bad of it is that the parents are not communicating with each other about their children's lives and activities. Their only contact with each other is during an emergency or serious illness. The rest of the time they don't want to talk to each other and they definitely don't want their kids talking about what happened when they were at Dad's house, for example.

Refusing to discuss things with or about your ex is terribly unfair to your kids. They're walking on eggs most of the time, afraid you may blow up if they mention any little thing at all. Think of parallel parenting as poisonous parenting and get over it! You're being selfish if you don't.

In the parallel parenting model, parents are much less communicative with each other, and they set their own rules for how to parent when the children are with them. Parenting tasks are divided: For example one parent takes care of all the dental appointments while the other takes care of all the medical appointments. The key value of this approach is the reduction of parental conflict! This can be confusing and very destructive for younger children; and yet, in situations where one or both parents are incapable of working together in the best interest of the child, parallel parenting may be the only sane alternative. With older children (high school aged), this approach can be similar to having several teachers with different classroom rules. As long as the children are loved, and the parents can reduce the tension between the adults, this model can be used effectively. It is not the best possible solution, but sometimes the "best solution possible."

Getting involved in your kids' activities

If your ex has custody of the children the bulk of the time, you may not realize how important it is for you to be involved in their lives. Here are ideas for you to think about:

✔ **Meet your kids' teachers.** Not only during a parent-teacher conference, but drop by after school one day when their teachers may have a little more time to talk about your kids.

✔ **Get to know your children's coach, karate teacher, band director, or Boy Scout leader.** Hang out during one of their practices or meetings so you know what and whom your kids are involved with.

✔ **Attend church with your children, even if it's only once in a while.** If your kids are involved in a children's program, such as AWANA Clubs International (www.awana.org), meet the directors and become familiar with what your children are being taught.

✔ **Start a family memory album that includes photos of your kids participating in different activities, along with treasured mementos from some of these activities.** Also, while you're attending your child's game or musical concert, hand the camera to someone and ask him to take a couple photos of you with your son or daughter. Add these photos to the album, and if you have duplicate copies, send a few home with him once in a while to display in his room at your ex's home.

✔ **Take your children to the doctor.** If you usually leave doctor and dental appointments to your ex, why not be the one who takes your kids to their appointments once in a while? That way you know what's going on with your children's health and what to expect in their growth and development. You also have fair warning that your daughter needs braces sometime next year! Ugh! Start saving now!

If you're a single dad who's interested in his kids' lives, you're in the rare minority. Most teachers, principals, and doctors say they rarely see a child's father, whether the parents are divorced or not. That's pretty sad! Think what it means to your children when you have enough concern to take the time to meet the important, influential adults in their lives. If you're willing to do this, we admire you! Chapters 6 and 7 give you more ideas about how to stay involved.

What's your take on discipline?

By *discipline,* we mean the setting up and keeping of certain rules you agree upon between you. These include basic house rules, such as bedtime and curfew on school nights. They also include major no-nos, such as use of tobacco or alcohol or attending all-night dance parties where Ecstasy is served up like after-dinner mints! After you've established your house rules and list of no-nos, you need to agree on a style of discipline, which is to be applied to each child according to his age and personality.

Children need a structured environment that establishes rules and what's expected of them. It's so easy to let things slide when your lives are in an upheaval over the divorce, but that's the worst thing you can do. Establish a routine, set up the rules, and stick by them. If you do, you all benefit and the structure helps re-establish a sense of security and stability in your kids' lives.

Basic house rules

It's important to establish a list of basic house rules that are followed uniformly in both homes. In other words, Saturday night bedtime isn't ten o'clock at Mom's house, and midnight at Dad's! Here are a few of the rules you need to agree on:

- ✔ Bedtime on school nights, weekends, and during school vacations
- ✔ Curfew for your teenagers
- ✔ Helping out around the house

  Agree on the number of chores each child is expected to take care of. (See Chapter 4 for more on this topic.) You also need to agree on the amount of weekly allowance the children are paid, if any.

- ✔ Homework and TV rules

  Designate a time and place for doing homework before watching TV in the evening. Then, limit what your kids watch and how much time they are allowed to spend in front of the boob tube!

Listing major no-nos: Nope, don't even think about it, nyet!

In addition to the basic house rules, you and your ex need to talk about the big stuff. When your kids reach the age of 10 or so, you need to sit them down and have frank discussions about drugs, alcohol, and pre-marital sex. These discussions are uncomfortable for all parents, but especially for divorced parents struggling with all aspects of their lives, and who would rather not have to deal with these subjects when their children are so young. However, as obnoxious as it is to think about, your children are being introduced to these subjects in elementary school.

Here are just a few examples of major no-nos established by many single parents:

- ✔ **No illegal drugs.**

  Drug pushers are out there in force, offering a colorful array of illegal drugs, including uppers, downers, and Ecstasy, the latest designer drug for teens. Table 9-1 lists some of the most popular street drugs and some of their street names. You can also check www.whitehousedrugpolicy.gov/streetterms for more information on drug names. If your child is using any of these illicit drugs, contact your child's school counselor for referrals to substance-abuse rehabilitation programs available in your city.

Table 9-1	Drugs and Their Nicknames
Drug	*AKA*
Amphetamines	Meth, crank, ice, bennies, speed.
Inhalants	Airplane glue, cleaning fluid, rubber cement. Also known as *huffing*.
Marijuana	Dope, grass, pot, chronic, weed.
LSD	Acid, haze.
Barbiturates	Bluebirds, goofballs, blues, reds, yellow jackets, nembies.
Cocaine	Blow, cake, free base, lady, nose candy, snow, toot, crack.
Heroin	Dope, horse, junk, smack, scag, H, brown, hombre.

✔ **No smoking.**

✔ **No pre-marital sex.** For some hints on talking to your kids about intercourse and oral sex, take a look in Chapter 6.

✔ **No alcohol.**

✔ **No cutting classes.**

✔ **No swearing.**

✔ **No reckless driving.**

✔ **No tattoos, body-piercings, or questionable hair styles without your permission.**

✔ **No charging on any of your credit cards or accounts without your permission.**

Agreeing on a style

After you've set the rules, you need to agree on a style of discipline.

Whatever style of discipline you choose, make an effort to praise your child when he exhibits good behavior — when he does something positive. Here are three common discipline styles:

✔ **Total permissiveness.** Total permissiveness is when a parent lets his child do anything she wants, suffering any negative consequences that happen to result. In fact, the parent makes no demands on his child at all. For example, if your child never cleans his room, changes his sheets, takes his dirty clothes to the laundry room, or hangs up clothes he wants to wear again, the obvious results are that he doesn't have clean clothes or clean sheets and he can't find his soccer shoes or his homework when he needs them. The reason many parents are permissive is because it seems easier to them than trying to enforce rules, and they think their children learn from the natural consequences of their behavior.

✔ **Strict discipline.** Strict discipline is the traditional philosophy that says if you screw up, you get punished. Each time your child misbehaves, you have a corresponding form of punishment. For example:

- You tell your daughter that she needs to stop watching TV and do her homework. Your daughter becomes angry because she wants to watch the rest of the program, so she grabs her school books and throws them against the wall.

  You tell your daughter to pick up her books, then you send her to her room for the rest of the evening commenting, "Do your homework and when you're finished, you may not return to the family room to watch television. Stay in your room until bedtime!"

- Your son defies you by coming home after your established school-night curfew — in fact, he's an hour late. When he finally gets home, he doesn't offer a word of explanation — just sulks off to his room, slams the door, and goes to bed. You come unglued, of course, as you follow him into his room and demand an explanation. When he offers something weak like, "I lost track of the time," and shows no remorse, you tell your child that you will call your co-parent and come up with an appropriate punishment, which may be grounding him for a week or taking away his driving privileges altogether for the time being.

If you prefer this strict style of discipline, it's important to decide ahead of time what types of misbehavior deserve what types of punishment. For example, if your child talks back or uses a swear word, you may agree this warrants a one-hour time-out. Or, if the problem is more severe, such as your teen taking your car without permission, you may decide to take away all car privileges for a certain length of time. In the case of a very serious problem, such as cutting school or smoking marijuana, you and your ex need to have a joint meeting with your child where you announce what discipline measures you have agreed upon between you in advance.

✔ **Non-punitive discipline.** Many children's psychologists believe non-punitive discipline is the best method of discipline; also known as *positive discipline*. Positive discipline is a happy medium between permissiveness and strict traditional discipline. The idea of a non-punitive style of discipline is to disciple your children, instead of using punishment for their misbehavior. By *disciple* we mean to teach, instruct, and guide your children by talking to them about their misbehavior. The idea is to sit down with your child and coax him into telling you why he did what he did, what he thinks he can do differently next time, and what he's learned from the incident. Here are a couple of examples of non-punitive discipline:

- Your kids leave their toys scattered over the family room floor. You ask them to pick up their toys and put them in their toy box. They ignore you. You quietly explain that if they don't pick up their toys you will place them in a box and store them until you see a change in attitude. Your kids ignore you, so you gather up their toys and place them in a locked storage closet in the garage. If the same thing happens the next night, add the toys to your bulging storage closet until your kids eventually run out of toys. If your kids ask for their toys, sit down with them and have a chat. When you see an attitude change, retrieve a few toys at a time to see whether they got the message.

- You're invited to Grandma's birthday party at a nice restaurant. Your child whines and complains about everything, from the coloring book and crayons the waiter gave him to keep him occupied, to the yucky food he refuses to eat.

  You calmly and quietly remove your child from his high chair, walk to the car, buckle him into his car seat and read the paperback book you've brought along just in case this kind of thing happens.

  You and your child do not return to the restaurant, so neither of you were able to finish your meal, which may seem like you're the one being punished. But — get this — after this little routine takes place a couple times in a row, your child doesn't act like a brat in the restaurant because he's got the drill down pat: Act like a brat and you're removed from the restaurant for good.

The experts favor this latter style of discipline because they feel that

- ✔ Total permissiveness results in children who are aggressive, immature, and have a poor sense of social responsibility.

- ✔ Strict discipline causes you to become the Sheriff of the house, on constant watch to see who's breaking what rules, then dealing out appropriate punishment. They also feel strict discipline puts you in a tough spot that can exhaust you over time, and that it's like treating a gaping wound with a band-aid. They say that a punishment style of discipline doesn't get to the root of the problem, doesn't produce lasting changes in behavior, and can damage your child's self-esteem.

- ✔ The non-punitive style of discipline helps the child monitor his own behavior because he discovers that his misbehavior always leads to unpleasant consequences.

Anything but heaven

As though these aren't enough, we also have the trendy new drug called Ecstasy, which is freely available during many rave parties (all-night dance parties). When your teens try to convince you that a rave is totally innocent and that, in fact, no alcohol is allowed, that sounds pretty good, right? Wrong! Ecstasy is often offered for free or for sale by clean-cut, baby-faced teens attending these raves. Ecstasy pushers promise the users that the drug is innocent and will cause no lasting or dangerous side effects. In truth, the drug often causes a coma and has resulted in death.

The ideas mentioned above are just a beginning. Parenting is a very challenging task for *all* parents, and it's worth getting some help, like taking a parenting class, reading one parenting book each year, and/or getting professional consultations about your situation.

Never discipline your child when you're angry. Do whatever you need to do to cool down first — then address the problem in a calm, quiet way.

Flexing your muscles: Are you a wimpy parent?

Most single parents are barely hanging in there, much less award-winning disciplinarians! Here are a couple of signs that your discipline techniques may leave something to be desired, by which we mean you might be a wimpy parent:

✔ Your fifth grader calls from school because he forgot his homework and wants you to deliver it to him. He's pretty sure you'll do this because you've always done it in the past.

Solution: If you've always delivered forgotten homework before, go ahead and do it one last time, but have a serious talk with him that night when you get home. Explain that you aren't going to run errands for him again, and hold true to your word. Next time he forgets his homework — tough! Let him suffer the consequences.

✔ Your daughter gets into a mean screaming match with her brother, which evolves into a punching match. You send your daughter to her room for a time-out, but she throws a tantrum, screams and sobs until you tell her she can come out of her room if she's good.

Solution: Don't reward you daughter for her temper fits! If she continues to carry on in her room, add a half hour of time-out for every five minutes of tantrum time!

The discipline philosophy you choose is entirely up to you. However, here are three crucial things to remember:

✔ You and your ex need to agree on the same style of discipline. After all, what's worse than one parent who's totally permissive and the other who's as strict as a Marine drill sergeant!

✔ You and your ex need to be sure that you haven't established a discipline policy that one of you cannot carry out when the situation presents itself.

✔ You and your ex need to be consistent in your discipline methods. In other words, don't punish a certain type of misbehavior one time, but let it slide the next.

✔ Never, never, never punish your child by refusing to let him spend designated time with your ex, or by telling your ex that your child may not attend the concert with him after all as a punishment for something your child did wrong during the week while he was with you.

After you've agreed on your discipline style, it needs to be customized for each of your children. In other words, you can't discipline each of your children in exactly the same way, so you need to make allowances for your children's individual personalities. Take a look in Chapter 6 for ways to deal with different ages and stages, and to get some information about birth order. You may also want to pick up a book entitled *Positive Discipline for Single Parents,* 2nd Edition (Prima Publishing), by Jane Nelson, Cheryl Erwin, and Carol Delzer, which goes into more detail on the philosophy of non-punitive discipline.

Creating new family traditions

Just think about it for a minute — your kids have gone from your pre-divorce rituals and family celebrations to living a dual life. One year they spend Christmas and birthdays with Dad, the next year they spend them with you. Or, your traditional family outing on the 4th of July has taken on a new twist with the split — one year you take them to the Pops concert and fireworks down by the river, just like you always used to do. But the next year, when they're with Dad, he stays at home with the kids as they watch the neighbors light a few firecrackers out in the street.

Kids thrive on tradition, and family traditions help bond the family together. In fact, their childhood traditions help determine what type of parents they will be someday. So, if your traditional family celebrations are pretty messed up because of the divorce, why not make a conscious decision to add a few new traditions. Get your kids together and talk about any upcoming holidays, birthdays, or family get-togethers and ask them what they think is special. Explain that you want these celebrations to be rich and wonderful for you as a family — fun times they remember for the rest of their lives.

No fudging here

We know a single dad who wanted his kids to understand the true meaning of Christmas, so he started a precious new Christmas tradition for his little family. About a week before Christmas he took the kids to Costco where they purchased sleeping bags encased in backpacks. The bags were dual-purpose: They could be used as sleeping bags, or unzipped and used as blankets. Dad wasn't much of a cook, so he and the kids also bought boxes of fudge while they were out shopping. Then — and here's the tearjerker part, so get out your tissues! — on Christmas Eve afternoon, Dad and his three kids went down by the railroad tracks where the homeless hang out and gave several men a sleeping bag/backpack and a box of Christmas fudge. Even the little 3-year-old went up to one of the unshaven men and handed him his gifts. We ask you — is that a sweet new family tradition, or what?

Here are a few suggestions just to get your creative juices flowing. It basically revolves around thinking up something new for your kids and thinking of those less fortunate than yourselves:

- ✔ **Christmas/Hanukah/Kwanzaa:** Before the divorce, your family may have always attended Christmas Eve candlelight service, followed by a Swedish smorgasbord at your in-law's house, with gifts delivered by Santa overnight and a spectacular breakfast Christmas morning while you opened the gifts around the huge tree in the living room. Well, now you and your two kids attend Christmas Eve service — no reason for that to change. Then, instead of going to your in-law's house (because that's where your ex and his new sweetie are enjoying the smorgasbord), get together with a couple of other single parents, close friends, or family members for your own Christmas Eve buffet. You can host it yourself with a little help from the other parents who can contribute a baked ham or a pecan pie, followed by caroling around the neighborhood after dessert. Carry lighted Christmas candles as you sing — kids love this — and what a lovely new tradition! You can even carol your way through the children's ward at your closest hospital, dropping off candy canes as you sing along.

- ✔ **Birthdays:** So, you and your husband always surprised your kids with a special daytrip for their birthdays? Your son has memories of a day spent skiing or riding the historic train to the Grand Canyon or trying out all the rides at Six Flags over Texas. Why can't you come up with surprises of your own?

  If you can't fit train rides and amusement parks into your less-than-thrilling new budget, you can at least plan something special. How about a day bodysurfing at the beach, followed by a fresh seafood meal on the wharf?

If your child insists on both of his parents attending his birthday party, try like crazy to accommodate him. If you're planning a little bowling party for your son and his friends, for example, and your ex doesn't feel comfortable joining in on the bowling, maybe she can arrive in time for the cake, ice cream, and gifts.

✔ **Vacations:** If your pre-divorce family always went to Ocean City Beach for summer vacations, why not consider something new and different? Come up with a few suggestions, then let your kids decide.

Maybe they'll choose a week camping in the mountains or renting a cabin at a national park. After they've made their decision, go for it full tilt! Call ahead for visitor information, or search the Internet for available activities. After you assemble all the info, have a little family meeting where you discuss the possible activities. Would your kids enjoy a white-water rafting trip down the Colorado River? Or would they prefer a sunrise breakfast followed by a horseback ride out into the desert? Many of these activities require advance reservations, so call ahead. When you're at your destination and you find out what everyone has enjoyed the most, reschedule again for next summer and guess what? You've established a new family tradition!

✔ **Other holidays and get-togethers:** Every holiday and family celebration can be given a new twist for your family. Take a look at what you've done in the past, then get your kids involved in new ways to celebrate.

For example, one single parent family decided to make Thanksgiving more special by writing handwritten thank-you notes to friends and relatives who were kind to them the previous years, especially when they were going through the angst of the divorce. A single dad decided to make Hanukah extra special by making gifts with his kids. Another family started the tradition of making homemade Valentine cards for elderly patients in nursing homes. The handwritten thank-you notes and the Valentine cards are both ways to reach out to others, which is a wonderful way to overcome your own hurts and sorrows.

By the way, if your child is spending his birthday or Thanksgiving with his other parent, you can easily have your own celebration a week or so before the event. Celebrate his birthday with neighborhood friends, decorations, birthday cake, and, of course, plenty of gifts to open. Or, in the case of Thanksgiving, do it up right with your own version of the traditional feast!

If certain holidays seem painfully lonely with your small little family, get together with other single parents and their children. If you don't know many, join a single-parent group so you can get to know others in your same predicament, plus the group will probably have holiday activities planned that you and your kids can attend each year as well.

More muscle than money

Amy and Jake had always been thought of as a well-balanced couple — a perfect example of opposites attract. Jake was an artist and a craftsman and Amy was a hard-driving Type A perfectionist. He enjoyed listening to music while he played with his daughter, Sarah. Amy enjoyed going over the budget while she was doing the laundry. After a while, their differences caught up with them — it was just too much, and they agreed to separate.

Because Jake isn't into fulltime employment and needed free time to be creative, he can't really be depended upon for regular child-support payments. What he was into, and what he did very well, was to spend lots of time with Sarah. He was available to babysit on a moment's notice, which Sarah loved and Amy really appreciated. Amy's work required frequent evening meetings

with prospective clients, so Dad tucked Sarah into bed almost every night of the workweek.

Another opportunity for Jake to help out, without contributing a lot of money, came up when Amy bought a house. She found a fixer-upper that was structurally sound, but needed some significant TLC. When Amy pulled up the old carpeting and found quality hardwood floors underneath, she was thrilled. During the remodeling, Jake continued to be there for Sarah and Amy, too. The little fixer-upper needed a lot of work and Jake dove right in to help out. He's done a great deal of the repair work, painting, and landscaping, which helped offset his lack of child-support payments. This opposites-attract couple has managed to maintain a respectful, workable co-parenting arrangement that suits their personalities and life styles.

Promise us you won't mope around feeling sorry for yourself on holidays or other special occasions! That's the worst thing you can do! We know it's heart wrenching for you as you face each holiday, birthday, and vacation after the divorce or the death of your spouse. On Valentine's Day, for example, it's impossible to erase the memories of the sweet, tender things your spouse used to do for you on this special day. Maybe he helped the kids create a one-of-a-kind heart-tugger of a card! Wow! And now, here you are, struggling to celebrate Valentine's Day without him! So, how do you cope with each holiday as it comes along? Get together with your kids and come up with something sweet you can do for someone else.

Avoiding the Biggest Mistakes Made by Single Parents

Single parenting is an incredibly difficult job. As a matter of fact, parenting is difficult for two parents in a traditional family unit, so trying to go it alone is even more difficult. In the process of trying to be the best parent you can be, it's easy to fall into one of these single-parent traps. See whether any of these ring a bell.

Heaping more onto their plates

If your child has one or two extracurricular activities at a time, that's plenty. But if you're like many single parents, you want your child to achieve, excel, and win, win, win! It's only natural for you to want the best for your child, but it's a mistake to overload her with activities.

It's trendy these days to enroll your child in way too many classes, clubs, and competitive activities. But your kid needs down time, time to relax and be silly, and time to do absolutely nothing! You see, he doesn't have to be busy with something constructive every single minute of his life — cut him some slack and stop the madness!

If you agree with us that a kid is a kid, not a small adult, and that he has the right to enjoy his relatively short childhood, then you need to ask yourself this question: Is your child's life well-balanced? In other words, does he get along fine in school, participate in one or two extracurricular activities, and still have time to relax and play with his friends? If so, he's probably doing okay. But if you can tell he's feeling stressed most of time, if he gets down on himself because he doesn't win every game or get all A's in school, or if he tends to get sick constantly, then his plate is full! Step in and toss out a couple of the activities. Chapter 4 helps you do that effectively.

Encouraging your kids to be private detectives

Don't pump your children for information about your ex, your ex's lifestyle, or your ex's squeeze, and don't ever suggest any creepy stuff they should watch for when visiting their other parent. If you say things like, "See if you can find out where she's going after work," or "Try to find out whether that junky car out in front of her house belongs to that guy she's been dating," you may put suspicious ideas in your kids' heads that may make them think poorly of your ex, and when they realize how you're manipulating them, they may think poorly of you. Also, do you really want your kids returning the favor and spying on you for your ex? This is not to say that your kids can't talk to you about what they do when visiting their other parent. Just try not to seem too inter-ested and inquisitive, even if you're dying to know!

Labeling your kids

Unfortunately many parents label kids, and it's very damaging. Don't say things like, "Well, she's the clumsy one — she can't walk down the sidewalk without tripping over her feet. She's been that way since she was a little kid," or "He'll never be any good at math — his left brain is disconnected most of the time!" These careless remarks not only hurt your kids, but guess what? They put the kibosh on your kids' confidence to the point where they believe what you say and never overcome the clumsiness or distaste for math.

Denying yourself a social life

If you're like so many single parents, you're afraid that dating or having a social life of your own can hurt your kids, especially if they've been through a painful divorce. You tend to carry guilt around with you and if you do date, it's on the sly so your kids don't find out about it.

Sure, you're a parent and you don't want the kids to feel jealous or hurt because you date and have your own friends, but you're a healthy adult and you can't let your children prevent you from having a life of your own. In fact, when you don't have friends your own age, you run the risk of becoming overly dependent on your kids. Something that's not good for you or your kids!

So, watch for social opportunities and take advantage of them — you need friends your own age. Take a look at Chapter 15 for ways to ease back into the social scene and date — if that's what you want to do. You aren't going to be a fulltime parent forever — your kids grow up and have lives of their own. So, we give you permission to have a social life!

Allowing your kids' traits to ring your bell

It's quite common for you to be disturbed when you recognize your ex's traits in your kids. Your ex may annoy the heck out of you, and some of her annoying behaviors may have been passed on to your children. If your ex really irritates you, it's possible you dislike things about her that are actually positive traits! So don't take it out on the kids — it's not their fault that your ex drives you nuts! Sit down and make a list of things about your ex that annoy you. If one of these behaviors pops up in your kids, you now realize why they bother you.

Expecting your children to deliver messages to your ex

We know it's easier for you to send a message with your kids than it is for you to call your ex or deliver the message in person, but it's not fair to your kids. Don't say to your son, "Tell your dad that the support payment was due last

Wednesday and I need it by tomorrow." And don't ask your daughter to let your ex know that you'll be late to pick the kids up next Friday because you have a staff meeting at five o'clock. What a burden to lay on your poor children!

Getting sucked into power plays

Kids pull power plays on their parents. A *power play* is a verbal struggle that develops when your child tries to bully you into backing down on something you've asked him to do or on a rule that you've established. His voice becomes louder and louder as you respond in kind. When you are sucked into one of these power plays, no one wins. It's much better to enforce a rule in a calm way, which protects your child's sense of dignity. To avoid these power plays, don't give in to your child's antics.

These struggles start when a child is in his terrible twos, and they escalate as your child becomes a teenager and establishes his independence. If you don't recognize a power play as it is developing and you inadvertently get involved, it can become an angry confrontation in no time and actually escalate into a screaming contest if it isn't brought to a halt!

When you see a power play in the works

- ✔ **Say, "I'm not playing."** Instead, listen patiently as your child rants and vents and then say, "Nevertheless, that's the way it is."

- ✔ **Say, "If that's the way you're going to be, I'm not listening."** Then walk away. Don't give a reason. Just say, "I'm sorry you're upset." Period!

Being a poor role model

Don't be like some professional athletes who have proudly stated that they aren't anybody's role model. You, as a single parent, are a role model for your kids, whether you like it or not. In fact, research shows that children are copycats as they imitate their parents.

If you smoke, your kids think it's not only okay to smoke, but way cool! And if you get drunk from time to time, your kids want to experiment with alcohol so they can see what it feels like to be on the same kind of high you seem to enjoy. And when it comes to swearing and bad-mouthing others, your kids pick up your choice expletives and think they're part of being an adult. If you have a teenager who's learning to drive, what does she think when she sees you fly into a fit of road rage on the freeway when someone cuts you off? She thinks it's okay to honk and display her middle finger too as she models your behavior.

Finally, don't fight with the ex in front of your kids! If you've fallen into this trap, put on the brakes! If your kids see you disrespecting each other, they may find it easier to disrespect you!

Watch for any bad habits that can poison your kids and strive to be the best role model you can possibly be.

Allowing your kids to con you

Kids can be consistent! They're known to keep on asking for what they want. Sometimes over and over and over and over again until their parents finally cave in to what they're asking for! You could call it a form of nagging.

Your children are miniature con artists — yes, they are! They know how to work you and when they want something they play on your guilt. Whether they're crying out for designer jeans or a McDonald's Happy Meal, you're the one who decides whether you want to buy it or can afford to spend the money. Spending your money is not the kids' decision — it's yours. So, be strong and stop being manipulated by the clever little characters! Just say, "No!"

Failing to establish boundaries

Don't be a wishy-washy parent who isn't consistent with what's okay and what's not. If talking back is unacceptable, then it must always be unacceptable. If your child throws his toys across the room every time he doesn't get his way, don't ignore him part of the time and punish him other times.

One of the biggest mistakes you can make as a single parent is to be lax in your discipline. It's interesting that a prominent psychologist in central California said that when he counsels teenagers, they often tell him privately that they want boundaries — they want a parent who says "No." So set up some basic rules in your home and stick to them.

Pushing your ex's buttons

This comes from maintaining your anger toward your ex-spouse. You are right, and your ex is wrong, so why not "push your ex's buttons"? As you endured the conflict that led up to the divorce and as you suffered through the divorce rituals, you earned your Ph.D. in button pushing! You know exactly what pushes your ex's buttons! And even though you're trying desperately to successfully co-parent your kids, you can't seem to resist those juicy buttons. If you do maintain this pattern, and keep the tension high between you and your ex, then do so knowing it will likely damage your child. If you're having trouble controlling the anger you feel toward your ex, consider joining a single-parent support group or seeking out the help of a professional therapist (see Chapter 14).

Here are a few words not to use: *never, always, should, shouldn't, every,* and *always.* For example don't say, "You're always late picking her up — you're never on time!" Instead calmly substitute something like, "I would really appreciate it if you could pick her up by 5:30 on Fridays because my class starts at 6:00. You probably weren't aware of that, but it would be great if you could come just a little earlier than you have been." And don't say, "Every single time you forget to pack her nightie! Do you think I have the money to buy her a new nightie every single week?" Instead try saying, "Jaimie loves wearing your tee shirts to bed as nighties — can you donate a couple to the cause? She thinks it's way cool to wear one of her daddy's shirts to bed." See? Problem solved!

You see how it works? Make a list of the buttons you tend to push and try to ditch them somewhere along the way. Also, be aware of the ways your ex tries to push your buttons.

Refusing to consider professional therapy

Depending on how you were raised, you may think of professional therapy as a crutch for the weak. Your parents may have fought things through without seeking counsel of any kind, so you've adopted this same way of thinking. However, you may be experiencing an incredible amount of stress as you strive to cope as a single parent, and sometimes a single parent needs a time-out from the kids.

Parental stress hot lines allow a frantic parent to reach a well-trained volunteer who can lend a calming influence or helpful suggestions. In some areas, trained volunteers can come over to your home to give you a break.

Crisis centers have also been established to assist single parents who realize they're near the breaking point and are unable to cope with the children. A mother can drop off her kids at a crisis center and they will be cared for until she recovers and is able to cope. Unfortunately, not as many parents take advantage of this help as they should.

Many other professionals are there to help you, including family therapists, psychologists, and counselors available through your church or single-parent support groups. You can muddle through by ignoring the problem or trying to solve it yourself, or you can get some help. Remember that help can free you and empower you to have a happy, balanced life. Take a look at Chapter 14 for signs that you may need the help of a professional therapist and how to locate one near you

Considering Your Kids' Bill of Rights

If you're taking the High Road in your co-parenting plans, your children's rights are protected. Here is a list of your children's rights — you can use it as a guideline for your written and unwritten goals for your kids.

Your child has the right to

- ✔ **Be told about the divorce by both parents at the same time.** He must not hear about it from someone else before you talk to him.

- ✔ **Hear why you divorced.** Explain this simply with as much or little detail as your child can handle at his age.

- ✔ **Be loved and cherished by both parents.**

- ✔ **Love and cherish each of her parents individually, without feeling guilty or being forced to take sides.**

- ✔ **Be protected from overhearing any arguments, verbal abuse, or bad-mouthing of one of his parents by the other.**

- ✔ **Live in a clean, safe environment that is nurturing to his growth and development.**

- ✔ **Have her own private space,** even if it's just her side of a shared bedroom.

- ✔ **Have his physical needs met,** including nourishment, exercise, medical, dental, and vision care.

- ✔ **Have her emotional needs met,** including praise, encouragement, and sympathy when your child has had a setback of some kind.

- ✔ **Expect both of his parents to be positive role models as he grows, matures, and copes with his future.**

- ✔ **Be treated fairly, courteously, and with respect.**

- ✔ **Have you welcome her friends into your home and treat them with respect.**

- ✔ **Receive an apology if you've made a mistake.**

- ✔ **Expect you to keep your promises to him.**

- ✔ **Lead a stable life that includes a sense of continuity as she divides her time between two parents' residences.**

Don't forget that many of the problems single parents face raising their kids are common for all parents. We recommend a marvelous book entitled *Parenting For Dummies*, 2nd Edition by Sandra Hardin Gookin and Dan Gookin (Wiley Publishing, Inc.). This book gives many pointers on satisfying your child's physical and emotional needs whatever her age. It also discusses health and safety issues, child care, traveling, and discipline problems. You might want to take a look at this helpful book when you need answers to general parenting questions.

Chapter 10

Coexisting Peacefully
with Other "Parents"

In This Chapter

▶ Sympathizing with your kids' grandparents

▶ Understanding the stepparent

▶ Relating to godparents and other relatives

▶ Handling family visits

*Y*our doorbell rings. You answer the door. UPS has delivered three huge gift bags: one for your son, one for your daughter, and one for you. The first bag is from Grandpa Watson — it's filled with $100 bills, his contribution toward your son's college tuition. The second bag is from your ex's new wife — it's filled with hugs for your 12-year-old daughter. The third bag is from your ex's brother and sister-in-law — it's filled with love.

Do you accept these gifts, or do you call back the UPS driver and demand he return them to their senders? Your answer depends on your relationships with your children's other relatives. When you divorced your husband, did you divorce his family, too? If your wife passed away, do you maintain a relationship with her family? Or are you willing to accept their gifts of love, support, and financial help because of their relationship to your kids?

Grandparents and other family members can be pretty intuitive when it comes to realizing that the kids need their emotional support and the sense of belonging that support can bring. However, grandparents and other relatives may not always be on the same page in the case of divorce. For starters, they may not believe in divorce. For seconds, they're your ex's family, and their loyalty is probably with him. The best advice is to withhold your judgment and give them time to get used to the idea. Just because they aren't ready to get involved in your kids' lives now, it doesn't mean that they won't come around eventually. Include them in every holiday or significant event in your child's life, including birthdays, award ceremonies, and sporting events. Ask your child to do the inviting by writing a note, placing a phone call, or asking relatives in person. How can they resist?

Remember your father-in-law? He's the magical Grandpa who hand-whittled those little farm animals for your children when they were little. And how about Grandma, your mother-in-law, who knitted those multicolored scarves and stocking caps for your kids at Christmas time? Well, Grandpa and Grandma are still around, and they miss their grandkids like crazy! Of course, you may not miss your father-in-law's nagging about the way you neglect your car, or the way your mother-in-law wrinkles her face as she scolds you about letting the kids stay up too late on weekends. But you can bear up under these minor assaults for the kids' sake, can't you?

And what about your ex's new wife, Mother Marie, as your kids call her when they visit their dad two weekends a month? Even though she's not your favorite person in the whole world, she can't be all bad — she likes your kids, after all!

Of course, you can't ignore your kids' godparents, even though they are your ex's brother and sister-in-law! Or can you?

Many single parents wrap the ex's family into one tight wad and drop-kick the whole bundle of them out the door. If you're like them, you enjoyed it too! How dare his relatives side with your ex when he was in the wrong? You're angry with them at the moment, but that's no reason to deprive your children of their love and support. Honestly, you don't have the right to cut them out. After all, this isn't about *you* — it's about your *kids*. So take a big breath and bite your tongue — for your kids' sake.

One of the greatest things that can happen when these relationships are kept intact after a divorce is that they help your child see that not everything has changed in his life. A divorce is so traumatic for a child that he may think everything in his life is strange and different, which can generate a sense of instability. However, when he still gets to spend a week in the summer at Grandpa's cabin at the lake, or when he's still invited to his cousins' birthday parties, he then knows that many things are the same. These contacts can be great stabilizing factors in his life.

In this chapter we encourage you to take a look at your situation through the eyes of your kids' grandparents, godparents, aunts, uncles, and new stepparent. These family members have sacks full of gifts for you and your kids — don't turn them away.

Agreeing to See Grandparents

Your kids' grandparents are important people. They can be vital to your children's emotional well being. The bond between grandparents and their grandkids is special, and your children need the warmth and love their grandparents have to offer. Even if you can't stand to be around your in-laws at the moment, don't cut them out of your kids' lives. Remember that you divorced your ex — you did not divorce her parents!

Of course, that's not to say that all grandparents are caring and supportive. Some grandparents can be dysfunctional, just like anyone else. However, if a grandparent's love is unconditional, it can often be very close to parental love. For example, Grandpa's love doesn't necessarily depend on his grandson's grades or how well he behaves — Grandpa loves him anyway. So do everything you can to encourage and maintain the loving relationships between your kids and their grandparents. Not only do your kids need this unconditional love, but grandparents can also be an awesome source of comfort and stability, especially immediately following a traumatic divorce. Maintaining positive relationships between a child and her grandparents provides one more constant in the midst of all the changes divorce brings.

Grandma and Grandpa can help

Here are just a few of the ways Grandma and Grandpa can be good for your children, especially during difficult times:

- ✔ If you're a single mother, your kids need the positive role modeling of Grandpa in their lives, and if you're a single father, they need the influence of Grandma.
- ✔ If Grandma and Grandpa sincerely love and care about your kids, they want to provide good things in their lives by demonstrating their love and helping the kids as they cope with the divorce.

Granny's got the goods

According to a recent survey conducted by AARP, grandparents spend an average of $500 per year for each of their grandkids. Many grandparents also help out with other expenses. Fifty-two percent reported helping pay for grandkids' education, and 45 percent helped pay for their basic living expenses.

- Grandma and Grandpa can provide a little financial help as they take the kids shopping for school clothes, treat them to a movie or a trip to Taco Bell, or even take the children with them on a little vacation trip.

- Grandma and Grandpa's home can provide a stable environment where your children can kick back, enjoy Grandma's homemade comfort foods, and get away with some of the stuff on your no-no list at your house! Getting away with stuff may upset you, but you need to relax and realize that the grandparents' influence is only in effect while the kids are at their home. Remember how great it was when you were a kid and your grandparents spoiled you once in a while?

- Grandma and Grandpa can fill in as counselors and therapists as your kids pour their hearts out and tell them stuff they might never tell you. Their grandparents have lived a long time and survived many crises in their lives, so their advice is golden. It's like having free psychologists in the family.

- Grandma and Grandpa can give you a break from time to time as they serve as loving babysitters. They may even have your kids for a weekend so you and a friend can get away for a little much-needed R and R.

- Many grandparents provide free child care for their grandchildren, especially those who are preschool age.

- Depending on your own personal relationship with your mother and father-in-law, they can give you needed emotional support.

- Here's one of the very best things Grandma and Grandpa can do for your children: If the two of them are still together and happy, they provide encouraging proof that all marriages do not fail and that it's possible for a man and woman to be happily married to each other for many years. When you're going through a divorce, your kids need to see and experience good marriages.

ANECDOTE

Heather's loving grandparents

Heather was almost four when her parents divorced. Heather's dad moved to Maine to be near his parents, and soon Heather began visiting her grandparents there. Summer vacations in Maine became something she looked forward to. She became very close with her paternal grandparents and considers her grandfather her best male role model. At age 16 she realizes that it was pretty amazing that her mother has always maintained a close and loving relationship with them, too.

One summer evening when Heather was about 11, she asked her grandfather why her parents divorced. He gently explained to her that her father had fallen in love with another woman, her stepmother. Heather was very proud of her mother when she remembered her mom had never talked negatively about her dad or her stepmom. Most of all, Heather is proud of her mother who has taught her the value of family, education, and friendships. She says proudly, "Mom is no 50s woman and I'm not either."

Grandma and Grandpa's legal rights

Did you know that most states have passed laws that grant grandparents the right to visit their grandchildren after a divorce? In fact, if any parent — divorced or not — refuses to allow a grandparent time with a grandchild, the grandparent may sue for this right (and they often win).

Being Civil to Stepparents

When you really stop to think about it, your child's stepparent is in a tough spot. She has become the infamous other woman, or he has become the horrible other man — just for marrying your ex. Attempting to be a good stepparent can seem like a thankless job. Studies show that it takes about two years for a positive relationship to develop between a stepparent and new stepchildren.

It's no fun when your children say things like, "Well, Dad never cooks hamburgers that way!" or "My real mom knows all about science stuff!" Some days the new stepparent probably wonders what the heck he was thinking when he married your ex and became a stepdad to such unappreciative, bratty kids!

Even if your children don't love their stepdad, it's important for them to respect him. Making a second marriage succeed is even more difficult than with the first marriage, so it's important to have harmony and respect between the kids and their new stepparent.

Put yourself in a stepmother's shoes for just a minute — we know that isn't easy, but try. Don't you feel sorry for her just an itty-bit? After all, what if she doesn't really have fangs after all? What if she's actually a very nice person?

If you absolutely loathe your ex's new husband or wife, and the whites of your eyes turn crimson when you're around this person, try your best to change your attitude. Try to forgive, get over it, and move on with your life. Remember that the best revenge is to go on and have a happy life! Here are some of the positive ways your children's stepparent can help the kids:

- ✔ **Provide a shoulder for them to cry on.** When your child needs a little loving care and understanding, he may feel free to open up and express his hurts, worries, or frustrations to his stepparent.

- ✔ **Be there by helping them with homework and complimenting them on achievements.** It doesn't hurt to write a thank-you note to your child's stepparent once in a while. For example, if he redecorated your child's room at your ex's residence, telling him that it looks great can do wonders to strengthen your relationship with your child's stepparent. If you went to all that work, wouldn't you appreciate a thank-you?

✔ **Cheer your kids on when attending games or other events with your ex.** No child can have too many cheerleaders, so provide her with pom-poms and let her cheer as long and loud as she wants. By the way, let her know about any awards your kids have received, or are to be presented at a school assembly, plus any other achievements that merit praise.

✔ **Act as a referee between you and your ex.** If you're nice to him and he gets to know you, he might decide that you're an okay person. Why do you care? Because every once in a while you might need someone in your corner — you know, those pesky times when your ex insists on having the kids even though its not her turn, or when you're trying to talk your ex into attending your daughter's piano recital. You never know, your ex's new husband might be the very one who convinces her that you're right and she's wrong! Stranger things have happened!

If you really want to take the high road and prove to everyone that you're a wise, mature, grown-up person, suggest a joint family meeting to settle any discipline problems the stepparent may be having with your kids. If your child's stepparent needs support while trying to follow through on basic house rules, such as weekend curfews for your teenagers, arrange a joint meeting where everyone is in attendance: you, your ex, the stepparent, and your kids. Chapter 9 explains, in more detail, how to conduct a family meeting.

Seeing the Good in Godparents

A *godparent* is a man or a woman who has agreed to sponsor a child at the child's baptismal ceremony and be available to support and nurture the child during his growing-up years. Your children's godparents and other extended family members can provide wonderful support to you and your kids after the divorce (if you let them).

You see, they loved your children dearly before your divorce, and that love hasn't disappeared just because you and your ex have split. Some of these people may be on your black list at the moment, and you may want as little to do with them as possible, especially those who are close to your ex: his brother, sister, aunt, or uncle. But what about your children? Did your ex's sister and brother-in-law adore your kids? Did they go out of their way to give them gifts and do thoughtful things for them, especially over family holidays? If so, they deserve a spot in your kids' lives if they want one.

Be aware that extended family members can sue for the right to spend time with your kids. The same laws that protect the grandparents' rights to visit your kids often apply to third-party members, such as a godparent, foster parent, or person who has been a primary influence in the child's life. In many cases, third-party members join in a lawsuit initiated by the grandparents, demanding the right to spend time with the children. In fact, many laws are written to allow visitation by any other person with an interest in the welfare of the child. Wow! That leaves it wide open, doesn't it?

In some states, visitation rights are granted to other persons, named specifically as

- ✔ Foster parents
- ✔ Stepparents
- ✔ Grandparents
- ✔ Great-grandparents
- ✔ Siblings

And when rights are granted to third parties, as custodial parent you must actually facilitate the visits. *Facilitating* means that you can't merely agree to a visit. You must actually set up the visit by making phone calls or communicating in some other way. Then, when it comes time for the visit, your child must be dressed and ready to go with Great-Grandpa or have time available for the visit at the child's primary residence. But remember that the law was established to protect your child and his relationships. Of course, the law doesn't have to be a factor if you work to keep your child's relationships healthy and intact.

Setting Guidelines for Family Visits

Sure, your ex's extended family members may have the right to visit your children or have your children visit them, but that doesn't mean that your kids think it's cool. So don't force these visits. Let them evolve naturally as your children heal from the traumatic effects of the divorce.

After everyone involved agrees on when and where these visits will take place, take these guidelines into consideration:

- ✔ **Don't assume you can drop your kids off with relatives without calling first.** Just because you suddenly decide to take the afternoon off to go shopping, don't assume that your ex's sister will be ecstatic to have your 2-year-old for a few hours. Relatives have lives, too, so be sure to call ahead to make arrangements.
- ✔ **After a visit is set up, try as hard as you can to keep it.** Don't let anything short of a crisis cause you to cancel a promised visit between your child and one of his relatives. If your child thinks that a visit can be canceled on a whim, he may lose trust in you and the relative who requested the visit.

Although your child may not say so out loud, he may feel guilty when he enjoys being with his stepparent, grandpa, or anyone else on your ex's side of the family. Your child may feel, subconsciously, that it's wrong to like or love someone other than his natural parent, because that means he's being disloyal to you. Because your child probably won't voice his feelings, give permission for your child to love his relatives by

✔ **Saying nice things about them.** Avoid saying anything negative in front of your child. For example, don't let him overhear you calling your ex's new wife "the wicked witch of the east," "little Miss prissy butt," or any other choice descriptions!

✔ **Encouraging the relationships.**

✔ **Reassuring your child that there is plenty of love to go around.** Tell him that no matter how much he loves one of his relatives, he still has plenty of love left over for you. Sit down and say, "Honey, did you know that your heart has lots of rooms, a great big room where you keep your love for Mommy and Daddy, but a lot of other rooms where you can store your love for Auntie Tonya, and Grandma, and Mommy Marie (your child's new stepmom)?"

Here are some tips that may make visits easier on everyone:

✔ **Be sure all your child's parents know that elaborate entertainment plans aren't necessary.** The most meaningful reason for the visit is for your child to bond with his relative, and they can bond just by spending time together. It can be something as simple as helping Auntie plant her vegetable garden or playing chess with Grandpa. Hopefully, any planned activities are the type where your child and his relative can chat and get to know each other a little bit better every visit.

✔ **Don't ask your child to deliver a message for your ex via your ex's parents.** Let the visit be relaxed and unstrained — don't involve your in-laws in your problems or communication with your ex.

✔ **While your kids prepare for a visit, feed a few positive thoughts into their heads.** In other words, when your children are asked about their week with you, they can talk about upbeat stuff that has happened, such as how they helped you repaint their bedrooms or that the tomato plants are getting bigger every day.

✔ **Schedule down time for your child when he returns from his visit.** Don't cut things so close that the minute he gets home from Grandma's you have to whisk him off to a church service or a movie that you've already planned to see.

✔ **Don't try to cram in several other visits at the same time.** Just because your child's other relatives happen to live in the same town, it doesn't mean that she should visit all of them in one weekend. If your in-laws want to invite your ex's brothers and sisters over to visit with your child, that may work out, but a series of quick stops so everyone can say 'Hi' to your child on his way to Grandma's just isn't a good idea — especially for a younger child who can only handle so much social confusion at once!

✔ **Preserve relationships with family members you like.** If you were quite close to your in-laws before the divorce, or if you and your ex's sister really have a lot in common and still like and respect each other, stay friends. Sometimes they still feel like *your* relatives, too. Maintaining the relationships is not only good for your emotional health, but it helps your child adjust to the divorce when he sees that it's okay to still love his old family.

Don't always plan on dropping your child off and making your escape. Stay for a little visit or plan something that includes your child, his grandparents, and yourself. Such visits are dynamite stabilizers for your child.

✔ **Feel free to invite other family members to your home.** Invite them to your child's birthday party, to watch your son play in a basketball tournament, to come see your daughter in the cheerleader competition, or to your children's graduation and the party that follows.

Don't let the divorce cut off perfectly wonderful relationships you had with your ex's family. Continue to include them in your kids' activities so that they don't always feel like they have to mastermind an activity when your child visits them.

✔ **Know what you're going to say when they ask certain questions.** Take a little time to think up the zingers they may come up with, such as, "Whatever made you leave Eugene in the first place? Do you think you might get back together?" or, "What do you think of that woman Eugene is dating now? Have you met her?"

Have plenty of gracious, noncommittal answers ready on the tip of your tongue. We can almost guarantee that they'll come up with the questions, so you might as well be prepared. Oh, yes, and be sure to smile when you're answering their questions! They'll be deliciously confused!

✔ **Don't say anything negative about the activities your child does elsewhere, even if it's something you're not crazy about.** Unless it's some nefarious or grossly unsuitable activity, try to ride with it. A good example might be the day at an amusement park planned by Uncle Dwayne who thinks your 7-year-old son will be thrilled to ride the Big Daddy Roller Coaster with him. If it were you, you wouldn't even take your son on the Little Dipper, much less Big Daddy. But zip your lip and let Uncle

Dwayne find out for himself whether your little David thinks this is a way cool idea or not. If Uncle Dwayne ends up with little David's second-hand lunch all over his lap, he'll get the message!

- ✔ **Don't let your child decide whether he wants to visit a certain relative.** After the plan has been made, let your child know that he can't let Grandpa down now because Grandpa's looking forward to seeing his favorite grandson. If you let your child manipulate you into canceling a visit, he may think that he's in charge of the visits!

- ✔ **Be aware of any legitimate reasons to refuse visits with certain relatives.** For example, if you know for a fact that one of your child's relatives is deliberately trying to turn your child against you, or if you suspect emotional, physical, or sexual abuse, put on the brakes! In the case of abuse, seek the advice of a family law attorney immediately and, if necessary, take legal action.

Chapter 11

Keeping Cool When Resolving Co-Parenting Problems

In This Chapter

▶ Easing transition anxiety

▶ Cutting your ex a little slack

▶ Dealing with dangerous co-parenting problems

▶ Seeking help in the right places

A co-parenting plan is like a car. When it's new, it looks good and runs fine. But after you've driven it for a while, the paint begins to lose its luster and, much as you try to protect it, a few parking lot dings begin to show up. If you never take it down to the garage, a great many things begin to go wrong: The headlights stop working, and you can only drive during the day; the battery gets weak, so the car has trouble starting in the morning; or maybe the tires are worn out, so you get no traction in a storm. Every once in a while a co-parenting plan turns out to be such a *lemon* that a major overhaul can't even fix it up. If your plan is a lemon, you might need to junk it and start over with a new plan.

How's your co-parenting plan running these days? If you've kept it maintained, it's probably running pretty well at the moment. If you haven't kept it tuned up, it's probably limping along, barely making it one block at a time. In any case, if you've been a single parent for a while now, you've probably realized that this co-parenting thing isn't nearly as easy as you thought it would be! Every day is a challenge.

For example, maybe yesterday was a bad day for you: Your ex chewed you out on the phone because she thinks that you're a lousy role model for *her* kids. As soon as you hung up from that maddening conversation, you received another phone call — this time from the principal at your son's junior high school, requesting a joint meeting with you and your ex over "several serious incidents involving your son!" Of course, your daughter is still begging to go *back home* to live with her mother, because she thinks you're way too strict with her!

A co-parenting plan needs regular tune-ups, just like a car. If your plan is running rough, it's not going to run any better by ignoring the problem. This chapter is full of hints to help keep your co-parenting plan running smoothly. You can find helpful ways to get along with your ex and model a calm, positive attitude in front of your kids. We also take a look at those pesky problems that crop up around the holidays, as well as a few remedies for the really serious breakdowns your plan may suffer. (Check out Chapter 9 for advice on creating a co-parenting plan.)

Easing Transition Anxiety

Transition anxiety can be a real problem, especially right after the divorce, when all of you are trying to adjust to the co-parenting plan you agreed upon. By *transition anxiety,* we mean the anxiety on your part and your children's part when transferring your children from one residence to the other. In other words, if the kids have been with you for the school week, and it's time for them to go to Daddy's house for the weekend, anxiety can set in for a number of reasons.

Table 11-1 shows a few common problems that often pop up during the two-home-shuffle and offers you ways to handle them.

Table 11-1   Common Problems and the Co-Parenting Solution

Problem	Solution	Example
You and your ex are not real comfortable with each other now that the divorce is final.	Arrange to have pick-ups and drop-offs that don't involve personal contact with each other.	Drop your children off at day care in the morning, and your ex can pick them up on the afternoon he takes the kids for the weekend. Or, if he's had the kids over the weekend, ask him to drop them off at day care or school on Monday morning.
Your children don't want to go to Daddy's house, and they beg to stay with you.	If your co-parenting agreement has a set schedule for the two-home-shuffle, stick by it unless you see serious anxiety setting in.	Just smile and tell your child that, "Daddy would be so disappointed if you didn't come see him — he has so much fun stuff planned for you this weekend. We don't want Daddy to feel sad." Then, take your child by the hand and walk him to your ex's car.

Problem	Solution	Example
You're feeling bitter.	Don't send your kids off to your ex's home with instructions such as, "Remember, don't let Daddy know that Mommy ordered new carpeting for the living room," or, "When Daddy gets a phone call, listen to see if it's from his new girlfriend — that Gloria person."	Smile and say, "Have fun with Daddy. I love you and I'll see you Sunday night." If this is almost impossible for you to do without breaking your jaw, you may benefit from professional therapy. See Chapter 14 for ways that a therapist may be able to help you get over your bitter feelings.

Take a look in Chapter 9, where we discuss ways to maintain continuity in your kids' lives. We include such strategies as establishing new holiday traditions, maintaining two *real* homes, staying in contact with your children's old friends, and calling your child the day before he's scheduled to come to your home. During that phone call, you can tell him about the fun stuff you have in mind while he's with you, and you can go over a list of what he needs to pack in his suitcase for the stay.

Here are some more tips for making the transition:

- ✔ **Reassure your children that everything is fine.** Tell your children that you have lots of things you need to get done this weekend and it's okay for them to go to Daddy's. This is a good time to also reassure them that you and your ex love them equally and it's okay for them to love each of you with the same amount of love.

- ✔ **Don't turn the transition into a series of tearful *goodbyes*.** You know, "Just one more little kiss for Mommy?" This is difficult enough for your kids, so don't put them on a guilt trip by prolonging the physical transfer of the children from your care to your ex's. Try to lighten up a little, smile, tell them to have a good time, and then *leave*!

- ✔ **Thank your ex for having the children.** Say something like, "I'm sure they had a lot of fun." Then, when your kids later tell you about some way cool thing they did with their Dad, send a thank-you note to him, e-mail him, or leave a voice message saying, "Thanks for taking the kids with you to the driving range — they had a blast!"

Feeling Fonzie-like

Why is it important to have a calm, positive attitude in front of your kids? Because they react to your moods. If you're in a frenzy half the time, complaining about your rotten ex, your hateful boss, and your life in general, your children will perceive that their lives are unstable, too. They can't cope with the trauma of the divorce and the two-home-shuffle unless they think everything is okay with you. So what do you do if everything is *not* okay with you? Get thee to Chapters 12 and 14 for ideas that will help you.

If transition anxiety seems to be getting worse instead of better, and you're seeing warning signs, such as loss of appetite, sleeping problems, long periods of crying, regressive behavior, or any noticeable change in your child's disposition, meet with your ex and talk it over. It may be that your co-parenting plan needs to be revised to accommodate your child's age and emotional stability. Sometimes the solution is something as simple as letting the child spend more time with his preferred parent than before, and then easing him into a more balanced schedule as he matures and gets used to the idea of the two-home-shuffle. In severe cases, seek advice from a family therapist.

Even though you and your co-parent have agreed on a co-parenting plan, including which parent will have custody of the children on which specific days throughout the year, it's good to have a little talk with your ex every few months, just to see how you each think it's going. It's also a good idea to talk to your children once in a while. Ask them how they like the schedule. Their input may influence any changes you and your ex may decide to make in your plan.

Taking That Hex off Your Ex

So getting along with your ex isn't getting any easier, even with this marvelous co-parenting plan you two put together? First of all, you need to realize that every co-parenting situation has rough patches, especially at first. But studies show that things tend to smooth out as the years go by, especially if you *really* try.

When you look at this thing honestly, it's a wonder any divorced couples work things through enough to come up with an organized plan for their kids. After all, you're obviously not going to get along: If you could get along, you would have stayed married, right? So don't be surprised if your ex's annoying, disgusting, and unacceptable qualities raise their ugly little heads after the divorce, when you're trying to accomplish the monumental task of agreeing how to raise your children. Maybe a little forgiveness is in order — what do you think? Maybe you need to examine a few innovative ways to negotiate with your cranky ex. Finally, accepting and respecting your ex's relationships with your kids can also be a great help.

Forgiving

If we started listing all the *unforgivable* things couples do to each other, we could fill a book. So we understand why you don't want to forgive your ex for those things he did to you before the divorce. When we talk about forgiveness, we mean forgiving from your heart — not just giving lip service. (If you're having trouble forgiving your ex, you can find encouraging help in Chapters 12 and 14.) You *must* try to forgive your ex for the reasons detailed in the following sections.

Hurting your children

Why will your kids be hurt? Because they're sensitive, intelligent characters, and they pick up on your feelings. You may think that you're doing a fantastic job of hiding the hatred and bitterness you feel toward your ex, and you may fool a lot of people, but you won't fool your kids. They know! And the tension between you and their other parent is omnipresent — something they have to cope with when they spend time around either one of you.

Your first impulse may be to sabotage your ex in any way you can — to make his life miserable. You can sabotage him by bad-mouthing him in front of your kids and anyone else, by refusing to cooperate with his co-parenting requests, or by undermining what he's trying to accomplish with your kids' emotional healing.

Jabbing him where it hurts the most feels pretty good, doesn't it? It's your just revenge after all! Isn't it? Whether it's your just revenge or not, you need to give this some thought: How does your behavior affect your children? We encourage you to take the high road and forgive your ex for the kids' sake. (For more information on taking the high road, see Chapter 9.)

Respect the relationship between your child and your ex. When your kids are with your ex, allow them to bond — without interfering. Your ex has his own ways of dealing with co-parenting responsibilities, and just because they're not the same as yours, it doesn't mean they're *wrong* or *unacceptable*. Give your ex the benefit of the doubt. If he's trying as hard as he can to develop loving, lasting relationships with his children, don't sabotage his efforts just because you don't approve of his methods.

Your kids may feel threatened by the ongoing conflict between you and your ex. Children whose parents fight all the time tend to feel stressed and have low self-esteem. Research indicates that it matters less the type of family a child grows up in than the amount of conflict (parental tension) the child must endure! So do whatever it takes to stifle the conflict — if you don't, you're not being fair to your children.

Hurting yourself

Do you have any idea what happens to a person who's filled with hatred, bitterness, and a spirit of revenge? Any person filled with these poisonous attitudes may catch every bug that comes along, have aches and pains he never had before, feel tired and run down, and even become seriously ill. And that's just the physical stuff. A bitter person can also become emotionally ill, which means that he may suffer depression, feelings of poor self-worth, and other psychological pain.

Hurting your co-parenting relationship

Think about your co-parenting plan — how on earth are you ever going to make it work if you're continually bickering with your ex over every little thing? If your ex brings your son home an hour later than he promised, is that really a reason to blow up? After all, he did pick up your son, *as promised,* and take him to the basketball game, *as promised.* So are you going to come down on his head like a pot of hot chili just because he brought him home later than he should have on a school night? Why not save your energy and be grateful that your ex is involved in your son's life in the first place?

Like the saying goes: "Don't sweat the small stuff!" Give your kids a break and forgive your ex! Your kids' future depends on it!

Negotiating

Okay — you've decided to forgive your ex and try to get along with him for your kids' sake. What now? The next step is to sit down with your ex for an open, honest, and private chat. If what you've been doing isn't working, and you're at each other's throats all the time, what can you change?

We're willing to bet that, if you take an honest look at your situation, you'll probably find that it all comes down to *who's in control?* If that's the case, one of you needs to be mature enough to give up some of your control and let the *other* parent take over once in a while. Look at it this way — you're no longer married, so don't wrestle with this power struggle any longer!

Reducing the amount of conflict almost always results in a win for your child, even if you don't get your way!

Ann's shameful behavior

Ann had the other single parents spellbound when she told them about the elaborate schemes she cooked up to discredit her ex and prevent him from getting joint legal and physical custody of their two kids. She was so vindictive that she even hired a private detective to follow him and photograph him in any compromising situation that might present itself. She met with her ex's new girlfriend and told her untruths to discourage her. She shamelessly questioned the kids about their time with Dad and implied that his rules were cruel and abusive.

Ann thanked the single parent support group for showing her that her actions were based on hurt, anger, and a desire for revenge. She admitted that she had been only thinking of herself.

She had tears in her eyes when she told them how one question from another parent helped her see what she was doing. Ann was asked how her actions affected her children and what would her kids do if they lost their dad. This woke her up, allowing her to see things from another perspective.

It was hard to do, but she sat down with her ex and told him of her shameful behavior. They both had a good cry and agreed to treat each other with dignity and respect. They agreed that what the children needed were two parents who put their children first. Ann confessed that this action has helped her to let go of most of her pain and resentment.

Here are a few helpful tips for successful negotiating:

- ✔ **Be polite and respectful.** Don't smirk or roll your eyes when your ex says something to you. Be as courteous as you are when talking to one of your kids' teachers about some problem at school. This means letting your ex talk without interruption. Interrupting your ex is a slap in the face — the ultimate show of disrespect.

- ✔ **Begin your sentence with the pronoun "I."** Instead of saying, "You're always late picking up the kids," say "I feel bad for the kids when you're late picking them up — they worry that maybe you forgot them."

- ✔ **Don't bring up unresolved issues from the past.** Stick to the problem at hand.

- ✔ **Repeat what you hear to be sure that you're getting it right.** If your ex complains that he's sick and tired of having the kids dumped on him at the last minute, verbalize his complaint. Say, "If I understand what you're saying, you're upset because I don't give you enough time to rearrange your schedule when I need you to take the kids with little notice. Is that correct?" If you've got it right, go on to discuss ways to solve the problem. Can you give him a little more time to change his plans? Or, can your mom keep the children once in a while if you have an emergency at work? Try hard to resolve the conflict.

✔ **Don't hesitate to *apologize!*** An apology will go a long way toward softening your ex's adversarial attitude.

✔ **Try not to let any negativity rub off on you.** If you let it, the negative energy pouring out of his presence can sour your happy, positive disposition. Don't let it happen!

✔ **If your negotiations aren't going well, and anger is building, call a *time-out.*** By calling a time-out before the conflict escalates, you give yourselves a chance to avoid the angry scene. You can try again after you both cool down. Remember that a cooling-off period can work wonders when negotiating a painful issue.

Sometimes conflicts can only be resolved with the help of a professional counselor or therapist, so don't hesitate to seek a little help if you can't reach an agreement. Seeking help is a gift for your child and a sign of strength.

What do you do when he's bad-mouthing you to your kids while they're in his custody? What do you do if your kids come home after their visit with all kinds of tales: "Daddy says you're a slob of a housekeeper," or "Mommy says you're not a very good parent to us"? Here are a few clear-headed, mature ways to handle this type of immaturity on the part of your ex:

✔ **As you listen to these tales, keep your cool.** If your kids don't get the rise out of you that they anticipated, they may soon lose interest in *tattling on Daddy.*

✔ **Never, never, never bad-mouth him back!** If you do, you'll be acting as immaturely as your co-parent, plus you'll set a bad example for your kids.

✔ **Turn the bad words back on your ex.** Say "I'm sorry Daddy feels that way about me — I would never say anything that hateful about him. I think that sometimes when someone says something mean-spirited about someone, he really doesn't feel very good about himself."

✔ **Contact your ex in private to talk to him about his bad-mouthing habits — but *only* if your kids are being affected by his rotten mouth.** If he has genuine complaints about your housekeeping or the way you're raising your kids on your own time, let him get it off his chest in person or via a private phone conversation.

✔ **Forgive your ex for the mean things he says.** If you don't, you'll only hurt yourself and your children.

Dealing with Co-parenting Problems

God forbid that you're forced to face any extreme problems in your co-parenting efforts. But if something disagreeable does come up, try to remember that you're not the only parent with problems. You may be having severe problems with your kids, or your ex may have become a danger to your children because of abuse, an addiction, uncontrolled anger, or, in rare cases, attempts to kidnap your children. These are all wrenching, heartbreaking situations that require immediate intervention.

All of these problems can be worked through with help. Take a look in Chapter 19 for an appropriate agency or support group that can help you work through these problems.

Resolving super-serious kid problems

As you struggle to survive your divorce proceedings, your change in residence, and your less-than-wonderful new single-parent income, you may be leaving your kids to fend for themselves.

Co-parenting is difficult enough when things are going relatively well with your kids, but when super-serious problems come along, you both need to be totally involved. By super-serious, we mean problems such as defying your authority, lying, getting involved with smoking, alcohol, or illegal drugs, becoming sexually active, or exhibiting signs of depression, eating disorders, or suicidal thoughts.

We hope that your child doesn't face any of these grave problems, but if he does, you and your co-parent need to take action:

- ✔ If your child is smoking cigarettes, confront him together. Ask for help from the school counselor, who may be able to offer you a quit-smoking program available through the school district. The American Lung Association, the American Heart Association, and the American Cancer Society also offer self-help programs for teens. Your family doctor can be a great help, as well.

- ✔ If your child is showing signs of depression or eating disorders, ask the school counselor for a referral to a child psychologist or a family therapist.

- ✔ If your child is having suicidal thoughts, get help immediately. See your family doctor or call the National Hopeline Network at 800-784-2433 (800-SUICIDE). The National Hopeline Network provides access to trained telephone counselors 24 hours a day, seven days a week. If you feel that your child's threats are an imminent threat to his or her safety, call 911. Always assume it's a matter of life and death — unless a professional tells you otherwise!

- ✔ If your child is involved with drugs or alcohol, arrange a joint meeting with your ex, the school authorities, and the law (if they're involved). Establish strict curfews. And if your child is addicted, seek the help of a therapist who may recommend in-patient or outpatient rehabilitation care.

✔ If your child is sexually active, arrange a joint meeting with your child, your co-parent, and yourself to establish moral and spiritual guidelines. Follow that meeting with another joint meeting that includes the school counselor or a family therapist. You may also need to enforce a stricter curfew.

If you feel in your gut that your child is in danger, take action: Call 911, make an appointment with a family therapist, keep your kid at home for the night — do whatever it takes! Trust your instincts!

Seeking help when your ex is causing trouble

When we start talking about child abuse (whether it's sexual or physical), neglect, parental addictions, kidnapping, and custodial interference, we've moved away from common, easily solved co-parenting problems. We're talking about the need for immediate intervention — physical or legal.

If your biggest co-parenting problem is that your ex isn't paying child support as scheduled, take a look in Chapter 5.

Dealing with child abuse

Any type of child abuse, whether it's physical, sexual, or neglect, is despicable behavior that requires immediate action! If there has been abuse, you child will benefit from working with a trained therapist.

Abuse is something you have to take seriously, which means you must take these steps:

1. **If your children are in immediate danger, call 911.**

2. **Seek a court order barring your ex from any contact with your children.**

   You can obtain this order through your attorney, a child advocate, someone at your local battered women's shelter, or any police officer.

3. **If your ex physically takes the children away from you before or after you obtain a court order, call the police.**

   Provide the police with

   • A description of your ex's car

   • Your ex's license number

   • The general direction he was heading

4. **After your ex has completed some kind of treatment program, do *not* negotiate with him regarding visits with your kids or partial custody.**

   All negotiations, including any written changes to your child custody agreement, should be handled by a court-appointed mediator, an attorney, or a court official trained to handle this type of negotiation. Depending on the type of abuse, your ex may be granted the right for safe visitation with his children in supervised facilities. In extreme cases, the visitation privileges may be revoked entirely. The changes and provisions are spelled out in detail in court-mandated revisions to your original child-custody agreement. These revisions are enforceable by law, providing you and your child protection from the abusive parent.

Seeking professional help for parental addictions

An addiction to drugs or alcohol is no different for a single parent than it is for a married parent or single person. Addiction is addiction, and it must be treated, especially when the addict is the co-parent of your child. Helping your co-parent overcome his addictions is in the best interest of your child. Fortunately, many programs are in place for any addict who *wants* to recover, including Alcoholics Anonymous.

If — and we say *if* — your ex *wants* to recover and become a whole, productive person again, you can help her do exactly that.

1. **Make an appointment for your ex with her physician.**

2. **Physically take her to this appointment!**

   Her physician will refer her for proper treatment.

3. **Get your kids involved in Al-Anon.**

   This support program for children of addicts can help them deal with their own lives as their parent deals with hers.

Warning the children

The jury's out on whether to warn your children of a possible kidnapping — it depends on the ages of your children and whether your ex has actually threatened to abduct them or if he's become unstable and irrational to the point of being unpredictable. If you're living under a realistic threat of abduction, warn your kids.

Help them memorize your address and telephone number, including the area code. And here's a precaution — if your younger child has trouble memorizing the full address or telephone number, be sure he knows the name of the *city* where he lives.

Enlisting legal help for a kidnapping

Parental kidnapping (also called *child snatching* or *out of state moveaway*) is when one of the parents disagrees with the terms of the Custody Order and decides to take matters into her own hands. This is what happened to Emily (see Emily's story in Chapter 8), and it's more common than you would think.

What type of parent abducts his child? Here are the most common characteristics of a parent who commits this illegal act:

- ✔ Has a history of violence and/or child abuse
- ✔ Is in trouble with the law or with creditors and wants to move out of state or out of the country
- ✔ Has just lost a heated custody battle
- ✔ Has a history of mental illness or has recently become mentally unstable
- ✔ Has threatened to kidnap his children

If you have any suspicions, or even a *gut feeling*, that your ex could take such a drastic step as this, here are the steps you should take:

- ✔ Keep a journal that includes information about your ex, including his social security number, driver's license number, bank account numbers, car license and registration, credit card numbers, cell phone number, and so on.
- ✔ *Tell others* about your suspicions! Talk to anyone who may be involved in a possible kidnapping, including your child's daytime care provider, school principal and teachers, school bus driver, church personnel, and anyone else who's in regular contact with your children.

If you have a legitimate reason to believe your child is in danger of being abused or kidnapped, or if you feel threatened by your ex, ask your attorney to request a *restraining order* from the court. A restraining order is just what it sounds like: an order to restrain someone from doing something. A common use for a restraining order is to prevent a parent from taking his children out of state.

If you feel in imminent danger

1. **Change the locks on your home.**
2. **Contact the police.**
3. **Remove yourself and your kids from your home.**
4. **Go to a safe place and stay there until you have received an *emergency restraining order.***

   This is issued when there is immediate danger of being harmed, kidnapped, or violated in some way.

5. **After receiving a restraining order, be sure a copy has been furnished to your local police department.**

Follow these steps if your child is kidnapped:

1. **Call 911.**

2. **File a Missing Persons Report.**

   Take a copy of your custody order with you.

3. **Call your lawyer.**

   Your lawyer can help you obtain a felony warrant against your ex and file it with the *Federal Parent Locator Service,* a federal organization that can help you track your ex.

4. **Contact *Child Find* at 800-426-5678 (800-I-AM-LOST) or** www.childfindofamerica.org/.

   This non-profit charity locates missing children through active investigation. This organization also helps prevent child abduction through education and resolves incidents of parent abduction through mediation (CAPSS/Mediation).

5. **Call everyone you can think of who may know where your ex has taken your children.**

6. **Contact the media.**

   Furnish photos of your children and your ex and invite them to your home for a live interview.

7. **As a last resort, if you can afford it, hire a private investigator.**

One of the best ways to prevent a kidnapping is to resolve your differences with your ex now. If he feels the custody order is unfair, get together with a court-appointed mediator and renegotiate the agreement. If your ex is seeking revenge out of hatred and bitterness over the divorce, coax him into joint sessions with a family therapist who may be able to help both of you overcome your anger and bitterness.

Resolving problems with custodial interference

Custodial interference is anything a parent does to prevent the other parent from having access to the children. It can include

- ✔ Major problems, such as physically preventing a parent from entering the residence where the children live.

- ✔ Minor infractions, such as subtle forms of cutting off communication between the children and their other parent. For example, the parent with custody may destroy letters to the children from his ex, or he may refuse to let his children speak to his ex on the telephone or communicate via e-mail.

✔ Petty things, such as delaying the other parent's visit with the kids by making her wait in the car outside the home for two hours while the custodial parent *gets the kids ready for the visit!*

It can be very difficult to *prove* custodial interference; however, these are the two steps you can take to try to enforce your rights to have visits or shared custody with your children:

✔ Hire a lawyer to file legal paperwork requesting that your ex be found in *contempt of court.*

✔ Go to court to request that civil action be taken against your ex. This can include fines, jail sentence, or suspension of child support being paid by you to your ex.

Looking for co-parenting help in all the right places

Don't beat yourself up just because this co-parenting thing isn't coming easy for you. Studies show that it takes between one and three years to adjust to the role of co-parent. However, if you feel like your co-parenting conflicts are on the increase instead of the decrease, you may need to seek a little help.

You can find many professional therapists, counselors, and mediators out there ready to help you, if you give them a chance.

Participating in a little professional therapy

You may want to start by contacting a family therapist or joining a support group. Your therapy may be individual, one-on-one between you and the therapist, or with you and your ex meeting in joint sessions. It's possible that your therapist will recommend family therapy where your children are also in attendance. Chapter 14 has tons of information about therapists and what they offer.

Accepting the decision of a court-appointed mediator

A court-appointed mediator works with you to resolve your conflicts by improving your communication, modifying your co-parenting plan, or ordering a *child custody evaluation* from a mental health professional. During a child custody evaluation, the mental health professional interviews the child, both parents, teachers, and anyone else who may help determine what is best for the child. After conducting personal interviews and gathering other evidence, the mental health professional makes a recommendation to the court to determine the terms of the custody order.

Before seeking the help of a court-appointed mediator, you have the option of hiring a private mediator. Take a look at Chapter 3 for info about the advantages and disadvantages of hiring a private mediator, what one of these mediators can do for you, and how to find the services of a mediator.

Letting a co-parenting counselor help resolve your conflicts

If you tried professional therapy and a mediator, but you're still in serious conflict with your co-parent, your attorney can ask the court to appoint a professional co-parenting counselor who'll work with each of you to help reduce your conflicts and avoid any legal action.

Depending on your state and county, a co-parenting counselor may also be called a *special master, parenting coordinator, or family court advisor.* Whatever her title, she's a person who's appointed to act like a judge. This person may be a mental health professional, an attorney who's experienced with high-conflict divorces, or a retired judge with experience in counseling divorced parents who are having trouble getting along.

After she gathers information, she looks to the court for precedents that have been set in similar conflicts and makes a decision. After her decision is made, you'll be required to abide by the resulting order established by the court regarding sole or shared custody of your child. Court-appointed counselors differ from private practice marriage and family therapists in that they are appointed by the court (the latter is hired by you privately). A private practice therapist is often able to resolve conflicts between the parents so that the court doesn't need to get involved.

Part IV
Living Well Helps Your Kids Bloom, Too

The 5th Wave® By Rich Tennant

"I'm looking for someone who will love me for who I think I am."

In this part . . .

Did you know that by becoming a strong person, you also become a better parent? That's why it's so important for you to take good care of yourself. First of all, you're happier once you've shed that grief you've been carrying around for so long. Whether your grief is the result of death or divorce, you need to heal so that you can be strong for your kids. You also need to give yourself a pat on the back and treat yourself to the good stuff once in a while, including healthy exercise, a few new threads, and a little good, clean fun, without the kids! If you need professional therapy to help you heal and be happy again, why not go for it? Your goal is to become a whole, balanced, fulfilled individual, which will help you be the kind of single parent you really want to be.

Chapter 12

You Don't Get Healin' without Grievin'

In This Chapter

▶ Handling grief with dignity

▶ Understanding the stages of grief

▶ Clearing yourself of blame

▶ Making peace with the past

▶ Understanding your child's grief

*B*ecause you turned to this chapter, we know you're probably hurting and our hearts go out to you. The grieving process can be horrible — we know all about it! We've suffered through grief ourselves through the years, so we not only sympathize; we empathize!

Loving a person fully and completely brings great joy to your life, but it also places you at risk for indescribable pain and grief if you lose that person through death or divorce. This kind of loss breaks your heart. Unfortunately, none of us can escape this life without experiencing the grief that comes from a broken heart.

In spite of your grief and your pain, we want to reassure you that you can heal — it may take time, and a lot of tears, but you can experience joy and peace again. We want to walk down the path with you for a while with the hope that you can find some reassurance and comfort as you strive for inner peace and the strength to move on.

We hope this chapter helps you understand the grieving process. We tell you why it's good to shed healing tears and how to forgive yourself and let go of your anger and jealousy so you can be a whole, happy person again and a better parent for your kids. It's possible — we promise!

Grieving with Grace: Good Luck!

Losing your love — through death or divorce — is one of the most painful experiences a person ever faces. Whether you're grieving because of death or divorce, you can expect a lot of ups and downs and unexpected twists on the road to recovery. You may have heard the term *good grief* before and never paid much attention to it. We want you to think about it now. You see, good grief is not a contradiction in terms.

We know that you may be trying to survive by putting up a good front — acting as if you're okay — which might get you by for a while, but over time your act breaks down. If you continue to stuff your feelings, bury the pain, and bravely march along as if everything is just hunky-dory, we're here to tell you that you're creating roadblocks to your healing.

Grieving is a long uphill climb on a road cluttered with unexpected detours. The sound of a certain melody, a glimpse at a heart-tugging snapshot, or watching your toddler do something for the first time, can slay you. Special occasions like birthdays, holidays, and anniversaries may seem like insurmountable hurdles on this climb. See Chapter 11 for more information on handling these special days. And as you experience these detours, hang onto this thought: The cure for your emotional pain is joy.

We don't know you personally, so we can't understand the depths of your own unique pain and grief. We do know, however, that it's possible for you to reach deep down into the depths of your spirit and eventually heal yourself in a natural way through good grief. Yes, good grief can bring the joy back into your life.

Loss is a loss is *not* a loss

Being deprived of the person who was your mate and partner may feel as if you've lost part of yourself. No, your life will never be the same again. Because death is so irrevocable, you are forced to deal with it directly. Slowly over time you'll begin to feel acceptance and some peace of mind.

With divorce, your loss, your pain, your guilt, and your shame are in your face every time you drop off the kids at your ex's home and every time he shows up at your door to bring them back to you again. Contrary to what you may have read, divorce is not death, although it sure feels like it. The period of adjustment and acceptance may take longer with the road full of stumbling blocks and pitfalls. Your ex is alive and grieving, too.

Good grief includes:

✔ Fully acknowledging your loss.

✔ Allowing yourself to experience your feelings. Don't put the kibosh on sadness or anger.

✔ Reaching out for a little help from your friends. It's important to express your hurt and confusion with people who really care about you and your children.

✔ Letting your broken heart mend gradually. Don't rush yourself. Savor your memories and remember all the good times — these are part of the healing process.

Grieving is the way to finally heal and survive your loss. The problem is that no one can hand you a clear, concise map that shows you how to maneuver up that steep road. Knowing the stages of grief is about as close as you get to such a map.

Scaling Grief's Stages

Elizabeth Kubler-Ross, a small woman with a great big heart, is a noted psychiatrist who defined grief in an effort to help you face the five major stages that take place after a death. We think they apply equally well to that other big loss, divorce.

✔ Denial

✔ Anger

✔ Bargaining

✔ Depression

✔ Acceptance

It's normal to cycle through these stages several times or to experience a couple of stages at the same time. Or, you may get stuck in one of the stages for a period of time. Your emotions will go through many ups and downs — like a roller coaster. For example, one day you may react with numbness and denial, and the next day be as angry as can be. This is okay — you'll eventually make it through all the stages once and for all. The most important thing is to realize that you can't avoid grief — you need to travel *through it*. If you're having trouble traveling through it, you can benefit greatly by seeking professional counseling.

Shedding cleansing tears

Cry as much as you want, whenever and wherever you want, even if you're a man's man. Why shed those cleansing tears? Because tears are a natural result of mourning, and mourning is a universal response to death and other losses, large and small. To embrace your mourning is to be good to yourself. Pent up or stuffed down feelings only make you feel heavy and weighted down with sadness. Allowing some of those pent up emotions to come out in the form of tears is healing.

Have you ever gone to a movie, cried your eyes out, and walked out of the theater feeling strangely lighter? If you find that you can't cry for yourself without a little inspiration, rent a tearjerker movie and spend all afternoon crying. This is a great tension reliever and somewhere, halfway through the box of tissues, you may finally start crying for yourself! Good grief! Repeat this cleansing exercise as often as you need to.

Your kids need to cry too, so don't worry about hiding your tears from them. The more you cry together, the more comforted you'll all feel. Maybe an age-appropriate tearjerker movie, such as *The Yearling, Sounder,* or *Bambi* would be suitable for your family. Of course, all of you need private time to cry as well. Find those times for yourself and be respectful if your child needs them, too.

Relating the stages to death

Grieving is a unique experience, colored by your personal situation, the type of relationship you had with your loved one, and the special circumstances of your loved one's death. The pain and disruption will affect you physically, emotionally, mentally, and socially. You may be questioning your faith and asking questions about the meaning of life. You may even experience extra sensory perceptions, such as hearing, smelling, or sensing your loved one in the room. You aren't crazy! This is just a sign of how profoundly you are feeling the pain. We go over Kubler-Ross's stages in more detail to help you understand what you're going through.

Denial

Denial is the defense mechanism that kicks in to help you buy time until the dreaded reality sinks in. In the case of a sudden, unexpected death, denial is a natural reaction to the shocking trauma. Even if the death is expected, following a prolonged illness, for example, denial mercifully shields you for a while.

Denial is not a sign that you've lost it. It just means you need time to adjust to the fact that your life and the lives of your children can never be the same again. Your children will probably take even longer than you will to get through this stage. This explains why they can go out and play, watch TV, or spend time with friends. Let your kids react naturally, without any *shoulds*. It's okay — there's no right or wrong way to go about it.

Anger

Anger is a positive sign that you're on the path to healing. Anger brings energy, which results in action being taken; and energy and action are both good signs. If your partner died suddenly in an accident or as the result of a crime, you have all the right in the world to be angry. You may even be shocked at how much rage you feel.

Don't quell this natural expression of emotion. Finding safe ways to ventilate your pent-up energy may help. Now is the time to rely on your friends and family, who are undoubtedly experiencing their own feelings of rage and anger. Their anger may seem offensive to you. What right do they have to feel like you do? However, they are confused and their anger may be because they feel so badly for you.

If your partner died after a prolonged illness, some of your outrage may be related specifically to the pain and suffering your partner endured. Your feelings are justified because standing by and feeling helpless while your partner suffered was excruciating for you. You might be angry because you feel that when your partner died, he abandoned you. In fact, here's the universal question asked by widows and widowers: *"How could you leave me when I need you so much?"* If you're asking such questions, don't worry about whether they make sense. You're experiencing a common reaction to the death of your mate.

Bargaining

Here's a technique that helps you stall for time. Bargaining may take the form of a fervent wish or prayer that the whole thing has been a terrible mistake. Vowing to be a better person may be part of your bargain. In the morning when you first wake up, you may think all is well. Then the reality hits you and you realize that the bargaining isn't going to bring him back. Now you're facing hard reality and you're allowed — even encouraged — to wallow in your pain! In fact, you're not real sure you're ready to rejoin the human race!

Depression

Depression is the natural result of your trauma and pain. In order to get on with the grieving process, you must give in to your feelings. Let the waves of depression roll over you, because you're in mourning. Flaunt your depression — you've earned the right by surviving a terrible loss. You need people around you now, taking care of you while you temporarily give in to your grief.

If your depression feels dangerous (you're considering suicide or hurting yourself in other ways) or others say they're worried, please see the signs in Chapter 14 that you may need professional help. It may be more difficult for you to detect your children's depression. The cardinal sign of depression in children, up through the teenage years, is irritability. However, they aren't trying to be difficult — they're just so down that they don't know what to do.

Here are signs that your children may be entering a danger zone in their grieving (additional signs are listed at the end of Chapter 8):

- ✔ Sleeplessness.

- ✔ Weight loss that is rapid and significant.

- ✔ Complete withdrawal and isolation from friends.

- ✔ Lack of taking care of their hygiene and appearance.

- ✔ Expressing the wish to die and thinking about ways and means to do it.

If your child is experiencing these symptoms, don't wait — get help now! Call your local suicide or crisis line or call 800-784-2433, which is the National Hopeline Network, a suicide and crisis hotline. This line provides trained phone counselors 24 hours a day. Post this number on your refrigerator (it's also on this book's Cheat Sheet), along with your local suicide and crisis hotline telephone number. Also, contact a professional therapist for an appointment, or if you fear suicide is imminent, call 911.

Acceptance

Acceptance slowly slips in, finally bringing some needed relief in a strange kind of way. Acceptance may be elusive, coming in tiny increments. One day you feel pretty strong and able to cope. The next you're wallowing in self pity again. But that's okay — hey, you're allowed to wallow! You're on the road to survival.

One sign of acceptance is being able to sort through and make decisions about your loved one's clothes and personal belongings. This is a big step and you may want to have someone with you when you decide to go through his closet or the garage. Whoever you ask to help you will be flattered, because this is truly a sign of a trusting friendship.

Another sign of acceptance is when you find you can talk about your loved one without losing it and crying your head off. Don't be surprised if you can do this one day, but can't talk about it at all the next.

One day you'll wake up and see beauty in your world again: the slant of the sun on your back porch, or the peace of your sleeping child. Deep down inside you know you can survive. You're grateful to be alive and able to look to the future.

Relating the stages to divorce

Grieving the end of a marriage is a long uphill process that will be experienced differently by you and your ex. If you're the one initiating the divorce, you may have done a great deal of anticipatory grieving already. If you're the one who didn't want this to happen — the one who ignored the signs all along the way — your emotional turmoil will be a roller coaster ride of ups and downs.

Acknowledging your pain and loss, experiencing your true feelings, and remembering the good and bad may take the form of the grieving cycles we list. Just know that you may experience some of these cycles simultaneously, or ricochet back and forth, before you come to *acceptance*.

Every loss brings up other losses. This is normal, too, so relax and accept the fact that your life is like a river — and you can't hold it back or hurry it forward. Your grief will take as long as it takes, so accept the ebb and flow of your grief as part of your healing.

Denial

Denial is a way to buy a little time before the reality of the divorce sets in. In fact, denial may have been a ghost in your relationship for a long time before you decided to split.

When a couple has agonized over the question of separation and divorce, actually making the decision is sometimes a relief because it means they can finally get on with their lives. Meanwhile, to postpone the pain, they muck around in a state of denial. This state of denial is not intentional, but just another normal way to ward off the inevitable.

Anger

Anger is an emotion mutually shared, because neither partner wanted your marriage to end in divorce. Anger, however, is a positive sign because it means you're on the path to healing. After you get through mentally beating up your partner, you turn on yourself. You browbeat yourself for all the things you did and didn't do. All the *should haves* and *if onlys* can really drive you up the wall.

Try this paper exercise to see how you each shared in the demise of your relationship.

1. Write down all the ways your partner screwed up and contributed to the mess.

2. On the other half of the paper, take an honest inventory of all the things you didn't get right.

You can see that it took two to tango. Sharing the responsibility can tone down some of the anger you're feeling.

Bargaining

Bargaining is a stalling technique. You may try to bargain with or pressure your partner by promising to do all the housework, offering to move in with your mother-in-law, or ordering new furniture for the living room. On the other hand, maybe your bargaining included agreeing to two or three trial separations, each one followed by the real trial of trying to get back together.

This pattern can become exhausting. At some point you both agree to tear up the bargain and get on with the divorce — and the rest of your life.

Depression

Good old depression is the natural response to your disappointment and your lost dreams. Nobody who's touched by divorce can escape some degree of down-and-out depression. Even small children sense something is wrong.

ANECDOTE

Delayed grief rears its ugly head

Glenn's wife died suddenly in a car accident. The whole family rallied around as they all grieved together. Eleven family members accompanied Glenn to the funeral home to make the arrangements, but he was in such deep shock that he just went along with all the decisions. The funeral itself was a catharsis for Glenn's daughter and all the relatives. In fact, the rituals of death seemed to give everyone something to do and a reason to be together.

Within a couple of weeks, Glenn had taken care of all the legal stuff and his family kept congratulating him on how well he was doing. In fact, he seemed to be recovering so well that his parents took his daughter home with them for a vacation and Glenn returned to work.

A friend from college days named Margie had come to the funeral and started calling Glenn to see how she could help. Because everyone else seemed to have disappeared, he was grateful to her for being there. He was able to talk a lot about his wife, Shannon, and it felt really good. Before long their relationship had become a little more personal and within a month he was spending most of his spare time with Margie. When his daughter returned home, she also took comfort from Margie's warmth and caring.

Still, Glenn was irritable and moody. He tended to withdraw and cancel plans at the last minute. Margie was very understanding, but she was falling in love with him. She wanted the relationship to develop, and Glenn seemed to really like her.

One day Glenn woke up with a horrible sore throat. He stayed home from work feeling miserable and alone. He found a card that Shannon had written to him several weeks before the accident. It was full of love, hope, and playfulness. Glenn curled up on the floor in the fetal position, crying his head off. He was almost afraid because he'd never cried like this in his life. He wore himself out, crying for more than an hour. He got back in bed, propping the card up next to his bedside. Later that afternoon he felt strangely better. He even felt calm and relaxed.

When his daughter came home from school she could tell he had been crying so he showed her the card and they both had a good cry. Glenn realized that he had been blocking out his feelings by staying busy with his responsibilities and spending time with Margie. He hadn't taken time to acknowledge his loss and let himself experience the strong emotions he'd stuffed away in his heart.

He talked it over with Margie, letting her know how her kindness had helped them. He explained that he was not emotionally ready or able for a new relationship and that he needed more time to himself. She was very understanding and encouraged him to join a bereavement support group. Over the next several months, Glenn set aside some time every day to think about Shannon and to talk about her with his daughter. This brought them closer and helped them begin to heal.

Recognizing depression in yourself or your children is an important reminder that you have to take care of yourselves now. You may need the help of a true friend, a support group, or psychotherapy. Plenty of help is out there, but you've got to reach for it.

If you're considering suicide, injuring yourself, or neglecting your children, call 911 immediately. Chapter 14 details other signs that you may need professional help.

Acceptance

Finally, acceptance comes, but not without a heavy dose of humility and wisdom. Yes, you're sadder and wiser now, but you paid a price for this knowledge.

One sign of acceptance is that you're able to talk about your ex without breaking up in tears. Also, you're able to reflect on the good times — perhaps, tell a friend about a great family vacation you had one summer at Yellowstone, or the time your ex won the MVP award for the summer softball league.

Another sign of acceptance is that you're able to sort through any leftover clothing your ex left hanging in the back of your closet, or you're able to give away that bucket of practice golf balls stashed in the corner of the garage.

Finally, you'll realize you've accepted your loss when you wake up in the morning and, instead of a heavy heart, you look forward to the day with anticipation. Your life is now fuller and richer because you're a survivor! With acceptance, you can finally begin to restore balance to your life. A new beginning is yours!

Forgiving Yourself

Do you feel as if you're carrying the weight of the world on your shoulders? Are you obsessed with negative thoughts about the past? Your poor overworked brain generates two to three thousand random thoughts a day. Some of these thoughts can heal, but others can drag you down. You need to realize that you have the power to respond to your thoughts however you want. You can act on them or ignore them — it's your choice.

Your guilt may have you stuck in the bargaining stage of grieving, where you keep reliving those things you didn't do and should have, or those things you did do and wish you hadn't. Monitor your thinking to weed out the negative, critical self-talk and give yourself permission to close the chapter. That was *then* — this is *now*!

We want you to choose to react by nurturing yourself with loving kindness, compassion, and a sense of humor. In other words, you have the power to forgive yourself big time. This means letting go, accepting that you did your best, and that the past is over and done with.

So, how do you let go of the past, forgive yourself and move on with your life? The answer is simple: Eliminate these typical culprits that crop up after a divorce:

- ✔ If only I'd been more tuned into my partner's needs.
- ✔ If only I'd taken the time to be a better listener.
- ✔ If only I'd paid attention to my intuition when he was out every night.

Here are typical thoughts that may fill your head after your spouse has died:

- ✔ If only I hadn't encouraged him to take the new job that required more travel.
- ✔ If only I'd cooked healthier meals.
- ✔ If only I'd insisted that we get more exercise and go on more vacations.

You can probably fill a book with your regrets and lists of *if onlys*. However, think of it this way: All those *if onlys* are only thoughts and they're in your past. You can choose to ignore them, and that's exactly what we want you to do.

Here's an exercise that helps you eliminate *if onlys* and forgive yourself. Grab a piece of paper and write down every *if only* you can think of. Write them as quickly and furiously as you can — don't worry about spelling or punctuation. Just write and write until you can't think of any more. When you're done, keep the list handy so you can add to it every time any new self-sabotaging, negative thoughts raise their ugly little heads! You can also indulge in a little biofeedback by wearing an expansion bracelet or a heavy rubber band around your wrist. Every time you feel a negative *if only* thought coming on, give your wrist a snap. Soon you become more lighthearted and optimistic in your thinking — although you may have a sore wrist!

Journal writing is another very effective technique for getting your thoughts in order. Choose a journal that suits you. It can be a simple spiral notebook, or one of those attractive, hard cover books with blank pages. Be sure that no one else will ever see your writing. Keeping it private and personal allows you to write down anything that enters your mind. Writing something every day or so will help you to look back and see where you've been and the progress you've made dealing with your outrage at fate.

Encourage your older kids to try journaling, too. Of course, you need to reassure them that you'll never read their journals. Explain to them that a journal is like a diary that contains secret thoughts, and that it's a great relief to transfer secret thoughts from the brain to the written page.

Letting Go of Anger and Jealousy

Divorce is like a bed of hot coals, stirred up by two people who may be very explosive. One of the hot coals may be teeth-clenching anger and the other may be jealousy. In either case, you need a couple of asbestos potholders, along with a few practical ways to get rid of them for good!

Puttin' out the fire

You're burned and your ex doesn't seem to care. Feeling incredibly hurt and angry may be justified, but it isn't going to influence anyone but you. The first hurdle is to grasp the concept that it's over when it's over! How to put out that angry fire is a personal issue that shouldn't even involve your ex.

For example, what if your ex seems to be carrying on with her life just fine? She's out there dating and claims to love her new two-bedroom apartment. Meanwhile, she doesn't even notice that you're angry. You try to show her by not cooperating with the care and feeding of the children, but that isn't working either.

Your children come first and you must do whatever it takes to release the crippling anger that's stifling your energy. Don't make the children suffer because of your hurt feelings.

Here are a few suggestions: Go to the gym twice a day, talk to friends every evening, or plan a trip to Bora Bora. Pamper yourself in every way you can afford. Attend a divorce recovery workshop. Join a couple of single parenting groups or hook up with Parents Without Partners. Try to will yourself to release your rage and if you aren't getting anywhere, get some individual therapy. It may be the best investment you ever make.

The best revenge is to go on and have a happy life!

Washin' that ex right outta your hair

What if your ex is marrying the woman he left you for? You were sure that relationship would backfire and he'd get dumped. At least you hoped so. Now the kids are going to be in his wedding. You see green! This is the limit! The other woman's getting your husband and your kids. It feels like you've lost and she's won.

But stop and think for a minute — would you really want your ex back if you could have him? Would you want someone who would marry so fast on the rebound? The one thing you sure don't want him to know is that you're so jealous. No way! You wouldn't give him the satisfaction.

So, here's the bottom line: Plan a fun weekend away when that wedding date comes up! When things get tough, the tough get going — to the beach, preferably with friends. Pamper yourself, stay busy, and think up clever ways to wash that man right outta your hair!

Write down all the things that are making you jealous. Then shred the list! This may help get those jealous thoughts out of your head. Just think, now his new wife has to put up with his self-centered, egotistical, bad tempered, blah, blah, blah. One of the best ways to wash that man right outta your hair is to be gracious to your ex and kind to yourself. That way you rise above jealousy because it just isn't your style!

If all the willpower you can muster still doesn't quell these jealous feelings, consider getting some counseling. You may go to your pastor, or join a support group. Reach out for some support and new ways of thinking. If you still can't stop keeping score, see your own personal psychotherapist to help you get on with your new, happier life.

Grieving at Three Feet Tall

What could be more heart wrenching than telling a little kid that his father is gone? If you don't give him answers that he can understand, he makes them up. He may think he wasn't the kind of boy his daddy wanted. He may think he said bad words, or didn't eat all his peas, so Daddy died. He may think that God got angry with him and took Daddy away.

Unfortunately, in spite of all the good books and excellent bereavement support groups at churches, hospitals, and community centers, our culture still doesn't handle loss very well. It's a fact that the way you cope with your loss depends on your cultural background, the community you live in, and the amount of support you receive.

Not only are you handling your own grief, but you're helping your children deal with grief, too. Keep these things in mind while holding their hands:

- ✔ Answer questions about death or divorce at your child's level of understanding.

- ✔ Include your kids in all the activities centered on the illness and death that seem appropriate. Children need to experience this transition gradually, just as you do.

- ✔ Be prepared to answer his questions as he brings up memories or reminisces about his parent. A child's grieving may go on for years. This process is helpful to you, too.

The intricacies of loss

Many families are unaware of the resources available to help them through the heart-wrenching ordeal of death. Most large hospitals have cancer support groups for patients, their families, and for children. Hospice organizations are skilled at guiding the family through the ups and downs of a terminal illness.

We know of a young man who joined a bereavement support group to mourn the loss of the father he never knew. His father had been killed in Vietnam before he was born. The other members of the bereavement group warmly embraced his pain and they found they all had a lot in common.

You may think you're protecting your child by shutting her out or sheltering her from the grieving process, so she doesn't have to grieve at all. Not so! Shutting your child out means her grieving process takes longer than necessary and that she is forced to cope without your support.

Support groups for children and teens who have a sick parent are very effective in connecting kids with peer support. Teams of counselors are also available to make home visits expressly to offer compassionate care to children. If you need these services, we hope that you search until you find the care and support you deserve. We want you to find renewed faith and the courage to care for yourself, to ask for help, and to survive so you can look forward to a full and happy life ahead.

Chapter 13

Giving Yourself a Break Because You're Worth It

In This Chapter

▶ Patting yourself on the back

▶ Relaxing once in a while

▶ Getting into shape

▶ Nurturing your sense of humor

▶ Adopting a pet

▶ Treating yourself like royalty

Do you feel like you've just come home from war? Single parenting can be quite a battle, and you may be to the point where you're a real mess! You need to give yourself a break!

How about a little R and R plus a good laugh once in a while? And honestly, you might feel a lot better when you get yourself in shape physically and emotionally with a makeover, a few new threads, and some special treats. For example, when was the last time you indulged in a fun, just-for-the-heck-of-it daytrip to someplace interesting? Or how about splurging on a really nice dinner — you know, one that requires something a little dressier than jeans and a T-shirt? If extras are a stretch for your budget, you'll find great money-saving alternatives in Chapter 5.

However you happened to become a single parent — through adoption, divorce, death of your spouse, or maybe by sheer accident — you've survived a mega-battle. It's time for some pampering. You need to take a little time for yourself, because when you take care of yourself, you're a better parent.

If after reading this chapter, you still find that you just cannot seem to find time to take care of yourself, that can be a "red flag" indicating self-esteem issues, and you might benefit from working with a professional counselor to help you help yourself (and your children). You are the most valuable asset you have!

Cheering Yourself On

The time has come — yes, it has! Time to congratulate yourself for what you've endured and survived during your battle! Just take a look at everything you've accomplished in the last year or so! In fact, grab a legal pad and make a list of all the difficulties you've dealt with and all the awesome ways you've coped with the enemy. The enemy, in your case, may have been the courts, your ex, or even your own friends and family members who criticized the way you handled your crises. Or the enemy may simply be having too much to do and not enough time in which to do it!

Well, to heck with that! You deserve a lot of praise and a pat on the back, along with a little self-nurturing. After all, you've been worrying over everything these last few months, and now it's time to nurture yourself. Don't be like so many single parents who feel they're being selfish when they give themselves a break. You're not being selfish! In fact, unless you fill your well, it can run dry and you don't have anything left for all those who are making demands on you — your kids, your boss, your parents, or even your ex.

Practice saying to yourself

- ✔ I'm a good person.
- ✔ I'm a wonderful, loving parent and I'm doing an awesome job raising my kids alone.
- ✔ I'm a fun-loving person with a great sense of humor.
- ✔ I'm an honest, trustworthy person.
- ✔ I'm a reliable person — I keep my word.
- ✔ I'm a darned good cook.
- ✔ I'm an excellent employee.
- ✔ I'm a dependable, caring friend.
- ✔ I definitely deserve a pat on the back!

Get this indelibly ingrained in your head — you can't be everything to everyone every minute of every day! And when you keep trying, you only make yourself sick. Take care of yourself first, then if you have anything left over — that's what you draw from to be everybody's everything!

It's not your responsibility to make everyone you know feel good and happy. That's just too much responsibility for one person! Give yourself a break and give yourself the gift of self-esteem — something no one else is equipped to provide for you. And don't feel like a selfish person when you treat yourself the way you deserve to be treated.

Putting Your Feet Up

If you're like most single parents, you're constantly on the run, trying to get here, get there, and get everywhere to do the next thing on your list! Listen, you've got to relax by indulging in the simple pleasures, such as regular massages, hot bubble baths, and stretching your body like a cat. Set aside days that can be spent doing things that are pleasing for you, and if you're having trouble freeing up time for yourself, see Chapter 4 for some time-saving tips. The key is to give yourself permission to put your feet up and kick back once in a while.

Pamper yourself with these relaxing pleasures:

✔ **Deep, hot bubble baths:** Take the phone off the hook, place lighted candles around your tub, play your favorite instrumental music, turn off the lights, and sink into a healing, relaxing pool of pleasure. Close your eyes and stay in that tub until the water begins to cool. When you're all done, give yourself a rubdown with a terrycloth towel, stretch out nude on your bed for 15 minutes and you'll feel relaxed and revived. We suspect the single dads may pass on the scented candles, but maybe not. Who's going to know what you do in that tub?

Instead of a bubble bath, add essential oils to the water for some aromatherapy. Visit your favorite bath-and-body shop to find a wide selection of aromatic oils. You can find oils for practically anything that ails you, including lavender and tangerine oils to relax your sore muscles, ylang-ylang and lavender oils to relieve jet lag, and chamomile and orange blossom oils to help you sleep.

✔ **Regular professional massages:** Any massage is beneficial — even an upper body treatment. You may be surprised how much tension can be worked out of your muscles in only 30 minutes. Here's a money-saving tip: Visit a massage school that offers affordable student massages. The cost will run about half that of a professional.

✔ **Stretching:** Whether you're at work or running errands with the kids, stop every once in a while and — *stretch!* Pretend you're a sleepy cat and stretch your limbs over your head. Roll your neck around, scrunch up your shoulders for 10 or 15 seconds, and then release them as you breathe deeply. These simple breaks can relax and revive you to an amazing degree.

✔ **Saying no:** Don't say yes to everyone! You may feel stressed because you can't say "no." By saying "no" to demands on your time, you give yourself a great gift. Many single parents have found it helpful to write the word "NO" in black letters on their calendar/day planner. Then, when asked for some commitment, the "no" reminds them to take care of themselves.

✔ **A healthy diet:** Drink less caffeine and eat more complex carbohydrates. A little caffeine is okay, but too much can make you jittery and anxious, so try cutting down a little. Instead, eat more whole grains, beans, seeds, nuts, fruits, and vegetables. These complex carbohydrates have a calming effect because they increase levels of serotonin, a chemical in your brain that induces relaxation.

✔ **Experience the moment:** Start making time for all those little daily experiences that you let pass by because you don't take time to enjoy them. Most people tend to rush through daily life, looking forward to a vacation day or some distant chance to finally relax — tomorrow, or maybe next week. Try enjoying something wonderful today!

✔ **Progressive muscle relaxation:** Progressive muscle relaxation is a proven way to remove tension from a person's neck, shoulders, back, arms, legs, and torso. This relaxation exercise is being taught to stressed-out employees, teachers, law officers, and anyone else who tends to tighten up when under stress. You can benefit from it as well by following these simple steps:

   1. Turn off the lights, pull the shades, and play soft instrumental music.

   2. Sit in a chair or lie flat and close your eyes; get ready to relax every part of your body.

   3. Start with your feet. With your eyes still closed, take in a deep breath and hold it while you scrunch your feet up tight.

   4. Hold your breath to the count of 30 and release your breath as you slowly release your feet.

   5. As you inhale, imagine that you're breathing in joy and contentment.

   6. As you release your breath, envision releasing the muscle tension, letting it escape from your body as you exhale.

   Repeat this process for the rest of your body: your calves, your thighs, your buttocks, your tummy, your hands, your arms, your shoulders, your face, and your scalp. When you get to your face, grimace as hard as you can, squinting your eyes tight, gritting your teeth, and tightening your neck. Now, as you exhale, slowly relax your neck, face, and scalp. The end result is allover relaxation.

✔ **Soothing music:** Create your own personalized cassette tapes or CDs, and listen to your favorite music with a headset even while you're taking care of mundane chores. Music affects the major systems of your body, increases blood circulation to your brain, and can even lower your blood pressure. Music can stimulate or relax you, depending on the type of music you choose. When you're tense after a hectic day, listen to the most relaxing music possible.

✔ **Visualization:** Think of a place or an experience that makes you feel calm and happy. Maybe it's a deserted white sand beach on a warm summer's day where you picture yourself walking barefoot along the shoreline without a care in the world, or perhaps you recreate the beauty of the drive you took last fall along Route 176 where the trees were turning a riot of reds, rusts, and burnt oranges. Picture yourself wherever you feel peaceful and relaxed. Some people call it their *happy place,* but whatever you call it, enjoy this great escape when it's quiet around the house.

Involve your senses in your visualization. Taste the saltiness in the air as you walk along the ocean; listen to the sea gulls call to each other across the sky; smell the seaweed that has washed ashore; and feel the sand crystals as they massage your bare feet. See how it works?

✔ **Join a yoga, T'ai Chi, or Qigong class:** Yoga combines muscle-relaxing stretches with deep breathing. T'ai Chi and Qigong involve slow, deliberate body movements that are excellent tension relievers. If you don't have time to attend classes, pick up a yoga video and enjoy the soothing exercises at home. Practice T'ai Chi and Qigong in a classroom under the supervision of a live instructor.

These relaxation techniques work best when your kids aren't at home. If you and the kids seem to be joined at the hip and you never break free of your parenting responsibilities, figure out a way to have some alone time. What about asking Grandpa to take the kids bowling for the afternoon? Or, trading playtime with another parent? When you need a break, leave your children at your friend's home for a few hours while you pamper yourself, then the next weekend take her children for a while so she gets a break. If you don't make this thing work, you never get off the hamster wheel. Ten years from now you'll still be going around and around!

Simple pleasures

What daily experiences do you let pass by? Well, how about the beauty of a double rainbow? How many chances do you and your kids get to pull off on a side road, turn off the car radio, and just stare at such a rare phenomenon? Or how about that box full of puppies for sale by owner in front of the grocery store? Are you really in such a rush that you don't have time to squat down and pet their soft little heads? A simple walk through the neighborhood can also provide precious opportunities to stop and experience the moment. For example, what about those exquisite lilac bushes spilling over your neighbor's wall? Why not take the time to inhale their healing, uplifting fragrance?

We miss so many little pleasures throughout our busy days because we don't take the time to experience the moment. Give it a try — this amazing awareness helps you relax and get through each day. This is also a wonderful technique to teach your kids!

Staying Fit and Frisky

Staying fit and frisky means maintaining a healthy weight and starting an exercise program. If you've been totally overwhelmed with your single parenting responsibilities, you may have said the heck with the weight thing — eat anything that brings comfort for the moment! And as for exercise, you're asking, "Yeah, exactly when am I supposed to find time for exercise?"

Well, in spite of your schedule, you can get down to a healthy weight and you can find time to exercise. Why is this important? Because you'll feel better physically, mentally, and emotionally. Being overweight is bad for your self-esteem and your energy levels, while lack of exercise makes you feel tired and lethargic, with very little endurance when you really want to sightsee on vacation or go bicycling with your kids on the weekend.

If you're one of those people who sees dieting and exercising as punishment, think of it as striving for a healthy lifestyle, which has countless rewards. The rewards are key to the *new you*.

Weighing in on health

Did you know that the majority of Americans aren't happy with their bodies? We think we're too thin, too fat, too plain, or too something! And unfortunately, with our national trend toward overeating, many of us actually are overweight.

If obesity is your problem, give yourself the great gift of weight loss. But don't go on a crash diet or set unreasonable goals for yourself! You need a healthy, consistent dietary plan instead. Before you jump on any of the fad diets, find a better way to lose the weight — and keep it off. Studies show that people who lose weight super quickly tend to put it back on at the same rate. And after all, even if you only lose one or two pounds a week (which is the maximum recommended), that's between 50 and 100 pounds in a year, which may be more than you need to lose in the first place. So, take it slow and steady. Whatever weight control program you use, combine it with some kind of daily exercise.

Here are a few intelligent choices:

- ✔ **Put yourself on your own program of eating less and exercising more.** Cut down on your food portions and get into a daily exercise routine. Check out www.WebMD.com for weight loss resources.

- ✔ **Go to your doctor and ask for a little help.** He may be able to set you up with weekly visits to a certified dietary nutritionist who can analyze your life style, calculate your body mass index (BMI), and come up with a healthy, effective eating plan customized just for you. You may be pleasantly surprised to find that these visits are even covered by your health insurance.

✔ **Join a balanced, healthy weight control program, such as Weight Watchers.** Weight Watchers is now available over the Internet if you don't have time to attend weekly meetings (though studies prove attending meetings results in success). For a reasonable fee, you can follow a given program and *weigh in* with them on weekly Web site visits. Check out www.weightwatchers.com. They also help you determine your healthy weight range.

Many personal trainers say that you shouldn't worry as much about your weight as the shape and condition of your body. In other words, if you eat a healthy low-calorie, low-fat diet in addition to a regular weight lifting and exercise program, your muscles may build to the point where you actually gain weight, but your clothes fit better.

So, instead of setting some ridiculously low weight you're determined to reach, strive instead to be able to fit into the size clothes you have in mind — maybe all those cool outfits you crammed into the back of your closet because they're too tight around the waist? Well, shake them out and hang them where you can see them every day and make it your goal to be able to fit into them again — to heck with being super thin. And even if you never get into your *skinny clothes,* the most important thing is to be healthy and happy, and feel good about yourself.

Don't forget to carry the 2

BMI is your *Body Mass Index,* a point value determined by measuring the ratio of your weight and height. It is considered to be one of the most accurate ways to determine whether or not an adult is overweight.

BMI can be calculated in two ways:

1. Divide your weight (in kilograms) by your height (in meters, squared).

2. Multiply your weight (in pounds) by 705, then divide by height (in inches) twice.

If this seems a little too complicated for you, go to Weight Watcher's Web site and click on the BMI hyperlink on the home page. This will take you to an easy fill-in-the blanks form that calculates your BMI automatically.

Members of the medical profession don't precisely agree on when a BMI calculation is considered to be underweight, healthy, overweight, or obese. However, here are general determinations:

✔ Less than 18.5 is considered underweight.

✔ 18.5 – 24.9 is considered healthy.

✔ 25 – 29.9 is considered overweight.

✔ Over 30 is considered obese.

Getting off your rump

You need to *move* every day, if only for your mental and emotional health. But if you're trying to lose weight, an exercise program is a must. Now, when we say exercise we don't necessarily mean working out at a pricey sports complex or having to set up an expensive home gym.

Consult your doctor before starting any exercise routine.

Here are some painless, affordable ways to get at least 30 minutes of exercise every day:

- ✔ Walk at about 3.5 miles per hour for half an hour.
- ✔ Swim — even if the pool isn't large, you can still swim steady laps from one side of the pool to the other for 30 minutes without stopping.
- ✔ Work out at home with an aerobics video.
- ✔ Shoot hoops or bang a tennis ball against a wall for 30 minutes straight.
- ✔ Bicycle or roller skate around the neighborhood with your kids for a half hour every evening after dinner.
- ✔ Combine 30 minutes of vacuuming, gardening, or climbing the stairs to your office instead of taking the elevator.

If you're a single mom, you may think that when a woman lifts weights she ends up with big, bulky muscles — but this isn't true! If you work out with weights on a conservative program, you build some muscle, all right, but that's exactly what you need to tone your body and maintain weight loss. You see, muscle tissue burns more calories each day than fat does, so after you develop a little more muscle, you burn more calories without even trying. In fact, strength training revs up your metabolism, which helps you lose weight quicker and maintain your loss.

Acting Like a Kid

Did you know that when you laugh your body secretes biochemicals that serve as antidepressants? (See Chapter 14 for more about that topic.) A big uninhibited belly laugh can do wonders when you're feeling tense or depressed, because laughter makes you breathe deeper, lowers your blood pressure, and releases endorphins, which stimulate the pleasure centers of your brain. Laughter also cuts down on the production of stress hormones from your adrenal glands.

So, how about acting silly once in a while? You know, something beyond your normal worry-worry-busy-busy self? Hang around funny people and avoid gloom and doom! Right now, you need as much humor in your life as you can get.

Ditch the serious stuff — like the evening news and the latest terrorist threats — and watch for humorous moments. For example, buy a Far Side desk calendar and read a page a day, watch Comedy Central on cable TV, rent a funny movie, attend a comedy club, or just try to see the humor in your day-to-day activities.

We know you're around kids all day long, and kids can be hilarious — you just have to appreciate their humor before it slips by unnoticed. For example, when your one-year-old smears red gelatin all over his face, then grins because he knows he looks adorable, why not smile, grab the camera, and take a photo for his baby book instead of coming unglued and running for a wet towel? Or, how about laughing out loud when your toddler makes a mad dash for the bathroom as he holds himself and cries, "Mommy, Mommy my tinkler needs to tinkle quick!" Kids do say the funniest things, and you can enjoy them if you just loosen up long enough to give your funny bone a chance!

When was the last time you played hide-and-seek with your kids after dark?

Getting a Fuzzy Buddy: Pets

If you don't own a pet, now might be a good time for a trip to your local animal shelter. Why? Because studies show that being around a pet helps reduce stress and can even add years to your life!

Of course, before adopting a pet you need to have the room for him, plus enough money in your budget to pay for his care. If you can manage a pet, go for it!

A pet enriches your life. A dog, for example, is always happy to see you at the end of a long, discouraging day. Even if you're in a super-grouchy mood, he doesn't care. He just wags his tail, licks your hand, and cuddles. You see, your puppy loves you unconditionally and as you stroke his fur, his love travels right up your arm and into your heart. An unconditional love relationship — such a deal!

Think twice before taking on a puppy or kitten because they require so much care and can't be left alone in the house for long. You might want to consider a full-grown, housebroken dog or a full-sized cat that knows how to use a litter box. Or, if the idea of a dog or cat totally blows your mind right now, with all your other responsibilities, how about a nice, quiet, self-contained fish? It's relaxing to watch fish swim around a home aquarium.

If you're in a no-pets-allowed apartment, or you just don't want the responsibility of caring for a pet, you can still benefit by borrowing a pet. You can offer to pet-sit for your friend's cat or dog while she's on vacation, or you can even borrow a pet for the day. Your local animal shelter may be delighted to let one of their pets spend a lonely holiday weekend with you — just ask! And besides, walking a dog in the park is a great way to meet people. Pet-lovers have an affinity for each other and, suddenly, you become approachable!

Giving Yourself Some Goodies

If you're the typical single parent, you've been spending all your time, money, and energy on your kids. Of course, you've been do-do-doing what your kids want to do, and go-go-going where your kids want to go for a long time! Admirable! But now is the time to treat yourself to a few of those pleasures you've been deprived of for so long. Try out some grown-up treats, including classy evenings on the town and a relaxing daytrip once in a while.

Pick up a few of your favorites at the grocery store for a change, instead of all those animal crackers and ice cream! And how about your appearance? You deserve a few new duds, a makeover, and a stylish new hairstyle.

Stocking up on yummy foods

Why do you bypass those special treats you used to keep on hand before you became a single parent? What rule says you must always shop wisely and prudently, making your money stretch as you pass by your favorite snacks to pick up your kids' favorite foods? You deserve a few gourmet treats once in while, too.

What's your thing? Chocolate éclairs? Well, why not once in a while? Or, how about that live lobster scratching around inside the freshwater tank at your local seafood market? Can't you splurge once in a while and boil up Mr. Claws for that special, melt-in-your-mouth meal?

Buying a few new threads

We don't care how *classic* your present wardrobe is, you still need a few new threads — just for the glow of it! Nothing feels quite so good as a few new outfits that not only fit and flatter, but are also in style for a change.

We know that some of you can't afford to spend money on new clothes for yourself. But even on a tight budget you can usually spruce up your closet with a few accessories, a new tie, or by coordinating pieces to bring an existing outfit up to date.

Watch for sales, of course, but don't be above shopping at some of the finer consignment stores. Ask around and check out your yellow pages, to find one of the many resale shops that feature name brand clothing. Pretend you're a fashion coordinator as you pull a Chaus jacket off one rack, a pair of coordinating Gloria Vanderbilt slacks off another, and combine them with a Liz silk shell. We've been fooling our friends with these types of purchases for years, and you can do it, too! Most of these resale stores also carry name brand clothing for men so all you single dads should take advantage of them, too.

Going in for that makeover

How about a makeover? If you can afford it, indulge in a day at the spa — complete with manicure, pedicure, a fresh new hairstyle, and a new face. If you can't afford a day at the spa — and oh, how we hope you can save up the money somehow — go for it in small doses. For example, make an appointment with an affordable hairstylist for a makeover-do. If you can't afford an expensive salon, you can still get the results you want if you bring in a photo or magazine picture with the style and color you're hoping for. And yes, single dads, even men can have their hair styled and colored. So, go for it!

The most economical way to have a new face is to take advantage of the free makeovers provided at the cosmetic counters in major department stores. Even though you may not be able to afford their cosmetics, you can still have your face made over, and then try to copy the effect with less expensive cosmetics from your favorite drug store.

Adults only: Dinner and a movie

You've probably seen enough Disney movies with your kids to last a lifetime, and now you're ready for some grown-up entertainment. Grab a friend — another single parent, your cousin, your neighbor, or a member of your support group — and have a dress-nice-look-fabulous evening once in a while.

What's your favorite thing? Dinner at the Four Seasons followed by an evening at a live theater performance? Or, have you been deprived of big-people-entertainment for so long that something as simple as Mexican food and a visit to a comedy club sounds like giddy delight?

The key is to have a social life away from your kids. We know your kids are a lot of fun, but you need a night out to be your own person.

Taking a daytrip

Take a day off now and then for some grown-up fun, without the kids. Run away from home with a friend, or spend the day all by yourself!

Taking time for yourself gives you a chance to ponder, reflect, and take stock of your life. This restful interlude revives you and makes it easier for you to cope with your single-parenting responsibilities when you get back home. The important thing is to plan these escapes and actually take them!

Depending on your interests, you may enjoy a day poking around a ghost town, hiking through a canyon, or taking in a professional ballgame. If you're divorced and your co-parent has custody of the kids every other weekend, devote your free weekends to such pleasures as a camping trip or a stay at a bed-and-breakfast on the ocean.

ANECDOTE

Lisa reaches out

Lisa was a devoted mother. In fact, her son was the center of her universe. She had a challenging job as a public health nurse, but she was completely drained by the end of each workday. Even though she was exhausted, she always prepared dinner for herself and her son, Tommy, then helped him with his homework. Every other weekend Tommy went to stay with his dad's new family. He liked his stepbrother, and Lisa was glad that he looked forward to his weekends away, but she always felt a bit hurt and lonely on her weekends off.

Going to her first single women's group was an eye opener for Lisa. She had always assumed that most single moms spent all their time and energy on the kids. However, she found that the women in her new group were on the go and doing things she had never dreamed of. Lisa didn't dance and she even felt shy and out of place at potlucks. Gradually, Lisa opened up and began making friends with the other women. Soon her new buddies were insisting that Lisa go out to dinner and even attend a Thursday night dance class.

Because of all these new activities, Lisa had to hire a babysitter for the very first time, which was so frightening for her that she phoned home every hour. Actually, Tommy liked the babysitter and teased his Mom into going out more often. Lisa slowly realized that she needed to do some things on her own. The Halloween Dance was the first big challenge. All the women in her group were going and they wouldn't hear of Lisa bailing out. She had a great time in disguise — and even met a couple of nice guys!

Lisa's transformation was complete when three of the women from the support group invited her to go with them on a single's trip to Mexico. She talked it over with her ex, who agreed to have Tommy stay with him for the seven days Lisa was away. When she returned from the trip, she told the group that she felt like a brand new person. She missed her son while she was gone, but didn't worry about him. She was actually able to enjoy a real vacation for the first time in her life.

Chapter 14

Therapy Isn't Just for the Rich and Famous

. . . .

In This Chapter

▶ Realizing you may need help

▶ Finding out about therapy

▶ Joining a support group

. . . .

*W*hen you think about professional therapy, what comes to mind? Do you envision a celebrity, jewel-collared poodle in tow, emerging from her private limo as she arrives for her weekly session with her shrink? And how do you picture the shrink? A balding, brooding guru with a salt-and-pepper goatee who knows everything, says nothing, and makes you suffer as you spill your guts? And finally, how about the image of a *shrink,* which conjures up thoughts of voodoo and shrunken heads suspended from the ceiling? Now that's creepy!

Unfortunately, these stereotypical images of psychotherapy have been impressed into our brains by television and movies.

In the real world of the twenty-first century, however, psychotherapy is a wonderfully healing science that's now available for all of us — whether we're rich or poor, famous or unknown. Psychotherapy is the treatment of mental and emotional disorders through encouraging communication of conflicts, and insights into those problems. Because many health insurance providers pay for psychotherapy, and because low-cost and no-cost clinics are available to those of us who are definitely not rich and famous, therapy has become affordable and available to everyone in the United States. Therapy patients are often everyday people who just need a little help overcoming those times when they're temporarily off track and need to get their lives back on track.

Today's therapists are ordinary human beings, and most of them are warm, approachable, easy to talk to, and dedicated to helping people feel better about themselves. In addition, contrary to the stereotypical image, a therapist probably has a sense of humor. He meets you where you are, with no preconceived expectations about you; he does *not* sit in judgment, but listens to you, accepts you, and talks with you. He's on your side all the way — you have a need and he's there to help.

In this chapter we help you get a handle on what psychotherapy is and how it can help you. Look for self-tests to diagnose depression, anxiety, and to see how well you're handling the transitions in your life. We take a look at a quickie cram-course on the different types of therapists and what all those fancy titles stand for. We also consider mental health insurance and other payment options.

Facing Facts: You May Need Help

Many single parents just muddle along in their misery, hoping to wake up some morning to a brighter day where they feel good and everything's right side up in their world for a change. Oh, that it were that easy! Unfortunately, hoping doesn't always cut it. You may need to replace *hope* with *action.*

Before you can take action, however, you need to recognize your needs. Following are four signs that you could use some help. You may recognize signs of depression or anxiety in your life, or you may realize you're not transitioning well. You may also acknowledge subtle hints being dropped by family and friends. Take a look and see how many signs you recognize in your life.

Recognizing signs of depression

You may be suffering from major depression and not even know it. Until you recognize the signs, you won't seek out the professional therapy that can help you recover. Do you identify with any of the following feelings or behaviors?

✔ **Getting out of bed and making it to work takes all the willpower you can muster.** Your feet are encased in cement shoes. You're up to your hips in quick sand. Your world looks gray.

✔ **All anyone needs to do is look at you sideways or say a kind word and you burst into tears.** You cry in front of your kids and coworkers alike. You just can't control the tears.

✔ **The face staring back at you in the mirror is unrecognizable.** The dull eyes and frozen gloomy mask are foreign to you. When you force a fake smile, you're afraid your face may crack.

✔ **Nothing gives you pleasure anymore.** Even though you're an avid reader, you can't read more than a paragraph or two without forgetting what you just read. Golfers don't show up for a tee time much less hit a ball. Even spiritual folks can't say a prayer to ask for help. In fact, nothing and nobody can rouse you out of your isolated cocoon.

✔ **You can't eat because you have a big lump in your throat.** You also forget to eat because you don't recognize when you're hungry. You aren't even tempted by your favorite dark chocolate treats. Or, on the other hand, maybe you can't *stop* eating and you've gained so much weight that you have nothing to wear but a seedy old jogging suit.

✔ **Sleeping is an ordeal.** First, you can't get to sleep. You toss and turn for hours. You turn on the TV. You try to read something boring. Or, you go to sleep exhausted, only to awaken between 2 and 4 a.m. with your mind on fire. You have scary thoughts of remorse and revenge. Finally, you fall asleep and the alarm goes off. Nighttime is torture for you!

Or, on the other hand, you find that sleep is the answer to all your problems. You don't go out to lunch during your workday. Instead, you sleep in the employee lounge for an hour. You drag yourself home to get in a nap before the kids need some dinner. You go back to bed with a book you only pretend to read. You get up to brush your teeth and then climb back into bed and sleep through the alarm the next morning.

✔ **Your get-up-and-go got up and went.** You don't have the energy to feed the cat, let alone your kids. Catatonic is a descriptive word for your lack of energy and motivation. You seem to be "stuck," and reading books and getting good advice doesn't help.

✔ **Your nerves are frayed.** You have a short fuse and it takes very little to anger you. The sparks fly for no reason. In fact, you'd probably snap at the messenger who comes to your door to tell you that you're the next Reader's Digest millionaire.

And you can't stop the whirlwind of frantic activity. You're a human dynamo, performing every chore meticulously. All the while you're chattering away at a frantic pace. You're barely aware that your kids and coworkers have a glazed look on their faces as they try their best to stay out of your path.

✔ **You can't think or make a decision.** You open the fridge door and then can't remember what you're looking for. You notice that your car keys are sitting on top of a container of yogurt. The thought crosses your mind that you probably should ask for help, but you don't even know what it is you need help with.

> ✔ **You're really down on yourself.** You can't think of one positive quality or one good thing you've ever done. You're loaded down with guilt, self-criticism, and a pervasive sense of worthlessness. Harboring very dark thoughts of regret or revenge, you think about escaping from life. It's just too hard.

If you have thoughts about killing or hurting yourself, immediately call 911 or 800-784-2433, which is the National Hopeline Network, a suicide and crisis hotline. This line provides trained phone counselors 24 hours a day. Post this number on your refrigerator (it's on this book's Cheat Sheet), along with your local suicide and crisis hotline telephone number. Carry these numbers in your wallet if you feel vulnerable.

If you answered yes to five or more of these symptoms and they have lasted at least two weeks without relief, you may be experiencing *major depression*. Most people feel some or all of these things at one point. The key to depression is consistency; if you feel terrible more often then not then you need a little help, and we know how to steer you to just the help you need and deserve.

An important thing for you to know up front is that just because you're feeling depressed does *not* mean you're crazy or having a nervous breakdown. In fact, those two terms don't even appear in the *DSM IV,* a book that mental health professionals use to help them diagnose different mental conditions.

You're reacting to the confusion of going through the divorce or death of your partner, and these reactions are known as *adjustment disorders with depression and/or anxiety.* That sounds a lot better than *crazy,* doesn't it? In fact, isn't it normal and logical to have a mood change and feel depressed when something so devastating happens? Your depression is a sign of appropriate and necessary adjustment to very stressful circumstances in your life. The good news is that this response doesn't last forever and is not the same as *chronic, internalized depression.*

If you're feeling down, we're so sorry you're suffering, but the prognosis is good — if you seek the help of professionals and get a little support from your friends.

Recognizing signs of anxiety disorders

Anxiety is a state of intense, often disabling, apprehension, uncertainty, and fear caused by the anticipation of something threatening. It's the flip side of the depression coin and recovery may require the help of a professional therapist. Take this self-test to see whether anxiety may be your problem:

✔ Are you nervous as a cat in a roomful of rocking chairs?

✔ Are you restless and jumpy?

✔ Are you so stressed out and tense that your body is as tight as a corkscrew?

✔ Are you so irritable that you can't even stand yourself?

✔ Do you have butterflies in your stomach?

✔ Do you have constipation, followed by diarrhea?

✔ Do your thoughts race around your head to the point where you can't concentrate on the business at hand?

✔ Do your knees turn to jelly and do you have visible shakes?

✔ Do you sometimes wonder whether you're about to lose control? Crack up? Or, go crazy?

✔ Does your heart pound?

✔ Are your throat and chest tight?

✔ Are your hands tingling, cold, and clammy?

✔ Do you think you're going to choke?

✔ Do you sometimes feel strangely detached from your body?

✔ Do you wonder whether you're dying?

The last six symptoms are signs of anxiety or panic attack. They're *not* life threatening, but they *are* pretty upsetting! These problems are actually quite common and can be helped. Make an appointment with a professional therapist to get a little help *now!*

If you answer yes to five or more of these symptoms that recur over a two-week period, you have an anxiety disorder. This is easily treated and you can recover completely. Making an appointment with a professional is the first step.

You may find that your therapist wants to know a great deal about you that you have never even considered important. Candidly talking about your worst fears, how anxiety is affecting your body, and your coping skills may seem difficult at first. Your ability to disclose your feelings depends on how comfortable you are with the therapist. It usually takes two or three sessions to begin to feel some trust and to feel comfortable talking openly. Remember that while you may feel better after one or two appointments, your anxiety won't magically go away without some hard work.

Therapists use a variety of techniques that are tailored to your particular needs. They often help you identify that negative, self critical, self-doubting inner voice and to talk yourself out of self-defeating ways of thinking.

You and your therapist may decide that you could also use some help in the form of medication. A psychiatrist is the expert in medication for treatment of depression and anxiety. She may prescribe medication to be taken routinely every day or as needed. Ask a lot of questions and remember that it's your choice to try medication.

Transitioning: How well are you doing?

You may be having a hard time adjusting to recent events in your life. Do any of the symptoms below sound familiar? If so, you're probably experiencing significant emotional pain and can use a little professional help to get you through this time.

Here are a few symptoms that indicate you may need assistance:

- ✔ Your partner died a year ago, but you still feel overwhelmed with grief and aren't coping very well at all.
- ✔ Your divorce is signed and sealed, but you can't get her out of your mind.
- ✔ Your mind is cluttered with thoughts of how to get him back.
- ✔ You respond excessively and angrily to the wrong triggers.
- ✔ You worry that something is terribly wrong with you and that you'll never have a good relationship.
- ✔ You avoid friends and phone calls and invent excuses to stay home and feel lonely.
- ✔ You suspect people are talking about you behind your back.
- ✔ You begin to overindulge in alcohol, drugs, or food to calm your nerves.

Recognizing subtle hints from friends and family

Your friends and family members care about you. Some may come straight out and say they're worried about you and ask if you need any help, but many people are sensitive to your need for privacy and recuperation time. They may be dropping subtle hints that they're concerned.

See whether any of these caring acts sound familiar:

✔ Your daughter nags you to go swimming with her or to the mall for a little retail therapy. You notice that she comes up with these escape plans on a daily basis.

✔ Your teenage son gets your attention when he actually offers to go with you to the library!

✔ Your mom continually brings you casseroles and bakes your favorite cookies.

✔ Your dad takes you aside to ask whether you need a little money to tide you over. Of course, it's natural for him to be concerned about your finances immediately following the divorce or death of your spouse, but if he's still concerned six months or a year later, that may be a sign that he's worried about your ability to transition through your loss.

✔ Your coworkers invite you out to lunch, probing you with questions about what you did over the weekend. They make comments such as, "Do you think you need to get a complete physical and have your hormonal levels checked?"

✔ Your well-meaning friends try to encourage you with stories of other widows and widowers who had it even worse than you, but who recuperated much more quickly!

✔ Your best friend, who always seemed to be there for you in the past, listening, reflecting, and sympathizing, has now turned a deaf ear because you're beginning to sound like a broken record. He cares, but he can't fix your life.

✔ Your kids are bouncing off the walls. They're irritable, incorrigible, and scared silly, but you aren't there for them.

Some of your friends may not be quite as subtle. In fact, they may be giving you advice that's not only unsolicited but is actually dragging you down. For example, they might think they're being really helpful when they encourage you to try to find a new squeeze over the Internet. What they're really doing is depressing the stuffing out of you because you realize they have no clue how you really feel. This tends to make you feel defensive and lonelier than ever! We know a single dad who fell into one of these traps when his best friend's wife invited him over for what he thought was supposed to be a family barbecue. However, he became really morose when they introduced him to a single lady who just happened to drop by!

Be clear with your well-meaning friends and relatives that you're not ready to jump back into your life, let alone pick up with some other lonely, depressed soul. Every person must recover in his own unique way, in his own time; and there's no right or wrong way to get over a major loss. You need to communicate these concepts very clearly. Chapter 12 talks more about this process.

On the other hand, if you get the idea that your friends are really worried about you, you might ask them what they think you should do.

Benefiting from Professional Therapy

Okay, you're a bit down, a little anxious, a little discouraged, and yes, darn it, you admit you're depressed. You also realize that you might benefit from some professional therapy, but first you need to know what it is and how it works.

Mood changes, depression, and anxiety are experienced as emotional pain. This pain can be overwhelming and immobilizing. Psychotherapy with a licensed professional therapist empowers you to work through these painful feelings.

Make no mistake, therapy is hard work and you do most of it. You and your therapist put your heads together to fathom the depths of your present pain — and your past experiences. Some of your ways of coping in the past aren't working now and some of them were always dysfunctional. Through the therapist's insatiable curiosity, open mindedness, and positive regard, you begin to see your situation in a different light. Helping your therapist truly understand your feelings and perceptions allows you to recapture your emotional energy and equilibrium.

Here are the techniques used by a licensed, professional therapist, along with translation into everyday language:

- ✔ **Skillful interviewing.** Translation: He asks questions and lets you answer without interrupting — what a refreshing concept!

- ✔ **Astute reflection.** Translation: She not only listens to you but also hears and values your point of view.

- ✔ **Non-judgmental acceptance.** Translation: He accepts you as you are, with no preconceived judgments — nothing you say is a wrong answer.

- ✔ **Boundary-keeping.** Translation: The therapist places boundaries around her thinking, always keeping in mind that the therapy is about you — not about her or anyone else. The therapist won't tell you how awful she felt when she went through her terrible divorce. Instead, she wants to know what your experience is from your perspective.

- ✔ **Unconditional positive regard.** Translation: The therapist is always on your side — you can do or say nothing wrong.

Referrals by professional organizations

These professional organizations will be happy to refer you to a local therapist:

✔ American Association of Marriage and Family Therapy: www.aamft.org or 703-838-9808

✔ National Association of Social Workers: www.naswdc.org/ or 800-638-8799

✔ American Psychological Association: www.apa.org or 888-964-2000

Psychotherapy is not

✔ A walk in the park

✔ Magic

✔ Astrology

✔ Brainwashing

✔ A how-to guide

✔ A friendship

✔ Something for "crazy" people

It's a relationship like no other. You can say anything and everything to your therapist and it's confidential. Even if you've committed some serious crime, you can tell your therapist all about it, and he will keep it to himself. However, if you tell your therapist you're planning to knock off Joe Blow, this is *not* confidential information because the therapist has a duty to warn Joe Blow, a clearly identified potential victim.

So, let's say you decide to make an appointment with a therapist. How do you go about it, you ask? Who are you going to call? Ghost busters? In a real sense, a licensed professional mental health care expert may indeed become your ghost buster. Especially if you've been struggling unsuccessfully with a repetitive, self-destructive, shoot-off-your-foot tendency, like always choosing the wrong type of partner. Or, if you have a ghost in your past that holds you back from becoming the centered, self-accepting, fulfilled person you can be.

TIP

Non-network what?

If the therapist you want to work with is not on the preferred provider list

✔ Ask your insurance carrier whether they can reimburse you for the cost of treatment. Be sure and ask how much they reimburse as well.

✔ Ask that therapist to consider participating in your plan. This can take some time, depending on the insurance company.

Taking the first step by placing a call to a therapist is evidence that you *can* and *will* take care of yourself. Just making that first appointment may actually make you feel a bit better because you're taking action. Remember, *you* are in charge, and it can be helpful to interview several therapists to find the right match for you! Ask questions and find out if they are experienced working with people going through a divorce.

Three FAQs about therapy

After you decide to seek help from a therapist, you find that you have questions about your decision. Here are answers to the three most common questions asked by patients of psychotherapy.

✔ **What am I getting myself into?** The psychotherapy relationship is like no other. It's not a friendship and your therapist isn't necessarily the warm fuzzy type. In fact, a therapist may seem neutral at first, like a blank screen. He answers your personal questions only if they seem therapeutic, but by the same token he gives you permission not to answer his questions if you don't want to, don't know the answer, or are not ready to go there. You are in charge.

✔ **How long does therapy last?** The length of time you may spend with your therapist depends entirely on your needs. For example, if you're going through a temporary time of depression or anxiety due to something traumatic in your life, such as death or divorce, you may respond quickly to therapy. Usually, it takes three to six months of care until you're able to cope and feel good again. Take a look back in Chapter 12 for a more in-depth look at grief, loss, and bereavement.

✔ **Why are some people like the Energizer Bunny — they just keep going and going and going to their therapists forever?** Long-term therapy (more than six to twelve months) is usually for those folks dealing with problems like chronic depression or early childhood issues, such as abuse, neglect, or certain personality problems.

A professional doesn't keep a client in therapy longer than necessary to arrive at a satisfactory result the client is pleased with. However, if you feel your therapist isn't helping you the way you had hoped, tell her, and any professional therapist will be happy to refer you to other reputable counselors and wish you well.

Picking from a smorgasbord of therapists

As you choose your personal therapist, we don't want you to settle for any old generic shrink. Because knowledge is power, we want to provide you with a little helpful info you may not know about all those friendly psychology-types out there.

To assure consumer protection (that's you), each state regulates the education, training, and licensure of mental health caregivers. If you're seeing a licensed counselor, psychotherapist, social worker, psychologist, psychiatrist, or psychoanalyst, you can be pretty certain the person is a safe, well-qualified practitioner. Of course, your therapist must meet your particular standards and needs as well. You can ask to see your counselor's license; no reputable counselor balks at this. If she refuses to show her credentials, run to a different doctor. You can also call the BBB to see if anyone has filed complaints against any counselor you're considering.

Whenever the word *safe* is used in this chapter, as in safe therapy or a safe counselor, it means that the therapist is licensed and abides by legal and ethical guidelines. It also means that your therapy takes place in a safe environment where you feel comfortable and able to tell the therapist anything.

Table 14-1 reveals various therapists' titles and qualifications.

Table 14-1	Therapists Training and Specialties	
Therapist	*Training*	*Specialty*
LMFT or Licensed Marriage, Family, and Child Counselor	Master's degree (MS) in psychology or counseling theory and completion of 3,000 supervised hours of therapy with individuals, couples, children, and families. Successful written and oral examination.	Specializes in relationships. Training is almost entirely in psychotherapy and relationship counseling.

(continued)

Table 14-1 *(continued)*

Therapist	Training	Specialty
LCSW or Licensed Clinical Social Worker	Master of Social Work (MSW) degree and completion of 3,200 hours of supervised experience. Have passed licensing examinations.	Much of an LCSW's training is in social welfare agencies, hospitals, clinics, case management, adoption, and so on. Many practice psychotherapy.
Psychologist	Doctorate (PhD) in psychology, a post-doctoral internship, and successful completion of State Board examinations.	Trained in psychotherapy, with emphasis on psychological evaluation, testing, and research. LMFTs and LCSWs refer clients to psychologists for special personality, IQ, or other psychological testing.
Psychiatrist	Medical doctors (MDs) with additional internship and residency in psychiatry. They may or may not do psychotherapy. Research has shown that what works best for the treatment of major depression is a combination of therapy and medication.	Many psychiatrists consult with other therapists to diagnose and treat serious mental health problems. Some exclusively see patients to evaluate their need for medication. So, if your therapist refers you to a psychiatrist, it isn't because he thinks you're crazy!
Psychoanalyst	Most psychoanalysts are MDs/psychiatrists trained in Freudian Analysis. Jungian Analysts may not be MDs, but have spent many years training. All psychoanalysts undergo years of training and seven years of their own psychoanalysis. Woody Allen should be a psychoanalyst himself after all the years he's spent on the couch!	This is for long-term personal insight and growth.

Dealing with mental health insurance can drive you crazy

Cost is a significant factor in how much of therapy you get to enjoy, so you probably want to see a provider who's on your mental health care insurance approved provider list. Call your insurance company or check out their Web site, which often lists participating doctors.

After finding a therapist, remember these gems:

- ✔ Contact your insurance provider *before* seeing a therapist because many of them require prior authorization for psychotherapy.

- ✔ Your health care benefit probably has limitations on the amount of time spent receiving therapy.

  - • Know in the beginning how many sessions you can depend on. A typical contract provides 20 sessions per calendar year.

  - • The confidentiality is an agreement between you, your shrink, and the computerized world of PPOs, HMOs, and managed care.

Most large employers offer Employee Assistance Programs (EAPs). You may be eligible for up to six free sessions to help you through a crisis. In many instances, you can continue to see the same therapist privately, or under your own health insurance. This is very important if you've established a good therapeutic relationship and don't want to start over with someone new. You may have some legitimate concern about confidentiality with EAPs, especially when your boss or department manager refers you.

Many mental health care providers do not contract with insurance companies because of limitations of care and infringement on confidentiality. In other words, the mental health care providers refuse to work with certain insurance companies that limit the amount of care they (the insurance company) will pay for. They're also wary of loss of confidentiality between the therapist and patient, which means that the patient's personal information is revealed to third parties.

Considering your options

After you're armed with information, how do you decide whom to call? Here are a few helpful suggestions:

- ✔ **Ask a friend for a recommendation.** This is probably the best way to find a safe, affordable psychotherapist. If your friend had a good therapeutic experience, chances are you will too. Be sure to call the number on your health insurance card to see whether this highly recommended therapist is on their list. If she is, go ahead and make an appointment so you can check her out.

✔ **Find the most affordable care available.** Most therapists work on a sliding scale according to your ability to pay. Do not hesitate to ask about the fee when you make the first phone inquiry.

What if you're barely making it financially, but you know you need therapy? Don't despair:

- **Non-profit counseling centers:** Most communities, depending on population size, have several reputable non-profit centers where you can receive excellent therapy on a sliding scale basis. Interns who are collecting their 3,000 hours of counseling experience, along with volunteer lay counselors, perform the therapy. These highly motivated individuals have been carefully screened and are meticulously trained. Retired professionals and educated homemakers make wonderful, caring counselors. They have weekly supervision and training by licensed professionals. Check with your pastor or a friend for references, or read their brochures and then stop by to see how the place looks and feels to you.

- **A university master's or doctorate program:** Probably the best low-fee therapy you can find is through a university that has one of these programs for professional psychology. The students are often starting a second or third career. They may be doctors, lawyers, teachers, nurses, or clergy who have maturity on their side and a strong desire to do this type of intimate, heartfelt work.

- **Psychotherapy paid for by Welfare with Medicaid:** What if you're down and out financially? In fact, you may be on Welfare with Medicaid. Good news! You'll be able to receive the same psychotherapy from the same community therapist who usually charges $100 an hour in private practice, but who enjoys giving back to the community by helping a few Medicaid clients.

Evaluating the therapist

The best way to know whether you and your therapist are a good match is simply whether or not you build trust with this person over time. It may take two or three sessions before you feel you can speak freely. Can you bare your soul and know your therapist listens and cares? It sounds like a blind date, doesn't it? You aren't going to marry this person, but the personal risk and vulnerability feel similar.

Donna's successful therapy

Donna was a single mom who had just graduated from a university. She was driving through downtown on her motorbike when a confused motorist plowed into her. The next two years were an endurance contest of surgeries, bed rest, rehabilitation, and living on welfare. She felt as though she would lose her mind with the pain, immobility, and worry about her uncertain future. Her social service's caseworker recommended she get into therapy to help her cope.

Donna tried out two or three psychotherapists before she settled on someone in a convenient, wheelchair-accessible office, who seemed professional and approachable. Over the next two years, Donna received the support she needed to control her anxiety and lessen her depression.

At no time did the county mental health agency ask for unreasonable information or justification. The therapist appreciated this and enjoyed being able to work with Donna on a long-term basis. The therapist's lower fee was more than compensated by the satisfaction she received from seeing the client through from wheelchair to walker, to crutches and finally to walking on her own.

Here are a few important questions to ask yourself before settling on a therapist:

- ✔ Is the therapist's office location good for me? Is it near public transportation? Does it have an elevator and wheelchair access, if necessary?

- ✔ Does the therapist have appointments available that mesh with my work and child-care responsibilities?

- ✔ Does the therapist also work with children, teens, and families, in case the whole family needs therapy?

- ✔ Does the therapist explain everything to me in advance, including the rules of confidentiality and his fees?

- ✔ Do I feel more comfortable working with a male or female therapist?

- ✔ Does the therapist have experience dealing with divorce/single-parent issues?

Jockeying for Support

At this time in your life, you need all the support you can get, so you may want to consider joining an organized support group whose members can empathize with what you're going through and offer encouragement. You may

John's single-parent support group

John had always been a private person and a bit anxious in social situations. When his therapist suggested a support group for single parents, John knew it would be a stretch for him, but might be a way for him to overcome his self-imposed isolation. He agreed to attend the Monday night meetings and his two young sons took to the child-care group right away.

John was pretty aloof in the beginning. The facilitator explained that participants are under no pressure to talk or disclose anything unless and until they are ready. It surprised John that the 25 to 30 single parents who showed up each week weren't particularly looking for dates. In fact, what they talked about was how they needed to get their lives back in order and recover from some pretty painful breakups. In a strange way, John found it comforting that his problems were not as complicated as some that he was hearing about.

During the summer, the support group sponsored picnics for the parents and their kids, and slowly, John began to become friends with a couple other single fathers in the group. They took their kids to the beach or the water slides on weekends. One of the guys talked John into attending the Sunday night singles program at a church to hear a talk about communications. He reluctantly agreed at first, but soon found himself looking forward to both Sunday and Monday nights.

John realized that he was creating a life on his own. He and his boys even went on a family vacation sponsored by the singles program at the church. John has found that he gets a great deal of satisfaction from encouraging newcomers and he's overcome much of his social anxiety. The Single Parent Family Network became a true source of support for him and his family.

also benefit from getting involved with family therapy, which means that you, your children, and other family members meet together with a therapist who works as a facilitator to encourage family bonding and support.

Joining a group

When your heart is broken you may just want to crawl under the blankets and hide. Being around happy people who are perking along in their daily lives may be too painful for you now.

But misery *does* love company, so you may feel more comfortable in a support group where the members know what you're going through and want to be as helpful as possible. Joining a support group, scary as it may sound, can be empowering. Successful groups often offer open discussion sessions alternately with specific topics or guest speakers.

Your first step is to decide what type of support group you want to try. Table 14-2 shows a few options.

Table 14-2	What to Expect with Support Groups	
What the Group Is	*How to Get There*	*What It's Like*
Professionally sponsored therapy group facilitated by a licensed mental health care provider.	Talk to friends or check with your mental health insurance provider. Sometimes your therapist can refer you, when you're no longer receiving individual therapy.	These groups usually have no more than eight participants and confidentiality is safeguarded as much as possible, although it's difficult to maintain the same type of strict confidence you had with individual therapy. Be a bit more cautious about what you say during the meetings.
Support groups sponsored by community agencies, churches, synagogues, and singles' clubs. Facilitators may be skilled volunteers, interns, or licensed therapists.	Check out your local yellow pages under therapy, depression, divorce, death, and other key words. Call your local hospitals and ask whether they can direct you to an appropriate group. Local newspapers often have a community section that lists a variety of support groups and informational classes.	These groups are usually larger than those that are professionally sponsored, but they may be free or charge a very low fee. Child care may be included for an additional fee. Single-parenting groups may be co-ed or specifically for moms or dads. We know of divorce recovery groups where the participants attend both co-ed and single sex meetings to receive the maximum support.

It's a good idea to try out a few groups to see where you fit. Although you may feel a bit uncomfortable during your first meeting, we recommend you attend at least three sessions before you decide it isn't right for you.

Participating in family therapy

Going to a therapist as a family is a rich experience, full of possibility and a lot of uncertainty. You don't know *what* your two teenagers might say during the sessions, but it's better to be in the know. You might have a few things you want them to know about you, too! Family therapy with a skilled family therapist is a way for your whole family to pull together, rather than remaining at odds.

During your family therapy sessions, you begin to

- ✔ See the roles you all play within the family.
- ✔ See how you affect each other.
- ✔ Find ways to use your strengths.
- ✔ Consider new ways to work and play together.
- ✔ Support each other through the difficult transitions you're experiencing.

The renegotiated custody agreement

After a very rocky marriage and a failed attempt at marriage counseling, Carl finally threw in the towel and divorced his wife, Janice. At the time of the divorce, their only child, Matthew, was 6 years old. Their custody agreement called for Janice and Carl to co-parent their son on a fairly equal timetable, with Carl picking him up after school on Thursdays and dropping him off again each Monday morning.

When the custody arrangement was put into place, Carl was very pleased with the way it was working out at first because Matthew was a joy to have in his home. He was well behaved and responsive to Carl's parenting style. However, when Matthew was with Janice during the early part of each week he regressed and "turned into a monster," as Janice described it. As soon as Janice picked Matthew up from school every Monday afternoon, the fireworks began. Matthew threw tantrums and generally defied everything Janice tried to accomplish with him. After a

short time this behavior began to drive Janice nuts and it wasn't long before her health began to suffer, along with her performance at work.

According to Carl, the worst of the whole situation was that when it was Janice's turn to have custody of Matthew, Carl often received frantic calls from her and no matter where he was or what he was doing, she tracked him down, crying hysterically over the phone and demanding that Carl pick up Matthew immediately.

Carl was a loving, responsible father so he always dropped what he was doing — even if he was on his way to a party or to pick up his date to take her to a movie — and drove over to Janice's house to pick up his son. This pattern continued month after month and developed into a huge problem when Carl remarried. His new wife, Connie, tried to be loving, understanding, and supportive every time Carl received one of his ex's frantic phone calls, but after a while it grated on her that they were constantly expected to change their plans at the last minute, just because Janice couldn't cope with her son.

It all came to a head one Monday evening when Carl and Connie were on their way out the door to attend his company's annual dinner where Carl was to receive the Salesman of the Year Award, and Janice called in tears. And what did Carl do? He left Connie at home and headed over to rescue his ex from her motherly duties! On the drive over he called his boss to let him know a family emergency had come up and he wouldn't be at the dinner after all.

Connie was livid! How dare Janice deprive Carl of this very special evening? A few days later, after Connie finally cooled down and gave some sane thought to the problem, she suggested to Carl that he, Janice, and Matthew get some counseling from a Marriage and Family Therapist to see whether the therapist could come up with a solution.

Miraculously, Janice was agreeable to this and after six months of counseling, she and Carl took the therapist's advice and revised their custody and visitation agreement so that Carl became the sole-custody parent and Janice was given liberal visitation rights. Evidently, during the counseling sessions, it didn't take long for the therapist to realize that Matthew felt insecure and unstable when he was with Janice, and that Janice wasn't emotionally mature enough to raise her son.

The happy ending to this story is that with the new custody agreement, everyone is doing better: Carl, Janice, Matthew, and yes, even Connie! Connie has come to love little Matthew and she doesn't mind having him live with them fulltime — at least she and Carl don't have their schedule constantly thrown into chaos! And the loveliest thing of all is that Matthew has become quite attached to Connie, too.

If Connie hadn't suggested family therapy to get to the bottom of the problem, she and Carl would probably still be walking on eggs every minute Matthew was with Janice!

Family therapy is flexible and different members may be involved at different times. Take a look at the many possibilities:

- A single mother and her children
- A single father and his children
- A single mom, her ex, and their kids
- A single mom, her ex, her ex's new wife, and all their children
- A single dad, his ex, his ex's new husband, and all their children
- A brother and sister together, without their parents
- All the parents — blended and splendid — in the same room at the same time
- In-laws and all those caring grandparents may be included, if appropriate

Family therapy is *not* a way to manipulate people into better behavior. It is a way to understand each other better so everyone can be happier.

The reasons to decide on family therapy are as varied as the possible combinations of players. Maybe a family hasn't taken the time to find out just how hurt and sad each person is after a painful divorce. Listening to your children express their hurt and anger may not be easy, but it is the first step toward healing. The important thing is that you communicate in a safe place where everyone is seen and heard. The therapist makes sure everyone is allowed a chance to communicate, even the 4-year-old who's protesting loudly by throwing the new toys around the room.

Family therapy can empower the single parent who feels overwhelmed by all the responsibility with no cooperation from her kids. It's surprising how much more easily she can be heard in this kind of setting. On the other hand, the children can also tell their sides of the story. One practical outcome can be the development of a chore list everyone agrees on.

In the blended family situation, therapy gives the new family a chance to express concerns and make some decisions about living and sleeping arrangements. One single mom said that meeting the woman her children were going to spend every other weekend with was very helpful to her. Her worst misgivings were banished and she found a way to communicate without feeling resentful. The new stepmom felt empowered because the kids realized that she and their mother talked things over and made decisions together about their care.

Family therapy is usually goal-directed and short-term. Some families also use it as a safety valve. After setting up a good working relationship with the therapist, they can return for a tune-up or to put out a small fire whenever necessary. When children feel comfortable with family therapy, they may initiate a session or ask to see the therapist on their own. Family therapy is often covered by mental health insurance and many family clinics provide excellent care at an affordable cost.

Part V

Finding Those Other Fish in the Sea

The 5th Wave   By Rich Tennant

"I really can't have a relationship now. I'm afraid it might impact my 'needs analysis form'."

In this part . . .

Hey, are you in the mood for a little fishing trip? The ocean is full of fish, so why not grab your gear and enjoy the quest? The problem is that you're not as young as you were the last time you enjoyed the dating scene — in fact, you may find that the rules have changed since you dated last. The new, improved dating game may not be as hard to play as you feared. Of course, you need to learn how to trust again, plus it isn't easy finding the time and money to date, but we offer answers to all your questions in these chapters. If you think you've found the right person and you're considering remarriage, read about the dangers of the rebound thing, the advantages of a pre-nuptial agreement, and the tribulations of blending together as a family.

Chapter 15

Dating Tips for the Middle-Aged Teen

In This Chapter

▶ Taking some time to think dating over

▶ Figuring out what you want

▶ Beginning to trust again

▶ Taking a look at your fears

▶ Making time for someone other than your kids

▶ Coming up with the dough to date

*W*e can see you standing in front of the mirror mumbling to yourself: "What the heck have I gotten myself into?" or "Why do I have butter-flies in my stomach — I'm acting like a teenager!" or "I think my butt looks big in these jeans — maybe I should wear the khakis instead." or "I never noticed these lines before — they make me look ten years older!"

Dating is weird, isn't it? Especially after so many years of settling into the pre-dictable lifestyle of being a married person with kids. Whether you've been through a divorce or suffered the death of your spouse, you're not alone if the idea of dating again scares you. Widows and divorcees do carry different baggage, however, and if you're having problems transitioning through the loss in either case, you may want to take advantage of the help offered in Chapter 12 or Chapter 14 before getting back into the dating scene.

In this chapter we take a look at your fears and expectations, and give you some pointers on where to look for interesting people you might want to date. If you've already jumped back into the dating scene, read about how to make dating fun and how to begin to trust someone again.

Of course, when you start dating again after such a long time, you're probably wondering where to find the time and the money — a couple of major obstacles. We tackle these obstacles later in this chapter, and we're sure you agree with us that it's who you're with that really counts — not how much money you spend on your date.

We're just full of dating tips for all you middle-aged teens! This is an exciting time in your life and we want you to enjoy it.

Looking at the Big Picture Before You Leap into Dating

You need to look at dating from many vantage points. First, you need to see it from an adult's perspective, especially when it comes to sexual expectations, practicing safe sex, and finding the time to date. Next, you need to understand the difference between *dating* and having a *relationship,* and finally, you need to see it from a kid's perspective. How will dating or a relationship affect your child? What is your child thinking? How will he react?

Viewing it from an adult's perspective

You're considering calling up a grown woman to ask her on a date. Or you've been asked out — to dinner and a concert, no less. How do you get back into the dating groove after so many years? Have the rules changed? What does she expect from you? What do you expect from her? If dating seems like a struggle at first, hang in there — it gets better!

Here are some things to think about.

Differing sexual expectations

Research has shown that most single fathers expect to have sexual relations after dating a woman a few times; however, not all women are thinking the same thing, so this may be an unrealistic expectation until you find a willing partner.

If sexual relations are *not* in your immediate dating game plan, whether you're a man or woman, you might want to have a frank discussion with your potential dating partner to let her or him know about your expectations.

Sex while single

Remember that latex love is a fantastic thing! In other words, practice safe sex whether you're thinking of a long-term relationship or not. Please, please, please ask your friend about his or her sexual history. And if you're thinking of marriage, you should both agree to have lab tests for AIDS, the HIV virus, and venereal diseases. Planned Parenthood is a great resource for information, testing, and free condoms.

By the way, just in case you were wondering, people in the know say you should buy latex condoms with that contain a spermicide.

Talking it over with your kids

Single parents who have the best success transitioning back into the dating scene are those who talk it over with their kids beforehand.

1. Explain that you are a grown adult and enjoy socializing with other adults, so they shouldn't be surprised when you start dating.

2. Ask your kids what they think about the idea.

   They usually end up agreeing to the plan. If they don't, their resistance may be because they feel strong loyalty to their other parent. Let your children know that you'll always consider their best interests and that, although you're in no hurry to marry again, someday you may meet someone special and decide to remarry. Reassure your children that you love them now and always will.

Parents who date secretly or start dating with no warning may damage relationships with their children. Discuss the dating idea with your kids before taking the plunge.

By the way, your kids' biggest concern is whether there's any hope of you getting back together again with their other parent. If you can convince them to let go of this fantasy, they may be more open to your dating. Unfortunately, too many kids have watched *The Parent Trap,* the movie where the kids schemed and connived until they got their parents back together again!

Rushing in sets you up for failure

Take it nice and slow. Start out by playing it as low-key as you can, going on occasional dates that don't involve the children. By dating, we mean going out with someone for the fun of it, on a casual basis. In fact, you can date several people, none of them seriously. A relationship is more serious, however, involving only one person whom you're seriously interested in for the long-term. This type of close association with another person often leads to commitment and intimacy.

One of the biggest mistakes you can make is to welcome your new squeeze into your home and involve him in your kids' lives before you get to know him. Maybe he's a control-freak whose wife divorced him because of physical abuse! You sure don't want someone like that hanging around. If you realize you're dating someone with a questionable past, it's wise to dump him after a few dates anyway.

So, don't get too involved until you've dated her for a long time — at the very least six months! And, whatever you do, don't invite her for sleepovers with your kids in the house! The reason why sleepovers aren't smart is because your kids' emotions are extremely fragile and they think you might try to replace them with your new love. It's also a bad idea in a legal sense because a nasty ex can use this against you in a court of law to try to get custody of the kids.

Easing your new squeeze into your kids' lives

When you've dated long enough to know that you're pretty crazy about the guy and you think he'd be good with your kids, involve him in a few of your kids' activities from time to time. For example, does your son play in a basketball league? Well, how about inviting your new friend to attend a game and join the family for pizza afterwards?

See how it goes, and if your son seems to enjoy being around your friend, take it another step. Maybe you can plan a ski day together — you, your friend, and both of your kids. You get to know each other on the drive, plus you have a chance to see how you mesh throughout the day. Or, maybe you can pick up tickets to a concert or spend an afternoon at the county fair together.

Dating a dad?

We know a single dad who overcame his kids' jealousy by spending one-third of his free time exclusively with his children, one-third on dates with his new squeeze, and one-third of his time on family dates that included his kids and his new love interest.

Unfortunately, when a single mom starts to date again, her kids may be more offended than when

their dad dates. The reason for this is because children are more protective of their mom than of their dad. Don't give up on dating just because your kids aren't being cooperative — you're single, not dead! And by the way, this is the twenty-first century — it's okay for *you* to ask *him* out on a date.

Don't let dating interfere with your kids' activities

It can be pretty romantic and exciting when you fall in love with someone special, and you may want to spend as much time with her as possible. However, we're willing to bet your kids aren't going to be quite as thrilled as you are, because they need to spend time with you, too. What a dilemma!

Here are a few things you can do to keep your kids from feeling jealous of your new relationship:

✔ **Schedule one-on-one time with each of your children, whether it's at home or not.** When you're with them, be a good listener and don't talk about your new friend. Do everything you can to let your kids know how much you love and value them.

✔ **During your at-home time in the evenings or on weekends, try not to spend too much time on the phone talking with your new friend.** Your kids pick up on this immediately and even though the time you spend on the phone may not deprive them of "Mom-time," your kids feel that you would rather talk on the phone with your boyfriend than play cards with them.

✔ **Have a talk with your friend and come up with a time-sharing plan.** Maybe you two have a certain night out together each week, and any other time you spend together needs to include the kids, so they aren't emotionally deprived because of your new relationship.

✔ **When your girlfriend is visiting, be careful how much physical affection you show each other in front of the kids.** What seems playful and exciting to you may be devastating to your children as they notice all the hugging, patting, and kissing going on as you watch a movie together in the dark.

Viewing it from a kid's perspective

What goes on inside your kids' precious little heads as they watch your new relationship develop? Even though you may be over the top with joy because you've fallen in love with someone you're just sure will be a fantastic new stepmom or stepdad, your kids may not share your euphoria.

You see, your new relationship may be threatening to them, especially at first, because:

✔ **They resent the time you spend dating because they think you care more about the new person in your life than you do for them.** Try not to make a big deal out of dating. Tell your kids you're dating for the fun of it and that if ever it did become serious, you plan to let them know. If you *are* getting serious about someone, help your kids feel comfortable around this person by doing things as a group once in a while. The more your kids get to know your new friend, the more likely they are to accept him. Don't let your kids manipulate you or prevent you from having a serious relationship. If you sense that your kids are feeling really threatened by your dating, you may benefit from a couple of group sessions with a family therapist. Meanwhile, do everything you can to convince your kids that you love them as much as ever, and that you have enough love in your heart for them *and* the new person in your life.

✔ **Your kids may actually fear that you'll abandon them.** They don't understand that you would *never* do such a thing, so you need to reassure them constantly, plus occasionally plan your dates around activities that include your kids so that they feel included in your fun.

✔ **It's common for children to try to sabotage the relationship.** For example, your youngest may start throwing tantrums or sobbing hysterically when you leave her to spend the evening with your new love, your teenager may just happen to forget to pass along an important message from your friend, and beware of sudden illnesses that force you to cancel your dates. Wow! As though dating isn't stressful enough!

Dating isn't always a battle — sometimes the children fall in love with their parent's new friend and are thrilled about the possibility of a remarriage.

However, to prevent your kids from getting all excited prematurely, the best plan is to avoid introducing your new friend to your kids until you've dated for several months. This may mean that you have to meet your friend away from your home, so that your kids never see the person. Wait until you see the relationship developing into something permanent before you get your kids involved. When you do decide to introduce your friend to your children, arrange the introductions in a casual setting. For example, plan an activity that includes your friend and your kids, such as an afternoon at the beach or ice-skating together some evening at the lighted outdoor rink.

We know of cases where the person the parent was dating won his way into the kids' affections by developing relationships with them individually over time, by playing with them, talking with them, or praising their accomplishments. One potential stepmom won her way into the kids' hearts simply by letting them help her bake their favorite cookies once in a while!

If you have teenage kids who are also dating, be very careful not to compete with them. Don't try to out-do them in what you wear, in what you talk about after your date, and especially avoid talking about how intimate your relationship has become. Being competitive messes up your relationship with your teenagers.

Analyzing Your Expectations

When you think about dating again, are you aware of your expectations? Have you even thought about what they are? Are you hoping for a long-term relationship that may eventually lead to marriage? Or, are you soured on marriage, at least for now, and you just want to get away from the world of the little people and have some good, wholesome adult fun for a change?

Searching for someone to marry

We know from our experiences that many of you are not looking for small game! You want to marry again, as soon as you can find someone you love who is also good stepparent material.

However, is this the best way to go about it, or, is it better to date interesting people, have fun, and hope something develops if it's meant to be? The latter is a healthier attitude, where the primary emphasis is on finding a *quality* person, one with whom you have a lot in common. Get to know this person, find out what kind of person she is, and then you can figure out if you're dating someone with marriage potential.

By the way, if you're looking for interesting singles to date, take a look at the best places to find them discussed later in this chapter.

Beware of the rebound thing! Many single parents become way too social immediately after their divorces and this can lead to poor choices! Play it cool for a while until you heal from the trauma of the divorce — chances are your chosen playmate will still be around when you're finally ready for another relationship. If you find yourself making consistently bad or dangerous dating choices, seek a counselor. Chapter 14 can help.

Dating for the fun of it

A lot of single parents had such a rotten go of it the first time around that the last thing they want is to remarry. They do want a social life, however, including dating others who feel the same way.

You can have an active social life without the pressure of remarriage by dating a lot of different people, or hanging out with the same person year in and year out, if you like. You can look at it as a form of companionship, having a safe escort, or hanging out with someone who's a good friend, regardless of gender.

Another popular way for single parents to get together just for fun is to hang out in groups. One single-parent church club we know of meets every Sunday evening for a potluck dinner and fellowship, with an informal invitation for a casual get-together the following Friday night. They may meet at a certain pizza parlor for dinner, followed by an hour or so at the local comedy club, or they may agree to bring their kids, their volleyball gear, and a picnic basket to a park at a certain time. Then, whoever shows up, shows up — it's usually an uneven number of single dads and moms, but they have a great time with no strings attached.

Don't feel pressured into remarriage if your goal is to just have fun and enjoy life to the fullest in spite of your singleness!

Looking for love in all the right places

Many single parents marry people they knew before the divorce or the death of their spouse. Some marry friends from grade school; others knew their mates when they were each married to others. However, if you're someone who needs to *look* for love, you need to find the right time and the right place to meet someone.

So, where are all these right places? Here are a few of the most popular ways to find a new squeeze:

- ✓ **Take a look around your office or campus.** If you're working, keep your eyes open for someone interesting, and if you're attending college, sit next to a potential someone in class to get to know her. Offices and school campuses are definitely two great places for your hunting expeditions.

- ✓ **Join a biking, swimming, or running club.** A club is a lot cheaper than joining a gym, and while you're getting fit, you may meet someone equally fit. If you already belong to a co-ed health club, hang out there as often as you can — a health club or gym is a great place to find someone interesting to date.

- ✓ **Meet someone interesting while traveling.** You can find all kinds of travel packages, cruises, and travel clubs geared especially for singles. Call your favorite travel agent or watch the travel section of your Sunday newspaper for ideas. Here are a few organizations that cater to singles' travel:

    - **Travel Companion Exchange, Inc.:** www.whytravelalone.com

    - **O Solo Mio Single Tours:** www.osolomio.com

    - **All Singles Travel:** www.allsinglestravel.com

- **Travel Buddies:** www.travelbuddiesworldwide.com
- **The World Outdoors:** www.theworldoutdoors.com
- **Windjammer Barefoot Cruises:** www.windjammer.com
- **TravelChums:** www.travelchums.com

✔ **Hang out in a large bookstore.** This may sound bizarre, but lots of single people have met someone compatible in a bookstore — you know, those comfy, cozy, fun bookstores with the wide aisles and overstuffed easy chairs? Hang out in the aisles that have books of interest to you. So if you love to travel and you're into all those travel books, you're likely to meet someone who also enjoys traveling. Before you know it, you're carrying on a conversation about Fiji or cruising or scuba diving in the Caribbean. Another trick is to attend those free lectures hosted by larger bookstores. Stand around for a while before the lecture starts and watch for an intriguing person who arrives alone, then sit down beside the guy or gal and strike up a conversation. Sounds easy enough, doesn't it?

A wonderful side benefit of looking for love in the right places is that as you're looking, you make a lot of friends, not necessarily people you'd like to date, but people you enjoy socializing with and having fun with. Your life will be enriched. It's a win-win deal!

✔ **Museums and art galleries.** We have it straight from the mouth of an army sergeant — who met his wife at a museum cafe — that you can find more interesting singles hanging out at a museum than you'd find in 20 bars. Because he found the love of his life standing in line at a self-serve museum cafe, he's quick to recommend the concept to the rest of you.

✔ **Outdoorsy places.** If you're a nature lover, kick your bod out of the house and head for friendly places where you're likely to meet other single parents. Bring your kids or your dog along to the beach, spend the day hiking a nature trail, or flying a kite at a city park.

✔ **Libraries.** Hang out at a public library for an afternoon and see what you come up with. Offer to help someone use a computer terminal or strike up a conversation with someone in the reading area. We know one single mom who just happened to hang out in the law library of a prestigious law school and what do you know? She landed an attorney — he was just starting out, didn't have one single client and owed huge school loans, but hey, he was a hunk, and smart to boot!

✔ **Volunteer.** If you enjoy volunteer work, whether it's helping prepare and serve meals at the homeless shelter over the holidays, singing in the community chorus, or joining the campaign staff of an up-and-coming political candidate, go for it and you just might find someone interesting who's as altruistic as you are.

- ✔ **Clubs.** Get involved in clubs that are interesting to you and have at least a few members who are singles or single parents. The important thing is for the club to be fun for you in the first place or you turn into a turnip from sheer boredom while you're waiting to find Mr. or Miss Right. If you're into line dancing, for example, look for a line-dancing club. Or, if you enjoy reading and studying the classics, join a classics book club.

  Of course, it's a given that a singles club or single-parent club is crawling with eligibles. Look for the largest club you can find so you have a nice selection to choose from.

- ✔ **Kids' favorite places.** As a single parent, you naturally spend a lot of time with your kids at places they love. Even though you're not taking your children to these places for the purpose of meeting other single parents, it might happen — you never know.

- ✔ **School activities.** We know you already attend all of your kid's school events you can work into your schedule, including his class play, sports competitions, field day, and Halloween party. If you can spare the time, you also volunteer to help out with the school carnival or as a chaperone on a field trip. While you're there, take a look around for interesting singles. You never know who's out there unless you take advantage of every opportunity to mingle with other single parents.

- ✔ **Church activities.** Get involved in kids' activities, such as the Awana Clubs, single-parent support groups, or Bible studies. Volunteer to be a counselor at the summer camp your kids attend. Whether you find your soul mate right away or not, you can still meet some pretty nice people at your church and your kids benefit from the activities as well.

- ✔ **Large social functions.** Whether it's a wedding, a high school or college reunion, or a company Christmas party, keep your eyes peeled for other singles who may be lurking around. If you see someone interesting, introduce yourself or ask a mutual friend to do the honors.

- ✔ **Amateur matchmakers.** We all have a few amateur matchmakers in our lives. You know, those clever friends of yours who always seem to have someone special you just *have* to meet! As annoying as they may be at times, we actually know of match-ups that worked out, so you might give it a chance. Blind dates are something else entirely. If a friend tries to set you up on a blind date, insist on speaking to the person over the phone before committing to the date — if the person is as boring as a prune over the phone, forget it!

  Of course, the person can sound wonderful over the phone but turn out to be completely uninteresting in person. A single dad we know was set up on a date with a friend's sister. The guy took her to a decent restaurant for dinner, but all she did during the entire meal was pick her nose, plus she wouldn't look him in the eye! What a waste of time and money that turned out to be!

✔ **Professional matchmakers.** As far as the professionals go, we leave that decision up to you. We actually think you can meet someone on your own. However, if you're interested, look for matchmakers in the yellow pages, in the personals page in your newspaper, via radio stations, or over the Internet. In fact, according to a recent poll reported in *USA Today*, the number of computer users who visit Web site matchmakers has increased to 15.5 million, with the highest percentage of users in the 35- to 44-year-old age bracket.

When working with a matchmaker, over the Internet or otherwise, take precautions. Safety comes first, so never give out your home address or telephone number to your new date (leave contact names and phone numbers with family or friends). Always meet the person the first few times in a public place, such as a coffee shop, where either one of you can walk away if you want. After you meet and get to know the person, if you discover that the person has misrepresented himself or herself, break it off immediately.

✔ **Be an opportunist.** Frequent the spots where you know a lot of singles spend their time. For example, have you noticed the shapely single who walks her dog in the park every evening before sundown? Well, walk your dog in the same park at the same time! What? You don't have a dog? Borrow one! If you live in an apartment or condo complex, singles usually gather around the swimming pool or barbecue areas on weekends, or how about all those wineries along Highway 52 that offer free wine tastings? The trick is to notice where singles and single parents seem to spend their time, and then go there!

If you hear that the hunky single dad in your condo complex happens to be home sick, it wouldn't hurt to bake him a casserole, would it? Be sure it's in a quality baking pan so he has to return it to you when he's feeling better. You guys who don't know a casserole from a block of Gouda can always bring that sweet single mom a gallon of chocolate chip ice cream!

Mustering Up Some Trust

One of the downsides of dating again is that it can stir up negative memories. If your ex broke your heart with unfaithfulness, physical abuse, or addictions, you tend to notice anything your date does that reminds you of the past. If you did not want the divorce, did not initiate the divorce, and you're still having trouble accepting that your dream of a happy marriage was shot all to you-know-what, you may have tremendous problems trusting again.

However, your new friend is *not* your ex and even though some of his personality traits may ring a bell from your unhappy past, give the guy a break and don't kick him out of your life quite yet!

Whether you're a single dad or a single mom, you may need to date a lot of people over a long period of time before you dare give your heart away again! To speed your healing process, you may want to consider a little post-divorce counseling to help you over this annoying speed bump in your road to a new life with a special someone. Until you feel comfortable with yourself, you're more likely to damage a new relationship, so take a look in Chapter 14 to find out how therapy may be able to help you and how to locate a therapist who works well with you.

If your ex wigs out because you're dating someone, this probably means that your ex hasn't emotionally divorced you yet and he may benefit from a few meetings with a therapist. Also, after your ex meets your new friend and gets to know this person, the tensions may ease. After your ex discovers that your friend is okay and isn't a threat to the children, you may see a change in attitude. It's a good plan to ask your ex ahead of time if it's all right to drop by so you can introduce your new squeeze.

Looking Your Fear Smack Dab in the Face

If you're a little freaked out about dating, you're not alone. Almost all single parents face fears similar to those you're having, but it may help to take a look at some of your fears and how to handle them.

If your biggest fear is related to same-sex dating, we'd like to refer you to an excellent magazine entitled _The Advocate_. This magazine is available at a discounted subscription price at `www.amazon.com`. If you recently came out and are having trouble transitioning into same-sex dating, you may benefit from professional therapy with a therapist experienced in gay/lesbian psychotherapy.

Where would you like to go?

With all the fun stuff out there, much of it free entertainment, it's hard to believe that finding a place to go with that special someone is a problem, but it is. For some reason, we think of _dating_ as a formal thing where the guy invites the gal out to dinner and the theater. Then, to add to the angst, he feels obligated to present her with flowers or candy when he comes to pick her up. In actuality, a date can be as simple as getting together some morning for coffee and rolls at your favorite neighborhood coffee shop.

Getting back on that horse

Here's hope for all you single fathers who think you'll never feel comfortable dating again: Research has shown that only 1 out of every 16 single fathers *never* dates again, which means that almost 94 percent of you do eventually get back into the dating scene.

 Except for very special occasions, such as the night you decide to propose to her or a birthday celebration, think of dating as *hanging out* together. Does this make it easier for you? Glance through the newspaper and see what's happening in your town. Maybe your date would enjoy *hanging out* (get used to the term) with you at the street fair where you can pick up authentic ethnic foods as you walk around and enjoy the free musical entertainment. Now that sounds like a fun date to us! By the way, for fun and affordable places to take your date, take a look in Chapter 5.

Five outfits tried on and counting

You can ask your date what he or she suggests you wear, or you can use your common sense. If you'll be walking around a street fair on a chilly night, wear jeans and a sweater. If you'll be enjoying dinner at a nice restaurant, you're always safe with nice slacks, shirt, and a classic jacket if the weather is cool. Dress your outfit up or down with accessories, depending on where you're going. Of course, if it really is a formal night out — for example, you know he's taking you to the Top of the Mark in San Francisco, and you suspect he may pop the question — you never go wrong with good old basic black.

 The rest of the time, just use common sense — you know, don't wear shorts and a halter-top to a symphony concert and don't wear a tux to a casual dinner date! Just stay in your generic comfort zone of all-purpose pants and tops until you get to know your date a little better and feel comfortable thinking outside the box. If you do happen to dress more or less formally than your date and it creates an awkward situation, treat it lightly with a little humor, or suggest that you'd like to run back to your apartment to change clothes. Another way to handle this little problem is to come prepared with a jacket and a tie, if you're a guy. If she's dressed more formally than you are, you can always add to your attire. Or, if you're the gal and you realize you've overdressed, you can always ditch the expensive jewelry and take off the sequined jacket. If the two of you are at all compatible, it will work out fine.

Kevin's new beginning

Kevin and Shirley were married the day after they graduated from high school. They had been sweethearts since the sixth grade. By the time they were married ten years they had three children and everything was going along pretty well until Kevin lost his job. Jobs were tough to come by in their hometown, so he was forced to take a position 90 miles away. At first they managed just fine with Kevin staying in a rented room during the week and driving home for the weekends. But over time, the commute put an incredible strain on their relationship and their finances. Shirley didn't want to move away from her family and friends and they decided to get a divorce.

They managed to be quite civil through the divorce proceedings and agreed on joint custody of their children. The children stayed with their dad in his new apartment every other weekend, which was the best time for Kevin. He always felt lost and devastated every time he returned the kids to his ex. In fact, the weekends without the kids were really hard on him. He frequently became so depressed and withdrawn that he wouldn't even leave his apartment.

One weekend Kevin's brother took him fishing, which was a turning point in Kevin's life. He and his brother had several long talks and Kevin felt free to bare his soul — did that ever feel good! Through his brother's caring concern and feedback, Kevin came to see that his life had always revolved around his kids' activities and he had never developed any hobbies or interests of his own. He realized that now was the time to finally *get a life*.

The first thing Kevin decided on was to join the local YMCA to get a little exercise. He also bought a used mountain bike and became a real biking enthusiast as he explored the many bike trails in his area on his free weekends. He was feeling better all the time, but he was still lonely — he needed someone to share his life with.

Kevin noticed an advertisement for a cooking class for singles — something that sounded interesting, not only because it would give him a chance to socialize, but also because his cooking skills were mediocre, to say the least! The class turned out to be great fun, he made lots of single friends, male and female, and his phone actually rang once in a while as others in the class invited him to join them at a restaurant or for a beer after work.

One Saturday evening when he met with a few of the class members at an Italian restaurant, he happened to sit next to one of the single women. He had crossed her off his list in the beginning because he thought she was way too serious for him, but when he got to know her a little better that evening he discovered she had a great sense of humor. He also discovered that she owned a mountain bike and loved trail biking as much as he did. He asked her whether she'd like to ride with him the next Saturday, and before he knew it, he had a real, live, official *date* with a heck of a nice gal.

They had so much fun on their biking date that she invited him over the next week to work on one of their class recipes together — and, as they all say, the rest is history! Their relationship bloomed over the next year and, interestingly, his weekends with the kids became easier to plan and they all went bike riding together. The kids loved it! And the best part of the story is that the kids don't have to push their food around on their plates anymore — they actually enjoy Dad's cooking.

But enough about me . . .

One of the main questions single parents ask themselves when they jump back into the dating scene is, "What on earth will we talk about?" Many single parents are afraid to spend too much time talking about their kids — the only subject they're totally familiar with these days. We could say something trite like, "Just be yourself," but in the real world of dating, that doesn't always work! Being yourself is probably what you're afraid of!

So, here's some great advice:

- ✔ Ask your date questions about herself and then *listen* to her answers without interrupting.

- ✔ Respond to questions your date asks you and comment on anything of mutual interest that comes up during your time together.

- ✔ Avoid talking about your trials and travails, such as how

    - • Unruly your kids have become since the divorce (a *huge* no-no!)

    - • Financially strapped you've been lately

    - • Disgusting your co-worker is

    - • You dread getting phone calls from your ex

    You get the point! Even though your problems are *really* on your mind at the moment, don't poison your evening together by opening your poor-me-I-have-so-many-problems can of worms. He probably has his own can of worms and he doesn't want to hear about yours. So, talk about happy stuff, especially as it comes up naturally in your conversation. If you're unable to do this, you may be in the wrong state of mind to date. Perhaps you're still grieving for your lost mate and you can't let it go. If so, take a look in Chapter 12 where you'll find encouraging help. Or, if you're not over your ex and it's impossible to laugh and have fun, a little therapy may speed your healing — see Chapter 14.

- ✔ Remember your sense of humor? Well, why not let it out of jail for one night? You'll enjoy using it for a change and your date will love being around someone who's happy, fun, and not afraid to smile and laugh at the humorous stuff that may happen during your date.

- ✔ Here are a few safe topics:

    - • Trips you've taken in the past

    - • Trips you'd like to take in the future

    - • Places you've lived and what you liked or disliked about them

    - • Your favorite restaurants in town

- Your all-time favorite entertainer

- Interesting goals you'd like to accomplish some day

- Movies you've both seen

- People you know in common

- What types of college or professional sports you both enjoy

If this person is as interesting as you are, you'll find so much to talk about other than your kids that you'll need to *hang out* dozens of times just to scratch the surface!

In the process of carrying on a conversation, it's practically impossible to conceal the fact that you have an ex or that you have children, so don't try to hide this information. It's okay to talk about your past, but *do* try to keep things fairly upbeat. Don't put on an act when you're on a date — relax and be yourself.

Cramming a Date Into Your Hectic Schedule

We can hear you screaming: "What do you mean, finding time to date? When am I supposed to do that? Cram it in between work, cleaning house, taxiing the kids back and forth to their games, and grocery shopping? You've got to be out of your mind!"

Yes, we've heard it all, but surely you can free up a little time somewhere in your schedule for some adult fun once in a while? You can't keep living under house arrest, so to speak, sentenced by your kids to a life of cooking, ironing, and helping them with their homework!

You're an important individual — not just a single mother or a single father. You need a social life — without one you can turn into a nut case, which won't do your kids any good! So, carve a little time out of your schedule for some fun, even if it means your kids need to iron their own shirts and you eat off paper plates every weekend. Remember — where there's a will, there's a way! Chapter 4 gives more ideas on how to save that precious commodity: time.

Scraping Up Enough Bucks to Date

Money is a huge worry for a lot of you, especially you single dads who are up to your necks in custody payments, higher utility costs, private piano lessons, and a car that needs a new transmission any day now! Yes, we know you're drowning in expenses as you try to raise your kids on your less-than-wonderful salary.

But, hang on because we have good news for you. You're no longer expected to wine and dine your date in the style of the '70s or '80s! In fact, formal dates have long since been replaced with *hanging out* together any place that sounds like fun. Chapter 5 talks about money and how to save some of it, too. And you find lots of great ideas that veer off the movie-and-dinner dating path.

Chapter 16

Blended Can Be Splendid

In This Chapter

▶ Pulling up before you go for the rebound

▶ Taking a look at a prenuptial agreement

▶ Blending a family like a professional chef

▶ Looking into some stepparent guidelines

Strawberry monkey surprise is the name of a smoothie, a delicious party drink that's concocted in a blender. The ingredients are 1 cup frozen strawberry yogurt, ½ cup fresh strawberries, one banana, and one cup fresh orange juice. When you toss all this stuff into a blender and let it whirl together on high for one minute, you have a perfectly yummy smoothie. A no-fail, no-brainer recipe, right?

Wrong! You can probably screw up this simple smoothie recipe 50 different ways. What if you're not experienced with mixing fresh fruits together in a blender and you toss the banana in without peeling it first? Your smoothie will be lumpy and yucky, and the banana peel will probably clog up the blades and bring your blender to a screeching, smoking stop.

Or what if you ignore the recipe and just toss stuff in from memory — something like a quart of yogurt, two strawberries, and a jigger of orange juice? You'll have a blended drink all right, but it won't taste like the smoothie you set out to make. Or what if you forget to plug in the blender? Duh. That's pretty stupid, but a lot of us make simple mistakes all the time.

The point we're making with our smoothie story is that a blended family (like a smoothie) can be splendid, but it may not turn out right if you don't have the required ingredients, follow the directions, or use a blender that works properly. Of course, every family smoothie will be different depending on the ingredients. Your blend will be a combination of everyone's unique personalities, backgrounds, and talents. Who knows? Your blended family may result in a smoothie called a *moonbeam,* a *shamrock,* or a *Malibu tango,* each delicious in its own way.

In this chapter, we talk about the risky business of creating a blended family of yours, mine, and ours in haste. This may seem like the fastest way to get over your loss and loneliness, but in reality, you could be making the mistake of marrying on the rebound. We also present a recipe for success — the prenuptial agreement — that can prevent lumps from forming in your smoothie as the years go by. Our goal in this chapter is to give you directions for blending your new family together as smoothly as possible.

Avoiding the Big R: Marrying on the Rebound

If you think the first-time marriage divorce rate is high, take a look at second marriages: The divorce rate is over 60 percent. We understand that suffering through a bitter divorce or losing your spouse through death naturally makes things pretty exciting when you find someone wonderful who not only loves you, but also wants to marry you. In fact, becoming single after years of marriage may make you feel as if you've lost all your friends as well as your partner, so you become vulnerable to the first person who makes you feel alive again, and remarriage is a way to rejoin the human race. The problem is that you may be mistaking lust for love as you strive to escape your depression and the stress of being solely responsible for yourself and your kids. It's no wonder you glom onto the first person who's willing to take on a ready-made family.

Here's an important statistic: It can take up to three years to heal from your wounds and feel whole again after the death or divorce of your partner. Avoiding the necessary grieving and healing period may set you up for a rebound marriage.

As the saying goes, marry in haste and repent in leisure.

However, many folks fall for common traps when they marry on the rebound. They often

- ✔ **Marry the same kind of person as their first partner:** It's a depressing thought for folks who've been divorced, but unless you get some counseling or have such a level head on your shoulders that you can figure it out for yourself, research shows that you may fall into this trap by bringing unresolved problems with you to the second marriage.

- ✔ **Mistake sex for love:** When a relationship reaches a certain point, couples often mistakenly feel that having sex proves that they love each other. We all need love and affection, and single parents often miss receiving it from their previous marriage. So they subconsciously fall into this trap of marrying the wrong person just because they *need* to replace their loneliness with what they perceive to be true love. But this *true love* may only be the temporary satisfaction that comes from physical intimacy and sexual pleasure.

✔ **Marry for the sake of the children:** Avoid this pitfall at all costs. If you remarry for the sole purpose of providing your kids with a new mom or dad, it'll come back to bite you. Even though you're lonely and you think your kids need and deserve to have a new stepparent, wait until the right one comes along — even if it takes years.

✔ **Give into pressure to remarry:** Beware of well-intentioned friends and relatives who insist that you should remarry as soon as possible because the kids need a "complete family" again. Don't let this unfair pressure influence you or cloud your better judgment. You have enough stress in your life without being pushed into remarriage before you're ready. If you're a single mother who's dating a single father, you may find him pressuring you, too. Single fathers tend to remarry within 18 months of a divorce, but single mothers are more cautious and tend to wait longer. Most divorces are initiated by women, so they're much more hesitant to jump back into marriage.

The bottom line: Give yourself time to heal from the trauma of the divorce or death of your spouse. Play it cool, easing back into the dating game slowly. It's fine to have adult friends and contacts — just make it clear during the first year or two that you're not ready to remarry. Make good choices by socializing when and where you feel most comfortable. Don't feel pressured by friends and family members. Being happy with yourself needs to come first, then you'll be ready when the right one comes along. (Chapter 12 gets you on the road to grieving right.)

The opposite of marrying on the rebound is to develop a strong friendship first — one where you talk freely with each other about money, kids, sex, and your careers. This open communication is the best foundation for a successful remarriage. Remarriages that work out tend to be relationships in which the couple took things slowly, got to know each other really well, and in many instances, sought out an experienced counselor *before* marrying for the second time.

Considering a Prenuptial Agreement

Before plunging into marriage, you may want to consider a *prenuptial agreement,* a marriage contract between you and your fiancé that is drawn up and signed before you get married — a recipe for the success of the marriage.

Many people think that one of these agreements only applies to couples where one or both are quite wealthy and the couple needs to decide what will happen to their wealth in case of a divorce. In actuality, however, a prenuptial agreement can also pertain to transactions that need to be made as soon as the couple is married, pertaining to such things as ownership of property, business interests, inheritance payments, alimony, or child-support payments. If a prenuptial agreement is a good idea for a first marriage — and many financial counselors believe that it is — it could be an even better idea for a second marriage.

ANECDOTE

A beautiful love story

Forty-one-year-old Benjamin and 36-year-old Joanne met on a blind date. Both were widowed with a total of seven children between them. Both Ben and Joanne had also avoided the dating scene since their mates died, mainly because they were totally immersed in their kids' activities, but also because the chances of meeting anyone who would be willing to take on such a big family didn't seem likely.

Benjamin's older brother (who knew Joanne through his wife's floral business) played matchmaker by setting up their blind date. Ben called Joanne and asked her to go to dinner and a local theater production. Joanne had a suspicion he would call, and against her better judgment (because she enjoyed live theater), she accepted. Their evening was interesting — to say the least. Over dinner they discovered that between her four children and his three, they each had a 12-year-old and a 16-year-old. Their kids had similar interests that included soccer, camping, and playing in the school band. The night flew by as they talked about their kids and their own lives, including the trauma of having a spouse die.

Soon after their first date, Ben, a trial lawyer, became so involved in a case that he didn't have time to date or even think about anything other than his kids and the case. He explained his situation to Joanne and told her that he hoped they could get together over dinner again sometime after he had wrapped up his case. She took his

comments with a grain of salt, figuring that they were his way of easing out of the situation because he really didn't care to date her again.

A couple months went by. Then one Monday morning the doorbell rang and Joanne received a delivery from the florist she worked for. Surprised, she opened the box and found a dozen long-stem red roses with a note attached: "Shall we give it another try? How about dinner at On the Green Friday night? I'll pick you up about six o'clock. I'll call you. Thinking about you, Ben." She was totally surprised because she'd given up on him. She was also surprised that Ben's sister-in-law must have known that Ben placed the order for the roses, but she hadn't said a word.

Their next dinner date was fun, and it was followed by more dates off and on over the next six months. Everything seemed to be pretty platonic, at least in Joanne's mind, until one night Ben took her dancing and — what do you know? — a spark of physical attraction finally flickered and changed the complexion of their relationship completely. From that point on, they tried to spend as much time together as their crazy schedules allowed.

Bright and early on the morning of Joanne's birthday, Ben showed up at her door. She was wearing her robe and didn't have on a scrap of makeup, but she invited him in. He seemed awfully nervous as he handed her what he called an early birthday gift. She opened it and found a lovely pearl and ruby ring. She thanked him for the beautiful birthday gift, and he said, "Well, it isn't just a birthday gift. I was wondering if you'd wear it as an engagement ring?" She was totally astounded! All she could say was, "This is too complicated . . . this is too complicated." He asked her why, and she said, "Well, the kids. . . ." Ben answered with a twinkle in his eye, "What? You want more?"

That struck Joanne as so funny that she started laughing and couldn't stop. Ben started laughing too, and when the kids came downstairs to see what the racket was about, Ben and Joanne were sitting on the living-room floor dissolved in laughter. Joanne's kids asked what was so funny, and she replied, "We're going to get married!" Joanne's kids adored Ben, and were thrilled about the news.

All seven kids got involved in the wedding plans. Joanne's daughter made her wedding dress, a simple white-linen sheath, and Ben's two older sons built a portable altar that they placed in Ben's brother and sister-in-law's garden for the touching, tearful, summer-afternoon ceremony.

The kids are adjusting to their new Brady Bunch life, which will be a lot more comfortable when they all move into their new, larger home. Ben and Joanne know that raising a house full of seven teenagers won't be easy, but they're sure that their love is strong enough to handle it. And they also know that, as full as their lives are now with the kids and all their activities, their children won't be with them forever. Someday even their youngest will move on to college and a career, but Ben and Joanne will be able to spend the rest of their lives together. Thank goodness for blind dates!

Many people have misconceptions about a prenuptial agreement:

✔ **Only rich people need one:** You're not one of those couples with lucrative stock portfolios, summer homes, and rental properties.

✔ **It's a slap in your partner's face:** The agreement is concrete evidence that you think the marriage may not last.

When you examine the idea with a level head (without the emotions), however, you may realize that it only makes good business sense. After all, any marriage (whether it's a first, second, third, or tenth marriage) is a risky undertaking. Right? If your marriage should fail, as unlikely as that scenario may be, don't you want to emerge with your finances intact (for your own sake and for the sake of your children)?

Here are just a few of the issues a prenuptial agreement may address:

✔ Assets of each spouse before the marriage

✔ Assets accumulated during the marriage

✔ Child-support obligations from previous marriages

✔ Debts of each spouse before the marriage

✔ Debts accumulated during the marriage

- Life-insurance provisions
- Pensions, IRAs, and 401K accounts

Prenuptial agreements also usually include factors that determine the division of joint assets in the case of divorce, such as

- Length of time you were married
- Birth of children during your marriage
- Ages of children from previous marriages at the time of the divorce

If you're not sure how you feel about this idea, and you need more input before you decide whether to take this route, make an appointment with your tax lawyer. A lawyer can explain the process to you. While you're at it, talk to the attorney about drawing up a new will that protects your children in case of your untimely death — ooh, now that's a *really* depressing thought. As depressing as it may be to think about, however, it's smart to revise your will when you remarry because your estate will change and become more complex due to the community property laws of your state. You also need to consider what happens if your new partner dies and has not legally adopted your children, in which case they cannot inherit his estate unless a new will is drawn up naming your children as beneficiaries. Your current will may no longer be valid because the assets named may now become community property with your new spouse, so sit down with your attorney and draw up a new will to protect the rights of your children.

A prenuptial agreement is *not* for everyone. Depending on your emotional makeup and the mutual trust that you share with your future spouse, having a prenuptial agreement may not be your thing. We're just pointing out that it's something for you to think about, and if you and your fiancé have a trusting relationship, you'll feel comfortable talking it over with an attorney together.

Facing Blended-Family Struggles

When single parents remarry, a whole new cast of characters emerges:

- Stepmother
- Stepfather
- Stepsiblings
- Half siblings

✔ Stepcousins

✔ Stepgrandparents and other assorted relatives

✔ The ex-spouse and his/her family

Each character has his or her own personality and value system based on a lifetime of relationships and experiences, so when the characters are thrown together in the intimacy of a family setting, it would be surprising if everyone instantly got along. But research shows that blended families can develop loving, compatible relationships over time — it just takes a little know-how and a little patience.

With all the work that can accompany melding a new family together, the relationship that started the whole process can easily be forgotten. Here are four great ways to make your second marriage work:

✔ Continue courting each other after the wedding (and never stop).

✔ Keep the lines of communication open. Talk to each other.

✔ Don't let your career or your parenting duties crowd out spending relaxed, private time together.

✔ Don't allow your lives to get into a rut. Keep life interesting by taking up new hobbies, finding new interests, discovering new places to go on vacation, and starting new routines. Think outside the box.

The fairytale view of a blended family is that it's like a box of instant brownie mix. Take one marriage, add some kids, throw in a pet and an egg, and in no time at all, you have a wonderful warm family where the kids get along with each other pretty well. In real life, however, a stepfamily faces a lot of problems, especially at first. (In many cases, stepfamilies resemble homemade brownies — they take a bit longer to perfect.) We discuss some of the most common problems and possible solutions in the following sections.

Bonding with stepchildren

We know that bonding with stepchildren can be a difficult and frustrating experience for both you and the child. We also realize that unconditional love is reserved for your biological children and that it's unrealistic to think you can feel the same way about your new partner's kids. But take heart: Bonds will usually develop eventually. You can speed up the process by developing your own special connection with each of your stepchildren, which may evolve over time into genuine caring and love for each other.

For example, does your stepson enjoy playing golf? Treat him to a round of golf once in a while — just the two of you. You'll be surprised how a common interest can help with the bonding process. With the golf example, the natural opportunities for friendly chats as you walk along the fairway or share a meal in the pro shop cafe will also push the relationship along.

Both you and your spouse, regardless of your gender, can find *something* in common with each of your stepchildren. The possibilities are only limited by your imagination. From participating in a sport to cooking to sharing your love of movies, you can think of *some* way to connect. And, if you connect, a healthy, close relationship will usually follow. It's the adult's responsibility to take the lead at connecting, and it needs to be done at the pace of the child. This can take a much longer time than you think it should — particularly with older children.

One important thing you can do is to encourage and support your stepchildren's relationship with their non-resident parent. Unconsciously, you may want to compete with or show the other parent what a great new family you're creating. What you really need to do, however, is realize that your stepkids need both of their biological parents, in addition to your emotional support and nurturing as their new stepparent.

Another important step is to nurture your relationships with your own children. It isn't unusual in the months leading up to a painful divorce for the kids to feel a bit neglected, and in the thrill of the romance and excitement of a new marriage, your kids may often feel like the fifth wheel. So, you, as their biological parent, need to spend extra time each day talking with and giving emotional support to each of your children, especially if they lost their other parent through death. They may feel confused, withdrawn, and depressed, so they need you now more than ever.

If your stepchild lost a parent through death, he may also be experiencing these same feelings, so you need to be there for him, be attentive and ready to talk and help him through the grieving process. Don't make the mistake of trying to take the deceased parent's place. He isn't looking for a replacement for his mom or dad — so tread lightly as long as he still feels an emotional attachment to his deceased parent. As he heals and recovers, you'll be there for him, ready to bond when he's ready.

Battling stepsiblings

If only the kids would hit it off and get along from the start, oh what a wonderful world it would be. But we have news for you: It's as likely as someone walking up to your door with a wheelbarrow full of cash.

Don't be surprised if your new family takes a while to blend together. And for many families, a more realistic goal is creating a loving stepfamily where individual needs are honored and accepted. This would be a collection of individuals who can support the family rule and who agree to disagree. In fact, some authorities think of stepfamilies more as "fruit salad," rather than some kind of "smoothie." This metaphor allows us to value and accept each person as an individual within the family!

The good news is that kids are adaptable. They'll come around eventually — they just need time to get used to the new family structure. Some family therapists say that kids can take up to three years to adjust. During the adjustment phase, don't constantly force the issue by insisting that one sibling apologize to the other for something he said or did or by forcing the kids to talk about their feelings during a family meeting. And, whatever you do, don't expect the oldest child to serve as a free on-call babysitter.

One of the biggest problems you may face with your blended family is the reshuffled birth order. Your oldest son, who was also the first-born child, may now be third in pecking order behind his two older stepbrothers. Take a look in Chapter 6 for helpful info on birth-order problems and how to handle them. Try to treat all the kids fairly, according to their unique needs, as they settle in to their new roles within the blended family structure.

Try your hardest not to play favorites. Feeling more interested in your own child's school project, for example, is only natural, but try to show the same amount of interest in your stepchild's project. Be careful that you don't praise your own kids in front of your stepchildren. And beware of those gifts. If you buy something for one of the kids, buy something of equal value for all of them. You want *all* the children in your new blended family to feel equally loved and cherished.

If you introduce a half brother or sister into the mix, prepare the children in every way you can think of to prevent sibling rivalry and jealousy. Plan age-appropriate ways to include the children in the excitement of adding a new family member. You can take older children with you for the monthly prenatal checkups, let them help shop for all the baby necessities and fix up the baby's new room. You can also take the kids to the hospital for a *sibling tour,* where they get to see the room where the baby will be born and the nursery where the baby will be taken care of after the birth. All these ideas will help the kids think of the new baby as *their* baby, too.

After the baby's born, encourage his brothers and sisters to help care for him, depending on their ages and abilities. However, avoid making a responsible older child into a *second mother* or a permanent babysitter. Also, be careful not to goo and ga too loudly over the new baby in front of the rest of your kids, because the baby may be perceived as a threat to their security. Try to lavish all your kids with equal love and praise.

The addition of a new baby into a blended family can be just the perfect ingredient and focus for expressing love within the family. After all, who can resist those first smiles and the fun of watching a baby grow and develop?

Playing the name game

Trying to figure out what stepchildren are going to call their new stepparents is a common problem in blended families, especially at first. The answer to this one is relatively simple: Don't force the issue. Your new stepson may not want to call you Dad.

The important thing for the stepparent to remember is that she is not competing with or taking the place of the children's non-custodial parent. Having them call you by your first name in the beginning may be the simplest. When they're ready, they may dub you with an affectionate mom or dad term, or a name of their own creation, which will be your best reward.

Disliking a new stepchild

Wow! Being unable to stand the kid is a real problem because you're going to be living with him or her — in the same house — for many years to come. You need to take a good hard look at your feelings. What is it about the kid that bothers you?

Does he remind you too much of someone you had conflicts with in your past? If so, this isn't the child's fault. You could be letting your stepchild press your buttons, and he may not even realize that it's happening. Are you sure that junior is the sole source of the conflict? Are you blameless? Can you do anything to ease the negative vibes?

Not getting along with each other's children is a major reason why remarriages fail, so here's a way to lessen the tension when you don't really care for a new stepchild: Look for something good about the kid. Because you fell in love with his mom or dad, look for some traits or qualities the he shares with his parent. Go out of your way to notice the good that he does. If he keeps fresh firewood loaded beside the fireplace without being asked, thank him. Or, if he's a natural musician (even though you *hate* those drums), tell him how talented you think he is. Looking for and commenting on positive traits will help you change your attitude toward him, and he'll try harder to please you in the future because he'll see that you value him as a person. Give it a try.

Disagreeing on discipline policies

Disciplining the kids can be a huge problem if you and your spouse don't sit down and decide how you're going to handle it. Most blended families find that the best approach is for the natural parent to discipline the child for at least the first year, and for the stepparent to play a supporting role, always following through on the decisions made by the natural parent. Maintaining a united front prevents the kids from playing one parent against the other.

In addition to being supportive of your new partner, you (as the stepparent) can contribute to a mellow family environment by recognizing good behavior from the stepchildren, helping them with their homework, rooting for them at their ballgames, and establishing friendships by being a good listener and sincerely caring about them. (If you're having problems coming up with a shared discipline plan, take a look in Chapter 9 for some helpful ideas.)

Don't make your blended-family discipline plan up as you go along. You need to have a friendly family meeting as soon as you can to let the kids know that you and your spouse are like a well-oiled pro-wrestling tag team. After you establish the rules and show the kids that you're both committed to following through on them, you'll have fewer problems from the start.

Clashing about the cash

Figure this issue out *before* you remarry. But, if you're already married and you haven't addressed money until now because you assumed that you'd agree on the subject, it's not too late. Sit down together (with a financial counselor if necessary) and come up with a budgeting plan. If you both have 10-year-old boys, and one receives an allowance of $20 a week while the other gets $5, you have a problem. You need to sort out little discrepancies like this so that each child receives the same amount. Maybe you can settle on $10 per week per child.

You also need to decide who'll be the bill payer in the family. *One* of you must be in charge of the checkbook, or the bills won't be paid on time.

If the money issue has become a crisis in your new marriage, run (don't walk) to a financial counselor for some help. Don't let a financial problem fester. It's not worth the tension when you can easily solve the issue with just a little help. If the problem is a matter of making ends meet, you can start looking for a solution in Chapter 5 where we outline dozens of ways to live a quality life on less money. And remember that money represents power and there are often hidden issues related to this topic. In this case, an experienced marriage counselor may be helpful.

Dealing with all the relatives

In Chapter 10, we discuss practical ways to establish and keep strong relationships with all sorts of extended-family members, but here's the gist of it: At this time in their lives, your kids need all the love they can get. They also need to be around grandparents and aunts and uncles who can help your kids realize that most marriages do hang together for many years. Your ex's relatives and your new partner's parents and extended-family members need to serve as anchors in your kids' lives. Some days you may feel like drop kicking your ex's family out of your life, which we can understand, but for your kids' sake, suck it up and take advantage of all they can do for your children.

If your blended-family smoothie isn't gelling as well as you had hoped, you can find all kinds of help within your community. In addition to stepparent support groups, you can try stepparent classes or family therapy, which may be very helpful to your entire family. (Check out Chapter 18 for some resources.)

Longing for privacy

When single parents marry and set up their new blended household, privacy can be an enormous problem, especially when you and your new spouse are enjoying your lovely newfound sex life. How do you handle the bedroom-door thing? Do you leave it unlocked and hope like heck no one comes bounding in, or do you install a half-dozen deadbolts?

In our informal interviews on the subject, we found that some parents kept their bedroom door closed, but not locked, with the understanding that their kids must *always* knock and ask permission to enter. Other parents locked their bedroom doors during lovemaking sessions and then unlocked them during the rest of the night. Some couples we talked to (especially those folks with their children in fulltime residence) found the privacy issue to be so exasperating that they escaped during the day to a hotel for a little uninterrupted lovemaking.

Misfiring on all cylinders

If you feel like everyone has his or her own agenda and that you're not blending smoothly at all, a family meeting may help. Schedule regular get-togethers where every family member is present and encouraged to talk *without interruption.* Family meetings are a good way to both fix problems and perform routine maintenance.

Slapping on a "Hi my name is" nametag

If your family meetings don't seem to be turning up any mega-problems (thank goodness), use the time together to get to know each other. One new stepdad got his brood together and passed out index cards that he prepared in advance. Each card asked a question like "What's your favorite color?" "What was your favorite vacation?" or "If you had three wishes, what would they be?" The idea is to have plenty of cards so that each child chooses one or two during each family meeting. This exercise is a wonderful way to get to know each other.

Rotate the role of facilitator, including the children in the rotation. However, if you've been designated as the family-meeting facilitator for a particular meeting, toss out a couple of open-ended questions and see what develops. Here are a couple we came up with:

- How do you think things are going so far?
- What would you say are our biggest problems blending together as a family?
- What are some ways your mom and I can help out?
- What type of changes would you suggest?

If the kids sense that you're sincere and genuine in your attempts to solve any problems that exist, you may be surprised with their openness and willingness to be part of the solution.

A sense of humor can go a long way toward blending your family. One stepparent took a shoebox and converted it into a "Brady Bunch Suggestion Box." He encouraged the kids to write down their questions, problems, or anything else they wanted to discuss during the next family meeting. The suggestions could be anonymous, but at least the children knew that the subject would be covered during their next get-together.

Tripping over baggage

When couples remarry, each spouse comes with baggage from the past — ex-spouses, ex-in-laws, kids, pre-wedding debt, weird food preferences, and on, and on, and on.

How can you handle all this baggage? Go with the flow (or to use another common phrase, deal with it)! If you find that you just can't deal with all the suitcases and carry-ons, you need to figure out why. Are you jealous? Insecure? Resistant to change? Stuck in a long line at the ticket counter? After you uncover the reasons why you're stumbling over this baggage day in and day out, dealing with it will probably be a lot easier. If you still can't check the baggage, you and your new love may benefit from a little family therapy to help smooth things out. If it feels more personal, by all means go for some of your own individual counseling, as well.

Molly finds her way

Molly was 17 when she showed up at a family therapist's office. The visit wasn't her idea. Her stepmother had talked her father into it. He always did what she said — at least that's the way Molly saw it.

For the first therapy session, the entire family went in together. It was awful. Her brother wouldn't say a word, and Molly felt as if the whole family expected her to say or do something. She felt like throwing up. Ellen, Molly's new stepmother, did most of the talking, and she was brutal. She didn't like Molly's manners, her grades, or the fact that she sometimes stayed out all night and slept all day. Ellen and Molly's dad also suspected that she was drinking, and they even wondered if she was doing drugs. Molly had to defend herself, so she complained about the excessive rules and how Ellen and her dad expected her to be perfect.

The next therapy appointment was a one-on-one session between Molly and the therapist. The therapist told her she was curious and wanted to know everything about Molly's life. In spite of her reluctance, Molly started talking. She found that she could complain and say things about Ellen, the wicked stepmother, without shocking the therapist. She agreed to return the following week when, much to her own surprise, Molly talked about her mother. It was a relief to tell the therapist things she hadn't told anyone.

She told the therapist that she was 7 when her mother got sick. She didn't know what was wrong, but she felt as if her mom's illness changed everything in her life. Her father was quiet and seemed angry. Her mother was in the hospital and then at home lying on the couch all the time. Her grandparents came, but they weren't much fun. As Molly began to explore those fateful days, she became very sad and angry. Looking back, she realized that she was excluded from her own mother's funeral. She remembers going to the zoo. How could they make her go to the zoo when her mother was dead? Her father told Molly and her older brother that their mother had died and gone to heaven. He told them everything would be all right. He told them not to talk about it and to go to school and get good grades so their mother would be proud.

Molly remembers walking into her mother's room one day and seeing that all her clothes and shoes were gone. Something really hit her about not seeing her mother's slippers sitting in their regular spot. This memory was still very painful, and Molly shed tears. Then she told the therapist her dad had remarried, and they moved in with her stepmother's two kids. From the start, Molly felt that the new stepmother didn't like her. And besides, she always stuck up for her kids. They were angels. Her father always took her stepmother's side, too. He never stuck up for her when her stepmother corrected her at the dinner table. Molly decided that she just didn't care. She became more and more withdrawn and stayed in her room after school.

The psychotherapist encouraged Molly to bring in some photos of her mother and the family. She wanted Molly to think about how losing her mom felt — even though no one had ever talked to her about it. She encouraged Molly to ask her father about her mom's illness and what it had been like for him. She even told her to ask him why she didn't get to go to the funeral and why he had acted so strange.

Molly asked her father to go to the therapist with her. He seemed pretty reluctant but agreed to go. Molly did all the talking. She told her father how her life had changed when her mom died and how she didn't think anyone remembered that she was around. She told him how she guessed that her mother was dying and wondered what she had done to make her mother get sick — she had tried to be very quiet and good. She was scared and cried herself to sleep.

Dad was shocked to hear that Molly had been so aware of what was going on. He confessed

that he couldn't even remember who took care of her during that time. He recalled that no one wanted to tell the children about their mother, so he guessed that they just didn't. He also said that no one thought that they should be exposed to the funeral. It was all too unbearable.

Molly confessed that she had been very angry when he got remarried. She realized that some of her bad behavior was due to hurt and jealousy. She said it was like she had lost both of her parents. Dad explained that he had wanted his kids to have a woman around the house to take care of them in ways that he couldn't.

Needless to say, Molly experienced an avalanche of feelings, but she found that her anger and negative behavior didn't seem necessary anymore. Her father arranged to drive her and her friend to college in the next state. He wanted to have some time to get to know her better. They had a good trip and developed a new sense of ease with each other.

Molly arranged to phone the therapist once a month and to see her during vacations. The therapist urged her to join a bereavement support group because it's never too late to do the grieving that has been postponed for so many years.

Following the Ten Stepparent Commandments

A stepfamily *can* meld into a supportive, satisfying, happy unit, especially if the stepparents follow certain guidelines that have been proven to work.

Follow these commandments:

✔ **Allow your relationships with your stepchildren to develop slowly:** Research shows that letting the kids take the lead is the best approach. Don't force a warm, fuzzy relationship — let it come naturally. Be friendly, supportive, and available when they need you but go slowly with showing physical affection, making changes in their normal routines, and setting up house rules.

✔ **Let your stepchildren decide what to call you:** Don't force the kids to call you Mom or Dad. Allow them to call you by your first name if they're most comfortable with that.

✔ **Be strong as a couple:** Your kids will feel reassured if you show unity as a couple. You may have a blended family, but at least you and your new spouse are in cahoots. Your relationship will become a strong foundation for your new family. To be a strong couple, you also need to keep your loving relationship fresh. Schedule mini-honeymoons once in a while in addition to going on a date (just the two of you) at least once every two weeks.

✔ **Spend one-on-one time with each of your children and stepchildren:** Set up scenarios in which you can spend time with one child alone. You may ask him to help you fix the fence, run an errand with you, or go to the driving range to hit a few balls. Or you may actually find some quiet time (it can happen) when the two of you can sit on the patio and have an informal chat.

✔ **Treat every child fairly:** Don't show favoritism in any way. Following this commandment is tough, so think before you speak.

✔ **Keep your sense of humor:** Try to see the lighter side of parenting. Some of the predicaments your kids get into can be pretty funny. So instead of coming unglued when your 3-year-old stepdaughter gets into your makeup, take a photo of her instead. (Then you can figure out a more secure place to keep your beauty supplies in the future.)

✔ **Never badmouth your stepchild's non-custodial parent:** As tempting as blasting the absent parent may be at the time, try to speak kindly about and show respect for him or her — including comments you make to your new spouse about his or her ex when the kids are within hearing distance. And don't forget that little pitchers have *big* ears.

✔ **Let the natural parent handle discipline problems:** This commandment is especially applicable when families are just starting to blend. Be supportive of her disciplinary decisions unless they are abusive, but don't become directly involved.

✔ **Plan frequent activities that the entire family enjoys:** A little trial and error may be necessary, but try to find activities that all of you don't just enjoy, but live for. These activities can be as simple as backpacking, bowling, or simply taking in a movie together once in a while.

✔ **Be patient:** Enough said.

Part VI
The Part of Tens

The 5th Wave   By Rich Tennant

"I always speak to the kids in a quiet and respectful way, but occasionally I wear this to add a little punctuation."

In this part . . .

The Part of Tens is composed of lists that are helpful to you as a single parent. You can to read the ten questions single parents most frequently ask, along with practical answers to those questions. You can also read about some valuable resources that single parents need.

Chapter 17

Ten Questions Single Parents Most Frequently Ask

In This Chapter

▶ Taking time to heal

▶ Dealing with money matters

▶ Playing the dating game

Single parents are seeking answers to questions about everything from fitting in as a single parent, recovering from a divorce, and negotiating for child support and alimony payments, to such things as surviving on a single-parent budget, finding a therapist or a support group, and coping with dating and remarriage. In this chapter, we have assembled the ten questions single parents ask most frequently. We're sure that you'll find at least a couple of your questions answered here.

How Can I Adjust?

Being a single parent isn't easy in a world where couples seem joined at the hip. But what you need to do is to stop feeling sorry for yourself and look for ways to fit in. Get involved with a single-parent support group for the support and the fun. Reach out to other single parents who may feel like they're having problems fitting in, too. Invite them and their kids over for a potluck dinner or a picnic in the park. Chapter 2 has more ideas for making your way in the world as a single person. The better you feel about yourself as a person, the better you'll feel as a single parent.

How Can I Heal?

Whether your spouse died or you've just survived a painful divorce, we know you're going through a grieving process that includes denial, anger, bargaining, and depression and finally ends in acceptance. Get involved in a divorce or bereavement support group. You also need to try to heal by crying whenever you feel the urge, exercising, taking some kind of class, working on your hobby, socializing with other adults, and reaching out to others. Yes, believe it not, other folks are hurting and need your help. By helping others, you can actually help yourself heal faster. Finally, if a year has passed and you're still paralyzed by grief, seek out the help of a professional therapist. In Chapter 12, we talk in depth about grief, its stages, and how to cope.

How Can I Make Fair Child-Support and Alimony Payments?

If you're the potential *payer,* don't accept the first terms suggested by your ex's attorney as you negotiate your child-custody or alimony agreements. Hire your own attorney to help negotiate on your behalf, and if you still feel that you're expected to pay more than you should, request that the court assign a mediator to collect all the facts and make an unbiased decision. Courts usually provide a court-ordered mediator at no cost, but you can also pay for a private mediator who may be able to come up with an agreement that you and your ex both will both find acceptable. Chapter 3 talks about this topic in more depth.

How Can I Receive Fair Child-Support and Alimony Payments?

If you'll be receiving child support or alimony payments, stick up for yourself and your children by fighting for the support payments you deserve. Hire an attorney to help you negotiate terms you can live with or, if you and your ex are at an impasse, request that the court assign a mediator to assemble all the facts and make a decision that you must both abide by. When a court-ordered mediator gets involved, the terms are usually as fair and unbiased as you can expect to receive. Chapter 3 talks about these topics in more depth.

How Can I Make It on My Budget?

As a single parent, you're probably experiencing a money crunch because your income is less than it was before. In many cases, the income that was supporting one household is now supporting two households. Look for ways to increase your income. Try to eliminate or restructure your debts. Employ all the little tricks of living a quality lifestyle on less income, which we outline in Chapter 5.

How Can We Develop a Co-parenting Plan That Works?

You and your ex need to have a written co-parenting plan that addresses all the issues including living arrangements, shared expenses, religious training, schooling, extracurricular activities, discipline policies, and provisions for unexpected catastrophes. Take a look at the sample co-parenting plan in Chapter 9, which provides the clauses and wording you can use as a guideline for your own plan. As you talk about your plan, keep the best interests of your children at heart. This plan is *not* about you — it's about your kids and the best way to maintain continuity in their lives and give them the assurance that comes with both parents' love and care.

Where Can I Find a Single-Parent Support Group?

Single-parent support groups are everywhere. You can even find specialty support groups such as groups for single mothers only, single fathers only, and mixed singles. The diversity doesn't stop there. You can choose from groups that focus on religious support, bereavement support, or support for people who have recently divorced.

Ask for referrals from your therapist, religious institution, and community agencies. Ask around and watch your local newspaper for information about support-group meetings. We recommend that you attend at least three sessions before you decide whether a group is or isn't right for you. After you find a comfortable fit, you'll receive the support you need. Chapter 19 lists resources at your disposal.

Where Can I Find Counseling for My Kids and Myself?

Ask for referrals from your friends, family physician, religious advisor, or health-insurance provider. You can also locate free or low-cost therapy through community non-profit centers, local churches, and university master's or doctorate programs. Regardless of your income or health-insurance provisions, you *can* find professional counseling to fit your budget, so don't assume counseling is only for your wealthy friends. Professional therapy is now within everyone's reach. Chapter 14 gives the inside scoop on this topic.

How Do I Get Back into the Dating Game?

Whether you want to date just for the fun of it or you're looking for someone to marry, here are a few ways to find someone to date:

✔ Join a coed club or class.

✔ Hang out in bookstores, museums, art galleries, libraries, and any other place where singles frequent.

✔ Get involved in your church, synagogue, or mosque (especially their single-parent support groups).

The fish are out there — it's just a matter of having the right bait and fishing gear. Chapter 15 can get you out on the water.

What Factors Should I Consider Before Remarriage?

Before considering remarriage, think about these factors. More on this topic in Chapter 16.

✔ The longer you date and get to know your fiancé, the more likely your marriage will be a happy one that lasts.

✔ Avoid marrying on the rebound.

✔ Taking the dating thing nice and slow is the way to go.

Chapter 18

Ten Great Resources for Single Parents

* *

In This Chapter

▶ Finding a big brother

▶ Meeting other parents without partners

▶ Becoming a single parent by choice

* *

As we conducted our research for this book, we discovered many helpful resources for single parents. We chose ten of the best for this chapter, including resources that provide help for your child's depression, ways to find a marriage and family therapist, guidance if you're adopting a child, and groups that support and nurture single parents and those of you who have recently entered into a blended family relationship. We describe each of these resources briefly; however, you'll find the Web sites contain much more helpful information than we have room to describe here. The bottom line is that help is at your fingertips, so go for it!

American Academy of Child and Adolescent Psychiatry (AACAP)

This organization offers a "Facts for Families" information sheet that describes and explains children's mental-health problems, including depression. You can also contact them for a referral to your local council of child and adolescent psychiatry, which can refer you to a child psychiatrist in your area.

Address: 3615 Wisconsin Avenue NW, Washington, DC 20016-3007

Phone: 202-966-7300

Internet: www.aacap.org

American Association for Marriage and Family Therapy

The following contact info is for the national headquarters for this association. Get in touch with these folks, and they'll send you a list of clinical members in your area.

>**Address:** 112 South Alfred Street, Alexandria, VA 22314-3061

>**Phone:** 703-838-9808

>**Internet:** www.aamft.org

Big Brothers Big Sisters of America

This nondenominational organization with tons of local branches provides professionally supervised adult men and women to serve as role models for kids from single-parent homes.

>**Address:** 230 North 13th Street, Philadelphia, PA 19107

>**Phone:** 215-567-7000

>**Internet:** www.bbbsa.org

National Center for Missing and Exploited Children

This organization helps parents and law enforcement agencies locate kidnapped children. Their Web site also provides helpful information to prevent abduction or kidnapping, including School Safety Tips, Rules for Going to and from School More Safely, Rules for Children Who are Home Alone, plus ways to teach your children how to be safer when using the Internet.

>**Address:** Charles B. Wang International Children's Building, 699 Prince Street, Alexandria, VA 22314-3175

>**Phone:** 703-274-3900; 24-hour hotline 800-THE-LOST

>**Internet:** www.missingkids.org

National Council for Adoption (NCFA)

This charitable organization conducts research and provides information and educational materials on adoption. The NCFA also provides advocacy services on adoption issues, which means they offer support and guidance for anyone going through the adoption process.

>**Address:** 225 North Washington Street, Alexandria, VA 22314-2561
>
>**Phone:** 703-299-6633
>
>**Internet:** www.ncfa-usa.org

National Organization of Single Mothers

The National Organization of Single Mothers publishes a helpful newsletter for divorced, widowed, and never-married single mothers. The organization has local chapters, so use the following contact information to find a chapter near you. Their Web site also includes links to a lot of helpful information, including Dating Do's and Don'ts, Single Mother's Guide to Child Support, a Freebies Auction, and weekly columns.

>**Address:** P.O. Box 68, Midland, NC 28107
>
>**Phone:** 704-888-KIDS
>
>**Internet:** www.singlemothers.org

Parents Without Partners

This group sponsors activities for all kinds of single parents, including those who have been divorced or widowed. Contact the national headquarters, and the fine folks there can refer you to a group meeting close to your home.

>**Address:** 1650 South Dixie Highway, Suite 510, Boca Raton, FL 33432
>
>**Phone:** 561-391-8833
>
>**Internet:** www.parentswithoutpartners.org

RESOLVE

RESOLVE is a national organization that supports women who want to become pregnant. This group will refer you to a local chapter and provide you with the very latest info on fertility drugs and procedures.

Address: 1310 Broadway, Somerville, MA 02144-1731

Phone: 888-623-0744

Internet: www.resolve.org

Single Mothers by Choice

Single Mothers by Choice is a very supportive organization for single women who want to become single parents through conception or adoption. Use this contact info to find a local chapter.

Address: P.O. Box 1642, New York, NY 10028

Phone: 212-988-0993

Internet: http://mattes.home.pipeline.com

Stepfamily Association of America (SAA)

The Stepfamily Association of America is a national support group for step-families. Contact them to subscribe to their publication, *Stepfamilies*. You can also request their general information packet, which lists local chapters.

Address: 650 J Street, Suite 205, Lincoln, NE 68508

Phone: 800-735-0329

Internet: www.saafamilies.org

Index

• A •

AACAP (American Academy of Child and Adolescent Psychiatry), 315
acceptance stage of grief, 29, 232, 235
activities. *See also* fun
  dating and kid's activities, 278–279
  entertainment/recreation expenses, 77, 89–90
  getting involved with children's, 181
  overloading children with, 191
adjustment disorders with depression. *See* depression
adolescents. *See* teenagers
adoption, 24, 43–44
age of children
  birth order and behavior, 104
  co-parenting schedule and, 172–173
  divorce effects and, 136–142
  parenting guidelines, 102–103
  puberty stages in boys, 118–119
  puberty stages in girls, 120–121
  talking about sex and, 123–124
agency adoption, 43
Al-Anon, 219
alcohol, 103, 217, 219
alimony, 36, 46–47, 312
American Academy of Child and Adolescent Psychiatry (AACAP), 315
American Association for Marriage and Family Therapy, 261, 316
American Psychological Association, 261
Anecdote icon, 4
anger
  in children after divorce, 143–145
  disciplining children and, 186
  explaining yours after divorce, 154
  pushing your ex's buttons, 194–195
  releasing after divorce, 19, 20, 237
  stage of grief (adults), 28, 231, 233
  stage of grief (children), 147–148
anxiety. *See* fear or anxiety
appointments for chats with children, 109, 152
artificial insemination, 24, 45
assets, 36
attorneys. *See also* legal issues
  abuse by relatives and, 208
  adoption and, 44
  for co-parenting plans, 172
  expectations for, 35–36
  finding a divorce attorney, 34–36
  need for, 33
automatic wage attachment, 36

• B •

babies. *See also* children
  co-parenting schedule and, 173
  divorce and, 136–137
  tips for raising, 102
babying your children, 130
babysitting co-op, 66
bargaining stage of grief, 28, 231, 233–234
bartering, 92
becoming a single parent
  by accident, 26–27
  by choice, 23–26
  by death of spouse, 15, 21–22
  by divorce, 15, 16–20
  legal protection, 27
  signs of difficulty coping with, 27–28

bedtime chats, 107
behavior patterns of children, 105–107
"best interests of the child," 36, 41
Big Brothers/Big Sisters International, 133, 316
bill of rights for children, 196
bird nesting, 171
birth order, behavior and, 104
birthday traditions, creating, 188–189
blame. *See* guilt
blended families. *See also* remarriage
  baggage from the past and, 305–306
  bonding with stepchildren, 299–300
  cast of characters for, 298–299
  challenges, 12, 293–294
  dealing with relatives, 304
  discipline policies, 303
  disliking a stepchild, 302
  family meetings, 304–305
  financial clashes, 303
  privacy issues, 304
  stepsibling struggles, 300–302
  success story, 296–297
  ten commandments for stepparents, 307–308
  tips for success, 299
Body Mass Index (BMI), 247
bonding, 102, 174, 299–300
boundaries, establishing, 194
bubble baths, 243
budget. *See also* finances
  after-tax dollars as basis of, 75
  categories, 76–78
  defined, 74
  envelope system for, 78
  form for, 76
  overview, 11, 313
  sample for $24,850 after-tax income, 75
  talking to children about, 161

• C •

calendar, creating, 64, 65
carpooling, 64–66
cars
  carpooling, 64–66
  transportation expenses, 77, 85
CCCS (Consumer Credit Counseling Service), 96
census statistics, 13
challenges of single parenting
  adjusting to single parenthood, 7–8
  becoming a strong person, 9
  becoming inspired, 13
  budgeting, 11
  co-parenting, 10
  dating, 11–12
  getting along with your ex, 9–10
  getting professional help, 12
  helping kids cope with trauma, 8
  legal issues, 10–11
  realizing you're not alone, 13
  remarrying and blending families, 12
child abuse, 208, 218–219
child care, 66, 69–70, 77, 83–85
Child Health Insurance Program (CHIP), 82, 93
child snatching, 219, 220–221
child support, 37, 46–48, 94–96, 312
children. *See also* babies; preadolescents; teenagers; toddlers
  adjusting your schedule for, 110–111
  assuring about divorce, 17–18
  attention needs after loss of parent, 150–152
  behavior patterns, 105–107
  bill of rights, 196
  birth order and behavior, 104
  child-care alternatives, 69–70
  chores for helping out, 57–59

communicating with ex through, 192–193
conflict with your ex and, 213–214
criticizing ex's traits in, 192
daughters with single fathers, 119–121
daughters with single mothers, 121–122
depression signs in, 217, 231–232
dumping about ex on, 159–160
encouraging positive talk, 109–110
fun time with, 112–113
grieving by, 145–149, 238–239
guidelines for age groups, 102–103
helping heal from death of spouse, 21
home alone, 111
journal writing by, 236
labeling, 191–192
listening to, 107–109
medical release form for, 111–112
mistakes to avoid with, 128–132
power plays by, 193
private time with, 151–152
puberty stages in boys, 118–119
puberty stages in girls, 120–121
rebuilding emotional security after
    divorce, 143–149, 156
rebuilding physical security after
    divorce, 142–143
resolving serious problems, 217–218
role models for, 132–134
sons with single fathers, 118–119
sons with single mothers, 122–123
stages of grief for, 147–149
staying close to non-custodial parent
    after divorce, 149–150
stepchildren, 299–300, 302
stepsiblings, 300–302
talking about sex with, 119, 121, 123–124
CHIP (Child Health Insurance Program),
    82, 93
choosing single parenthood
  adjusting to parenthood, 25
  after accidental pregnancy, 26–27
friends and, 25, 26–27
methods of having a child, 23, 24
reasons for, 24
Christmas traditions, creating, 188
closed adoption, 43–44
clothing, 77, 90–91, 250–251
clubs
  cooking, 66–67
  meeting people in, 284
clutter, eliminating, 61, 63
communication
  about dating, 161, 277
  about death, 145–146
  about divorce, 17–18, 144–145,
      153–161, 180
  about grief, 146–149
  about money, 161
  about puberty, 118–119, 120–121
  about relatives and extended family, 206
  about sex, 119, 121, 123–124
  appreciating your ex's efforts, 179–180
  backing up your ex's decisions, 180
  on dates, 289–290
  encouraging, between you and your kids,
      176–177
  encouraging, between your kids and
      your ex, 177
  encouraging positive talk, 109–110
  with ex through children, 192–193
  with ex through ex's parents, 206
  family meetings, 178–179, 204, 304–305
  listening to children, 107–109
  negotiating with your ex, 214–216
  with non-custodial parent after divorce,
      149–150
  positive talk, 109–110, 143, 158
  presenting a united front, 178–180
  with relatives and extended family,
      207–208
  rules in co-parenting plan, 169–170
community property, 37

conception, 16–17, 23, 24, 45
congratulating yourself, 242
Consumer Credit Counseling Service
	(CCCS), 96
contempt of court, 222
contested divorce, 37
continuity, maintaining, 174–178
cooking. *See also* food
	children's complaints about, 158–159
	clubs for saving time, 66–67
	by single fathers, 118, 119, 124
co-parenting. *See also* ex-spouse
	ages of children and, 172–173
	bird nesting, 171
	child abuse and, 208, 218–219
	children's bill of rights, 196
	common problems and solutions,
		210–211
	custodial interference, 221–222
	defined, 10, 167
	discipline agreements, 181–187
	family traditions, creating, 187–190
	finding help for, 222–223
	forgiving your ex, 213–214, 216
	getting along with your ex, 9–10, 212–216
	godparents and, 204–205
	grandparents and, 199–200, 201–203
	guidelines for family visits, 205–208
	involvement in kids' activities, 181
	maintaining continuity, 174–178
	mistakes to avoid, 190–196
	negotiating with your ex, 214–216
	by opposites-attract couple, 190
	overview, 10
	parallel parenting versus, 180
	parental addictions and, 219
	parental kidnapping, 219, 220–221
	plan for, 168–172
	positive results from, 168–169
	with relatives and extended family,
		199–208

scheduling agreements, 172–174
	serious problems in children and,
		217–218
	stepparents and, 203–204
	transition anxiety and, 210–212
	united front for, 178–180
	visitation rights of relatives, 203, 204–205
co-parenting counselor, 223
co-parenting plan
	bird nesting, 171
	contents, 169–171, 172
	defined, 168
	filing with the court, 169, 172
	forgiving your ex and, 214
	importance of, 168, 313
	maintenance needed for, 209–210
	parents' rules of conduct and
		communication in, 169–170
	positive results from, 168–169
counseling. *See* professional therapy
court-appointed mediator, 40, 222–223
credit counselors, 96
crying, 157, 230
custody. *See also* co-parenting; schedule
	"best interests of the child" and, 41
	binding arbitration for, 41–42
	change in, 48–51
	in co-parenting plan, 170
	court-appointed mediator, 222–223
	custodial interference, 221–222
	custody evaluation report, 41
	explaining to children, 161
	family therapy and, 270–271
	joint, visitation rights and, 42
	sole-custody single fathers, 126–127
	temporary modification, 51
	transition anxiety, 210–212
	types of, 36–37
cutting, 162

• D •

dating
  adult's perspective on, 276–279
  analyzing your expectations, 281–285
  anecdote, 114
  conversational tips, 289–290
  denying yourself a social life, 192
  dressing for, 287
  fears about, 286–290
  finding time for, 290
  for fun, 281–282
  gender differences and, 276, 278
  going slow, 277–278, 280
  hanging out versus formal, 286–287, 291
  involving kids with your date, 278
  jealousy from kids and, 279
  kid's perspective on, 279–281
  meeting people, 282–285, 288, 314
  money concerns and, 290–291
  overview, 11–12
  relationships versus, 276
  searching for someone to marry, 281
  sexual expectations and, 276
  talking to children about, 161, 277
  trusting again after divorce, 285–286
daytrips, 252
death of spouse
  answering children's questions about,
      145–146
  children's needs for attention after,
      150–152
  children's wounds from, 135, 145–149,
      306–307
  coping with, 21–22, 29–30
  helping children heal, 21, 145–149
  legal and financial advice after, 42
  stages of grief, 28–29, 230–232
  as top life stressor, 15
denial stage of grief
  adults, 28, 230, 233
  children, 147, 230

depression
  after death of spouse, 231–232
  after divorce, 157, 234–235
  chronic versus adjustment disorders, 256
  serious, 29, 231–232
  signs in adults, 254–256
  signs in children, 217, 231–232, 235
  stage of grief (adults), 28–29, 231–232,
      234–235
  stage of grief (children), 148, 231, 235
diet
  healthy, 244
  special treats, 250
  for weight control, 246–247
disciple, 185
discipline
  after divorce, 141
  anger and, 186
  backing up your ex's decisions, 180
  basic house rules, 182
  blended families and, 303
  crucial points about, 187
  defined, 181–182
  establishing boundaries, 194
  major no-nos, 182–183
  non-punitive, 184–185
  for power plays, 193
  signs of laxity, 186
  strict, 184, 185
  styles, 183–185
  total permissiveness, 184, 185
divorce. See also co-parenting; ex-spouse
  anecdotes, 144, 159
  answering children's questions about,
      153–161
  assuring children after, 17–18, 156
  avoiding going to court, 40
  babies (birth to 2) and, 136–137
  children feeling put upon after, 158–160
  children's needs for attention after,
      150–152

divorce _(continued)_
  children's wounds from, 135, 138,
    150–151, 152–153
  contested, 37
  coping with, 18–20, 29–30
  crying after, explaining to children, 157
  definitions of terms, 36–38
  dumping on children about ex, 159–160
  emotional, finalizing, 19
  explaining custody agreement to
    children, 161
  finding an attorney for, 34–36
  forgiving your ex, 213–214, 216
  forgiving yourself, 235–236
  getting children to express feelings about,
    144–145
  grandparents and, 199–200
  guilt about (children's feelings), 154–155
  guilt about (parent's feelings), 18–19, 143
  mediation for, 38–40
  moving after, 160
  name change after, 160
  no-fault, 38
  preadolescents (6 to 12) and, 139–140
  professional help for children after, 143,
    161–163
  questions raised by, 18
  rebound from, 281, 294–295
  rebuilding children's emotional security
    after, 143–149, 156
  rebuilding children's physical security
    after, 142–143
  releasing anger about, 19, 20
  removing the wedding ring after, 19–20
  requests to live with other parent, 157
  shock of, 16–17
  son's difficulty with, 122, 144
  stages of grief, 28–29, 232–235
  staying close to children after, 149–150
  support group for single mothers, 18
  teenagers and, 140–142, 155
  toddlers (2 to 5) and, 137–138
  as top life stressor, 15
  uncontested, 34, 38
Divorce For Dummies (Ventura, John and
    Reed, Mary), 17, 33
donated sperm, 45
drugs
  alcohol, 103, 217, 219
  children involved with, 217
  discipline rule for, 183
  discussing with children, 103
  Ecstasy, 186
  parental addictions, 219
  street names for, 183

• E •

eating disorders in children, 217
Ecstasy (drug), 186
emancipation, 37
employment. _See_ work
entertainment/recreation expenses,
    77, 89–90
envelope system for budgeting, 78
EOPS (Extended Opportunities for
    Programs and Services), 93–94
errands, structuring to save time, 59–60
exercise
  for coping with death of spouse, 21
  for coping with divorce, 19, 20
  painless and affordable, 248
  stretching, 243
  for weight control, 246, 247
expenses. _See_ finances
ex-spouse
  addiction in, 219
  appreciating efforts of, 179–180
  backing up decisions of, 180
  child abuse by, 218–219
  children don't want to go to, 210

communicating through children with, 192–193

communicating through ex's parents with, 206

criticizing traits in your children, 192

discomfort with, 210

dumping on children about, 159–160

encouraging communication between kids and, 177

forgiving, 213–214, 216

getting along with, 9–10, 212–216

kidnapping by, 219, 220–221

negotiating with, 214–216

promises not kept by, 108

pushing buttons of, 194–195

spying on, through children, 191

Extended Opportunities for Programs and Services (EOPS), 93–94

● _F_ ●

facilitating visitation rights, 205

family. _See_ blended families; relatives and family

family court, 37

family court advisor, 223

family support, 46

fear or anxiety
  about dating, 286–290
  after divorce, children's, 17–18, 156, 160–161
  children's loss of parent and, 146, 148–149
  fearful behavior pattern, 105, 107
  separation anxiety, 148–149
  signs of anxiety disorders, 256–258
  stage of grief (children), 148–149
  transition anxiety, 210–212

female role models, 132, 133–134

finances. _See also_ budget
  after death of spouse, 42
  attorney payment, 35

bartering, 92

blended families and, 303

car expenses, reducing, 85

challenges of, 71

child care, affordable, 83–85

collecting child support, 94–96

credit counselors, 96

custody and income changes, 49

dating and money concerns, 290–291

entertainment/recreation expenses, reducing, 89–90

financial advisors, 96–98

food expenses, reducing, 86–89

goods and services expenses, reducing, 90–91

government assistance programs, 93–94, 98

help from grandparents, 201, 202

housing expenses, reducing, 79–81

insurance expenses, reducing, 82–83

medical/dental expenses, reducing, 86

money mistakes of single parents, 72

professional therapy, affordable, 266

rethinking your career, 73–74

retraining for better work, 74

utility expenses, reducing, 80–81

financial advisors, 96–98

first-born personality, 104

food. _See also_ cooking; diet
  budget category, 77
  reducing expenses, 86–89
  shopping for, 60

forgiving
  your ex, 213–214, 216
  yourself, 235–236

friends
  choosing single parenthood and, 25, 26–27
  concerns about you, 258–260
  finding new ones for children, 176
  finding new ones for you, 30–31

friends *(continued)*
  maintaining children's old friends, 176
  as role models, 133–134
  therapist recommendations from, 265–266
  trying to be your teenager's best friend, 131
fun. *See also* activities
  with children, 112–113
  dating for, 281–282
  for yourself, 250–252

• *G* •

godparents, 204–205
government assistance programs, 93–94, 98
grandparents, 199–200, 201–203
grief
  in children after divorce or death, 145–149, 238–239
  coping with, 21–22, 29–30
  crying from, 157, 230
  delayed, 234
  divorce versus death and, 228
  good, 228–229
  over death of spouse, 21–22, 28–29, 230–232
  over divorce, 28–29, 232–235
  positive talk and, 110
  stages of (adults), 28–29, 229–235
  stages of (children), 147–149
grocery shopping, 60
guardian ad litem, 37
guilt
  about divorce, 18–19, 143, 154–155
  about working, 131
  forgiving your ex, 213–214, 216
  forgiving yourself, 235–236
  spending on children and, 72
  stage of grief (children), 148

• *H* •

Habitat for Humanity, 80
Hanukah traditions, creating, 188
health insurance, 77, 82–83, 262, 265
health issues, custody and, 51
helping others (volunteering), 30, 283
holiday traditions, creating, 187–190
housing
  bird nesting, 171
  budget category, 76
  custody and residence changes, 50–51
  establishing two real homes, 175–176
  reducing expenses, 79–81
  smoothing the transition between, 177–178
  uncluttering, 61, 63
  working from home, 69
Hungelmann, Jack (*Insurance For Dummies*), 83

• *I* •

icons in margins of this book, 4
illegitimate label for babies, 1
in vitro fertilization, 23, 24, 45
independent private adoption, 43
injunction, 38
insurance, 77, 82–83, 262, 265
Insurance For Dummies (Hungelmann, Jack), 83
ironing, eliminating, 62
irreconcilable differences, 38

• *J* •

jealousy, 237–238, 279–280
jobs. *See* work
joint legal custody, 37
joint physical custody, 37

• K •

kidnapping, 219, 220–221
Kwanzaa traditions, creating, 188

• L •

labeling children, 191–192
laughter, benefits of, 248–249
laundry, streamlining, 61–63
LCSW (Licensed Clinical Social
    Worker), 264
legal issues. *See also* attorneys; custody;
    visitation rights
  for adoption, 43–44
  after death of spouse, 42
  alimony, 36, 46–47, 312
  for artificial insemination, 45
  becoming a single parent, 27
  biological fathers and single mothers, 46
  child abuse, 208, 218–219
  child support, 37, 46–48, 94–96, 312
  co-parenting plan filed with the court,
    169, 172
  court-appointed mediator, 222–223
  custodial interference, 221–222
  divorce terminology, 36–38
  divorce without going to court, 40
  explaining divorce legalities to children,
    153–154, 161
  guilt and divorce settlement, 18
  kidnapping, 220–221
  mediator, court-appointed, 40, 222–223
  mediator, private, 38–40
  overview, 10–11
  prenuptial agreement, 295–298
  restraining orders, 38, 49, 220–221
  for surrogate motherhood, 45–46
  Uniform Parentage Act, 48
  for in vitro fertilization, 45
Licensed Clinical Social Worker
    (LCSW), 264

Licensed Marriage, Family, and Child
    Counselor (LMFT), 263
listening to children, 107–109
loss. *See* grief

• M •

maintaining continuity, 174–178
makeovers, 251
male role models, 133–134
marital settlement agreement, 40
Martindale-Hubbell Law Directory, 34
massage, professional, 243
matchmakers, 284–285
mealtimes, 174, 176
mediators, 38–40, 222–223
Medicaid, 82, 266
medical release form for children, 111–112
medical/dental expenses, 77, 86
mental health insurance, 262, 265
middle-child personality, 104
mistakes
  allowing kids to con you, 194
  avoiding warmth and affection, 130–131
  babying your children (mothers), 130
  being a poor role model, 193–194
  common mistakes, 128–129
  communicating with ex through children,
    192–193
  criticizing ex's traits in children, 192
  denying yourself a social life, 192
  expecting your child to improve your life,
    131–132
  feeling guilty when working, 131
  labeling kids, 191–192
  living vicariously through your kids
    (fathers), 129–130
  money mistakes of single parents, 72
  not establishing boundaries, 194
  overloading children with activities, 191
  power plays with children, 193
  pushing your ex's buttons, 194–195

mistakes *(continued)*
  refusing to consider professional therapy,
    195–196
  remarriage on the rebound, 281, 294–295
  spying on ex through children, 191
  trying to be best friends with your
    teenager, 131
money. *See* budget; finances
music, soothing, 244

• N •

names
  change after divorce, 160
  for stepparents, 302
National Association of Social Workers, 261
National Center for Missing and Exploited
    Children, 316
National Council for Adoption (NCFA), 317
National Hopeline Network, 217, 232, 256
National Organization of Single
    Mothers, 317
natural conception, 16–17, 24
negative talk, avoiding, 109–110
negotiating
  with your employer, 68
  with your ex, 214–216
no-fault divorce, 38
non-punitive discipline style, 184–185

• O •

obesity, weight control program for,
    246–247
open adoption, 43–44
organization
  calendar, 64, 65
  desk, 63
  laundry, 61–63
  uncluttering the house, 61, 63
out of state moveaway, 219, 220–221

• P •

parallel parenting, 180
parenting coordinator, 223
Parenting For Dummies (Wiley Publishing),
    113, 197
Parents Without Partners organization, 317
perfectionism, 59
permissive discipline style, 184, 185
pets, stress relief and, 30, 249–250
physical security, children's, 142–143
positive discipline, 184–185
positive talk, 109–110, 143, 158
positive thinking, 29, 110, 206
potty training, 102–103
Potty Training For Dummies (Stafford,
    Diane and Shoquist, Jennifer), 103
power plays, 193
praising yourself, 242
preadolescents. *See also* children
  co-parenting schedule and, 173
  divorce and, 139–140
  puberty stages in boys, 118–119
  puberty stages in girls, 120–121
  talking about sex with, 123
  tips for raising, 103
prenuptial agreement, 295–298
prioritizing responsibilities, 56–57
privacy, blended families and, 304
private time with children, 151–152
professional matchmakers, 285
professional therapy. *See also*
    support groups
  affordable care, 266
  choosing a therapist, 263, 265–267
  common questions about, 262–263
  for co-parenting, 222–223
  divorce and children's need for,
    143, 161–163

evaluating the therapist, 266–267
family therapy, 270–272
finding, 314
health insurance and, 262, 265
overview, 12, 260–262
psychotherapy defined, 253
referrals by professional
    organizations, 261
refusing to consider, 195–196
signs of anxiety disorders requiring,
    256–258
signs of children's need for, 162
signs of depression requiring, 254–256
signs of transition problems
    requiring, 258
stereotypes versus reality, 253–254
for suicidal children, 162, 217, 232
techniques of, 260
for teenage daughter with single father,
    116–117
therapist titles and qualifications,
    263–264
therapists not on preferred provider
    lists, 262
progressive muscle relaxation, 244
psychiatrist, 264
psychoanalyst, 264
psychologist, 264
psychotherapy. *See* professional therapy
puberty
  boy stages, 118–119
  girl stages, 120–121

• R •

rebellious behavior pattern, 106
rebound from divorce, 281, 294–295
Reed, Mary (*Divorce For Dummies*), 17, 33
regressive behavior pattern, 105
relationships, dating versus, 276

relatives and family. *See also*
    blended families
  abuse by, 208
  children's needs and, 199–200
  concerns about you, 258–260
  family meetings, 178–179, 204, 304–305
  family therapy, 270–272
  family traditions, creating, 187–189
  godparents, 204–205
  grandparents, 199–200, 201–203
  guidelines for visits, 205–208
  moving in with, 79
  as role models, 134
  stepchildren, 299–300, 302
  stepparents, 203–204, 302
  stepsiblings, 300–302
  visitation rights of, 203, 204–205
relaxation techniques, 243–245
remarriage. *See also* blended families
  custody and, 49
  as dating expectation, 281
  issues, 12, 314
  prenuptial agreement, 295–298
  on the rebound, 281, 294–295
  tips for success, 299
Remember icon, 4
residences. *See* housing
RESOLVE organization, 318
restraining orders, 38, 49, 220–221
rights of children, 196
role models, 132–134, 193–194

• S •

SAA (Stepfamily Association of
    America), 318
sadness stage of grief (children), 148
schedule. *See also* time
  adjusting for children, 110–111
  ages and, 172–173
  calendar for, 64, 65

schedule *(continued)*
 for co-parenting, 172–174
 errands in, 59–60
 fitting dating in, 290
 prioritizing responsibilities, 56–57
 saying no to activities, 55–56
 simplifying, 55–64
 typical day for single parent, 54–55
second-born personality, 104
security, rebuilding children's
 emotional, 143–149, 156
 physical, 142–143
self injury (SI), 162
self-esteem, bolstering yours, 242
separation, 153
separation anxiety, 148–149
settlement conference, 40
sex
 dating and expectations for, 276
 safe, 277
 sexually active children, 218
 talking about, 119, 121, 123–124
Shoquist, Jennifer (*Potty Training For
  Dummies*), 103
SI (self injury), 162
single fathers
 bonding by, 102
 with daughters, 116–117, 119–121
 described, 115–116
 frequently asked questions, 311–314
 likelihood of dating by, 287
 living vicariously, 129–130
 providing female role models, 132,
  133–134
 resources for, 315–318
 sole-custody, 126–127
 with sons, 118–119
 statistics, 13, 27, 126
 stereotypical behavior and, 124–125
 teenage daughter with, 116–117, 120

single mothers
 babying your children, 130
 biological fathers and rights of, 46
 with daughters, 121–122
 described, 116
 frequently asked questions, 311–314
 providing male role models, 133–134
 resources for, 315–318
 with sons, 122–123
 statistics, 13, 27
 stereotypical behavior and, 125–126
 super mom myth, 127–128
 support groups, 18, 252
Single Mothers by Choice organization, 318
SingleMOTHER organization, 18
smiling, 30
smoking, by children, 217
social life, 192, 251. *See also* dating
sole legal custody, 36
sole physical custody, 37
sole-custody single fathers, 126–127
special master, 223
sperm, donated, 45, 48
spousal support, 36
spouse. *See* death of spouse; divorce;
  ex-spouse; remarriage
spying on ex through children, 191
Stafford, Diane (*Potty Training For
  Dummies*), 103
stages of grief
 for adults, 28–29, 229–235
 for children, 147–149
 cycling through, 229
 death of spouse and, 230–232
 divorce and, 232–235
stepchildren, 299–300, 302
Stepfamily Association of America
  (SAA), 318
stepparents, 203–204, 302, 307–308
stepsiblings, 300–302

stereotypical behavior
  avoiding, by single fathers, 124–125
  avoiding, by single mothers, 125–126
  sole-custody fathers and, 126
  super mom myth, 127–128
stress release, 30, 243–245, 249–250
stretching, 243
strict discipline style, 184, 185
suicide
  danger signs in teenagers, 162–163
  help for adults, 235, 256
  help for children, 162, 217, 232
super mom myth, 127–128
support groups
  for bereavement, 239
  for children of addicts, 219
  for divorce, 20
  finding, 313
  joining, 268–269
  for single mothers, 18, 252
  therapy groups, 269
  types of, 269
surrogate motherhood, 45–46

• T •

tantrum behavior pattern, 105–106
teenagers. *See also* children
  co-parenting schedule and, 173
  daughter with single father, 116–117, 120
  divorce and, 140–142, 155
  puberty stages in boys, 118–119
  puberty stages in girls, 120–121
  rebellious behavior pattern, 106
  suicide danger signs, 162–163
  talking about sex with, 124
  tips for raising, 103
  trying to be best friends with, 131
temporary restraining order (TRO), 38
therapy. *See* professional therapy

time. *See also* schedule
  babysitting co-op for saving, 66
  carpooling to save, 64–66
  cooking clubs for saving, 66–67
  delegating chores to children, 57–59
  grocery shopping and, 60
  organizing to save, 60–64
  perfectionism and, 59
  prioritizing responsibilities, 56–57
  required for therapy, 262–263
  structuring errands to save, 59–60
  for yourself, 252
Tip icon, 4
toddlers. *See also* children
  co-parenting schedule and, 173
  divorce and, 137–138
  talking about sex with, 123
  tantrum tent for, 105–106
  tips for raising, 102–103
total permissiveness discipline style,
    184, 185
traditions, family, 187–189
transition anxiety, 210–212
transportation expenses, 77, 85
travel organizations for singles, 282–283
trial separation, communicating about, 153
TRO (temporary restraining order), 38
trust, dating after divorce and, 285–286

• U •

uncontested divorce, 34, 38
Uniform Parentage Act, 48
utility expenses, reducing, 80–81

• V •

vacation traditions, creating, 189
Ventura, John (*Divorce For Dummies*),
    17, 33

vicarious living through children, 129–130
visitation rights
  facilitating, 205
  of grandparents, 203
  issues requiring agreement, 42–43
  joint custody and, 42
  of third parties, 204–205
  visitation defined, 38
visualization relaxation technique, 245
volunteering, 30, 283

Warning! icon, 4
Web sites
  auto buying information, 85
  drug street names, 183
  government assistance programs, 94
  Habitat for Humanity, 80
  Martindale-Hubbell Law Directory, 34
  professional organizations for therapist
    referrals, 261
  resources for single parents, 315–318

  self injury information, 162
  travel organizations for singles, 282–283
  weight loss resources, 246, 247
wedding ring, removing, 19–20
weight control, 246–247
work
  custody and changes in, 49–50
  guilt about working, 131
  health insurance benefits, 82–83
  from home, 69
  negotiating with your employer, 68
  rethinking your career, 73–74
  retraining, 74
writing
  about anger over divorce, 20
  journal writing, 236
  to non-custodial parent after divorce, 149
  what you like about yourself, 30

• **Y** •

youngest-child personality, 104

Notes

Notes

Notes

Notes

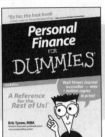

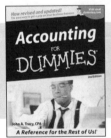
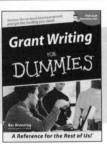

FOR DUMMIES®

A world of resources to help you grow

HOME, GARDEN & HOBBIES

Feng Shui

0-7645-5295-3

Gardening

0-7645-5130-2

Guitar

0-7645-5106-X

Also available:

Auto Repair For Dummies
(0-7645-5089-6)

Chess For Dummies
(0-7645-5003-9)

Home Maintenance For Dummies
(0-7645-5215-5)

Organizing For Dummies
(0-7645-5300-3)

Piano For Dummies
(0-7645-5105-1)

Poker For Dummies
(0-7645-5232-5)

Quilting For Dummies
(0-7645-5118-3)

Rock Guitar For Dummies
(0-7645-5356-9)

Roses For Dummies
(0-7645-5202-3)

Sewing For Dummies
(0-7645-5137-X)

FOOD & WINE

Cooking

0-7645-5250-3

Cookies

0-7645-5390-9

Wine

0-7645-5114-0

Also available:

Bartending For Dummies
(0-7645-5051-9)

Chinese Cooking For Dummies
(0-7645-5247-3)

Christmas Cooking For Dummies
(0-7645-5407-7)

Diabetes Cookbook For Dummies
(0-7645-5230-9)

Grilling For Dummies
(0-7645-5076-4)

Low-Fat Cooking For Dummies
(0-7645-5035-7)

Slow Cookers For Dummies
(0-7645-5240-6)

TRAVEL

Italy

0-7645-5453-0

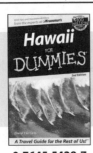

Hawaii

0-7645-5438-7

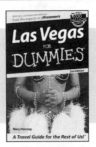

Las Vegas

0-7645-5448-4

Also available:

America's National Parks For Dummies
(0-7645-6204-5)

Caribbean For Dummies
(0-7645-5445-X)

Cruise Vacations For Dummies 2003
(0-7645-5459-X)

Europe For Dummies
(0-7645-5456-5)

Ireland For Dummies
(0-7645-6199-5)

France For Dummies
(0-7645-6292-4)

London For Dummies
(0-7645-5416-6)

Mexico's Beach Resorts For Dummies
(0-7645-6262-2)

Paris For Dummies
(0-7645-5494-8)

RV Vacations For Dummies
(0-7645-5443-3)

Walt Disney World & Orlando For Dummies
(0-7645-5444-1)

Available wherever books are sold. Go to www.dummies.com or call 1-877-762-2974 to order direct.

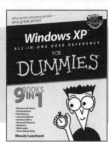
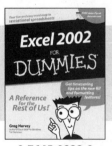

FOR DUMMIES®

Helping you expand your horizons and realize your potential

INTERNET

The Internet For Dummies
0-7645-0894-6

The Internet All-in-One Desk Reference For Dummies
0-7645-1659-0

eBay For Dummies
0-7645-1642-6

Also available:

America Online 7.0 For Dummies
(0-7645-1624-8)

Genealogy Online For Dummies
(0-7645-0807-5)

The Internet All-in-One Desk Reference For Dummies
(0-7645-1659-0)

Internet Explorer 6 For Dummies
(0-7645-1344-3)

The Internet For Dummies Quick Reference
(0-7645-1645-0)

Internet Privacy For Dummies
(0-7645-0846-6)

Researching Online For Dummies
(0-7645-0546-7)

Starting an Online Business For Dummies
(0-7645-1655-8)

DIGITAL MEDIA

Digital Photography For Dummies
0-7645-1664-7

Photoshop Elements 2 For Dummies
0-7645-1675-2

Digital Video For Dummies
0-7645-0806-7

Also available:

CD and DVD Recording For Dummies
(0-7645-1627-2)

Digital Photography All-in-One Desk Reference For Dummies
(0-7645-1800-3)

Digital Photography For Dummies Quick Reference
(0-7645-0750-8)

Home Recording for Musicians For Dummies
(0-7645-1634-5)

MP3 For Dummies
(0-7645-0858-X)

Paint Shop Pro "X" For Dummies
(0-7645-2440-2)

Photo Retouching & Restoration For Dummies
(0-7645-1662-0)

Scanners For Dummies
(0-7645-0783-4)

GRAPHICS

PowerPoint 2002 For Dummies
0-7645-0817-2

Photoshop 7 For Dummies
0-7645-1651-5

Macromedia Flash MX For Dummies
0-7645-0895-4

Also available:

Adobe Acrobat 5 PDF For Dummies
(0-7645-1652-3)

Fireworks 4 For Dummies
(0-7645-0804-0)

Illustrator 10 For Dummies
(0-7645-3636-2)

QuarkXPress 5 For Dummies
(0-7645-0643-9)

Visio 2000 For Dummies
(0-7645-0635-8)

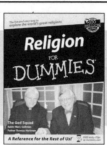
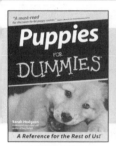

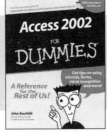

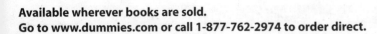